IPv6 Socket API Extensions

Extensions

Programmer's Guide

Qing Li
Blue Coat Systems, Inc.

Tatuya Jinmei
Toshiba Corporation

Keiichi Shima
Internet Initiative Japan, Inc.

ELSEVIER

AMSTERDAM • BOSTON • HEIDELBERG • LONDON
NEW YORK • OXFORD • PARIS • SAN DIEGO
SAN FRANCISCO • SINGAPORE • SYDNEY • TOKYO
Morgan Kaufmann Publishers is an imprint of Elsevier

MORGAN KAUFMANN

Morgan Kaufmann Publishers is an imprint of Elsevier
30 Corporate Drive, Suite 400, Burlington, MA 01803, USA

This book is printed on acid-free paper. ∞

Library of Congress Cataloging-in-Publication Data
Application Submitted

British Library Cataloguing in Publication Data
A catalogue record for this book is available from the British Library

ISBN 13: 978-0-12-375076-1

For information on all Morgan Kaufmann publications,
visit our Web site at *www.elsevierdirect.com*

Typeset by: diacriTech, India

Printed and bound in the United Kingdom
Transferred to Digital Printing, 2010

Contents

About the Authors

Li, Qing is a senior architect at Blue Coat Systems, Inc., leading the design and development efforts of the next-generation IPv6 enabled secure proxy appliances. Prior to joining Blue Coat Systems, Qing spent 8 years at Wind River Systems, Inc., as a senior architect in the networks business unit, where he was the lead architect of Wind River's embedded IPv6 products since the IPv6 program inception in 2000. Qing holds multiple U.S. patents. Qing is a contributing author of the book *Handbook of Networked and Embedded Control Systems* (2005, Springer-Verlag). He is also author of the embedded systems development book *Real-Time Concepts for Embedded Systems* (2003, CMP Books). Qing participates in open source development projects and is an active FreeBSD src committer.

Jinmei, Tatuya, PhD, is a research scientist at Corporate Research & Development Center, Toshiba Corporation. (Jinmei is his family name, which he prefers be presented first according to the Japanese convention.) He was a core developer of the KAME project from the launch of the project to its conclusion. In 2003, he received a PhD degree from Keio University, Japan, based on his work at KAME. He also coauthored three RFCs on IPv6 through his activity in KAME. His research interests spread over various fields of the Internet and IPv6, including routing, DNS, and multicasting.

Shima, Keiichi is a senior researcher at Internet Initiative Japan, Inc. His research area is IPv6 and IPv6 mobility. He was a core developer of the KAME project from 2001 to the end of the project, and he developed Mobile IPv6/NEMO Basic Support protocol stack. He is currently working on the new mobility stack (the SHISA stack) for BSD operating systems, which is a completely restructured mobility stack.

Introduction

1.1 Introduction

The transition to the Internet Protocol version 6 (IPv6) has begun, driven largely by the persistent Internet growth in developing regions resulting in the gradual and steady depletion of the available Internet Protocol version 4 (IPv4) address space. In anticipation of the eventual migration, based on our own IPv6 product development experience, we see that enterprises, Internet service providers (ISPs), managed service providers (MSPs), and various governments throughout the world have been actively gathering the requirements and evaluating challenges of deploying IPv6 in the existing infrastructures. ISPs and MSPs have been actively conducting trial markets to create viable business models and build value-added services around IPv6. Enterprises have been building test networks with focused deployments to perform feasibility studies on how to provide existing applications and services to users in the IPv6 space. All indicators suggest that demand for developers who have the knowledge of and the experience in developing IPv6-capable applications is inevitable.

In this chapter, our focus is on providing a high-level overview of the IPv6 application programming using the BSD socket interface. The usage of the various IPv6-related BSD socket application programming interfaces (APIs) is illustrated by examples. Comparisons are made between IPv4 and IPv6 with regard to how these APIs are invoked, the types of parameters, and how these parameters are initialized when calling the functions.

Developers must understand how to write portable applications that can operate in both IPv4 and IPv6 environments. The knowledge of how to convert and how to migrate the existing applications through least intrusive design approaches is one of the essential elements to the successful adoption of IPv6. Support for the IPv4-mapped IPv6 address introduces complexity inside the network stack. In general, using IPv4-mapped IPv6 address over an IPv6 socket to communicate with an IPv4 node is a discouraged practice, but we show how it is done for completeness.

Although we provide an overview, we omit the details and assume readers have the basic understanding of the general BSD socket APIs and programming model. Readers who are new to this area are encouraged to read the references section at the end of the book. We also assume readers have the basic understanding of the Transmission Control Protocol (TCP), the User Datagram Protocol (UDP), and IPv4 and IPv6. In this chapter, when we refer to the IPv6 stack and kernel, we mean the KAME implementation and the FreeBSD operating system.

1.2   Socket Programming Overview

By design, transport protocols such as TCP and UDP are independent of the network layer protocols, such as IPv4 and IPv6. Therefore, by and large, writing IPv6 programs is identical to writing IPv4 applications. Figure 1-1 shows a typical socket API call sequence (in the simplest form) for a simple TCP server and also a call sequence for a simple client application. Each side of a TCP connection is called an end point or a peer. A TCP or UDP connection is represented by the connection 4-tuple *<local IPv6 address, local port, remote IPv6 address, remote port>*.

Both the client and the server application must create a socket as a first step. The socket() call creates a socket object of a specific protocol type, for example, a connection-oriented TCP socket.

Next, the bind() call is issued to associate an IP address and a port number with the local end of the connection. On the server side, the bind() call allows the server application to wait

FIGURE 1-1

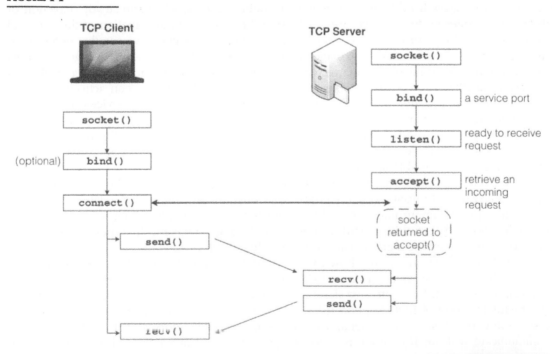

Socket API call sequence for TCP.

for requests on a specific port. This service port can be a well-known port, such as port 21 for File Transfer Protocol (FTP) and port 22 for Secure Shell (SSH). The service port can be a user-defined port that is outside the well-known port range.

The client application then calls connect() to issue a TCP request to the server application. The connect() call will initiate TCP protocol three-way handshake between the client and the server's TCP/IP protocol stacks. In the normal case, the connect() call returns as soon as the TCP protocol connection between the client and the server is fully established. The bind() call is optional for the client application. If the client application calls connect() immediately following the socket() call, then the client TCP/IPv6 protocol stack will automatically choose a source IPv6 address and generate a local port for the local end point.

On the server side, the listen() call is made to enable the server socket to receive incoming requests and set the socket in ready mode.

When a client TCP connection request arrives at the server, the server TCP/IPv6 protocol stack creates another socket internally using the listening socket as the template. The server TCP/IPv6 protocol stack then returns this newly created socket to the caller (the server application) of the accept() call. On UNIX-like systems, the server application may spawn off a child process, and this child process handles the just arrived TCP request.

Both the client and the server applications call the recv() and send() APIs to transmit and receive data, respectively.

Figure 1-2 shows typical socket API call sequences for a simple UDP server and client application. Similar to TCP, the UDP server listener first binds to a specific UDP port on which data will arrive. Because UDP is a connectionless protocol, the sendto() and recvfrom()

FIGURE 1-2

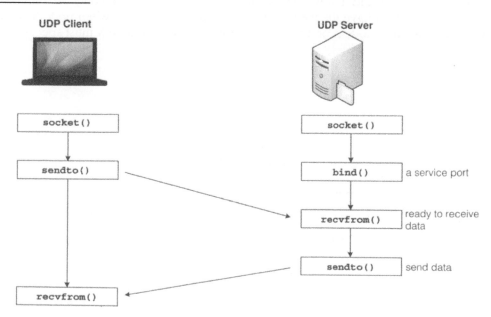

Socket API call sequence for UDP.

APIs are used to transmit and receive data, respectively. The `sendto()` caller must provide the IP address and port number of the remote node. In this example, the client application provides the server IP address and the service port number to the `sendto()` call.

In addition to receiving data from the client application, the `recvfrom()` call can return the IP address and port number of the client end point to the server application upon request. The server can then send data to the identified client using the address information returned by the previous `recvfrom()` call.

Although the `sendto()` and `recvfrom()` functions can be used on TCP sockets, such practice is uncommon in normal applications. The reason is obvious: For a connected TCP socket, the IPv6 address and port number remain constant for the lifetime of that connection.

1.3   IPv6 Addressing Overview

IPv6 address is 128 bits long and has three address types: unicast address, anycast address, and multicast address. The anycast address has the same format as a regular unicast address, and it can be distinguished from a regular unicast address only in a given context. Broadcast address does not exist in IPv6.

An IPv6 address is more structured than an IPv4 address. Both unicast and multicast addresses have *address scopes*. For example, unicast address has the link-local scope and global scope. Address scopes introduce ambiguity and are a source of confusion for developers new to IPv6. For example, a link-local address is unique only on a given link, and that same link-local address can exist on other links. Figure 1-3 illustrates this ambiguity. In this example, a node X is connected to both link A and link B. Because link-local address is unique only on a single link, both node A and node B have the fe80::a address assigned. Therefore, when node X wants to communicate with either node A or node B, the application within node X must specify exactly

FIGURE 1-3

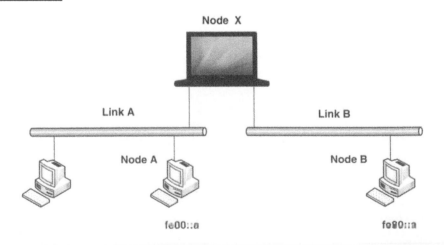

Link-local address Ambiguity.

which node the address fe80::a is meant for. To do so, the application must specify the *scope zone index*, which typically maps into an interface identifier.

For example, on the FreeBSD OS running the KAME implementation, the SSH application on node X wanting to connect to node A has the following command format:

```
ssh fe80::a%em0
```

The "%" character delimits the address and the scope zone index that is represented by the interface identifier "em0".

The textual representation of an IPv6 address is written in hexadecimal values of eight 16-bit quantities delimited by the ":", as in x0:x1:x2:x3:x4:x5:x6:x7. The following is an example of an IPv6 address:

```
2001:0db8:0123:4567:89ab:cdef:0123:4567

  x0    x1    x2    x3    x4    x5    x6    x7
```

It is not necessary to write the leading 0's. In this case, the same address can be written as

```
2001:db8:123:4567:89ab:cdef:123:4567

  x0   x1  x2   x3   x4   x5   x6   x7
```

Consecutive zero valued fields can be combined and written in the compressed form "::". The compressed field can appear only once in an address. For example, the IPv6 address

```
2001 :  db8 :  123 :    1    :    0    :    0    :    0    :    1

  x0      x1     x2       x3         x4         x5         x6         x7
```

can be written as

```
2001:db8:123:1::1
```

IPv6 introduces the IPv4-mapped IPv6 address to help the transition from IPv4 to IPv6. An IPv4-mapped IPv6 address represents an IPv4 node in IPv6 form. An example is

```
::FFFF:192.0.2.1
```

As can be seen, the last 32 bits is an IPv4 address.

1.4 Address Selection

We previously discussed that when the user application does not explicitly call `bind()` to assign an address and a port to the local end of a socket, the IPv6 stack in the kernel will automatically choose an IPv6 address and an ephemeral port for the local end point.

Because IPv6 introduces the concept of address scopes, and multiple IPv6 addresses can be assigned to a node, the IPv6 stack performs what is known as *source address selection* algorithm to choose an appropriate source IPv6 address. The selected source address will have the best matching scope to that of the given destination address.

When an application explicitly binds an IPv6 address to a socket, and provides the server address information as a hostname when calling `connect()`, the domain name server (DNS) will be involved in resolving the hostname into IPv6 addresses. The DNS may return multiple IPv6 addresses for a given hostname. In this case, the IPv6 stack in the kernel must perform what is known as *destination address selection* algorithm to choose an appropriate address from the return list based on the given source address.

The address selection algorithms conform to the address selection rules and policies that are configurable by the system administrator. On the FreeBSD OS, the **ipaddrctl** command manipulates the address selection policy table. For more information on address selection algorithms, see [LiCore06].

1.5   Socket Creation

The difference between creating an IPv6 socket and creating an IPv4 socket is the address family type given to the `socket()` call. The address family is `AF_INET6` for an IPv6 socket. The following code fragment shows how to create a TCP-over-IPv6 socket:

```
s = socket(AF_INET6, SOCK_STREAM, IPPROTO_TCP);
```

As can be seen, this call is identical to the IPv4 version except for the first parameter. Similarly, creating a UDP-over-IPv6 socket is done by the following code:

```
s = socket(AF_INET6, SOCK_DGRAM, IPPROTO_UDP);
```

Raw socket is typically used to handle transport protocols that are not implemented by the network protocol stacks on the host system. For example, the FreeBSD kernel implements TCP, UDP, and Stream Control Transmission Protocol (SCTP) by default. There are a number of differences between IPv6 raw socket operation and the IPv4 raw socket. For example, data transmitted or received over a raw socket must be in network byte order. With IPv4 raw socket an application can specify the `IP_HDRINCL` socket option to supply a complete IPv4 header for outgoing packets. There is no such equivalent option in IPv6. Instead, *ancillary data* is used to specify IPv6 header and extension headers. Also, checksum calculation handling is more flexible with IPv6 raw socket. Chapter 2 discusses this topic in greater detail.

1.6   IPv6 Address Structure

Socket APIs such as `bind()` and `sendto()` require the caller to supply address information. This address information structure is `sockaddr_in{}` for IPv4. For IPv6, the equivalent data structure is `sockaddr_in6{}`. The following code fragment gives the exact definition for `sockaddr_in6{}`:

```
struct sockaddr_in6 {
        u_int8_t        sin6_len;       /* length of this struct(sa_family_t)*/
        u_int8_t        sin6_family;    /* AF_INET6 (sa_family_t) */
        u_int16_t       sin6_port;      /* Transport layer port # (in_port_t)*/
        u_int32_t       sin6_flowinfo;  /* IP6 flow information */
        struct in6_addr sin6_addr;      /* IP6 address */
        u_int32_t       sin6_scope_id;  /* scope zone index */
};
```

The `sin6_len` is set to the size of the structure. The `sin6_family` field is set to the `AF_INET6` family type. The `sin6_port` field contains the port number used by the local end of a connection. The `sin6_flowinfo` field maps to the 20-bit flow label in the IPv6 header. The topic of flow label is outside the scope of this chapter. The reader is encouraged to read the reference text [LiCore06] for more detail. The majority of the applications seldom explicitly initialize it to a specific value.

The `sin6_scope_id` field contains the address scope. This field is unique to the IPv6 protocol. For example, when an IPv6 application communicates with another node using an IPv6 link-local address, the `sin6_scope_id` field must contain the scope zone index. For APIs such as `recvfrom()`, which returns address information to the caller, the IPv6 stack will set the `sin6_scope_id` to the appropriate value for the caller to read. Unlike IPv4, where the `sockaddr_in{}` structure is used mostly by the applications, in IPv6 the `sockaddr_in6{}` structure is shared between the IPv6 stack inside the kernel and the applications. In particular, internally the IPv6 stack stores the scope zone information differently and does not utilize the `sin6_sope_id` field. This difference is the source of confusion for many developers new to the KAME implementation. For more detail, see [LiCore06].

The 128-bit IPv6 address is stored in the `sin6_addr` field. The definition of `in6_addr{}` is shown in the following code fragment:

```
struct in6_addr {
        union {
                u_int8_t    __u6_addr8[16];
                u_int16_t   __u6_addr16[8];
                u_int32_t   __u6_addr32[4];
        } __u6_addr;                        /* 128-bit IP6 address */
};
```

The IPv6 address can be access in units of 8 bits, 16 bits, and 32 bits, respectively. The following illustrates an IPv6 address when accessed in 16-bit units:

```
          2001 : db8 : 1 : 2 : 0 : 0 : A : B
s6_addr16  [0]    [1]  [2] [3] [4] [5] [6] [7]
```

1.7 Assign IPv6 Address Information to Local End Point

The `bind()` system call is used to assign an IPv6 address and a port number to the local end point of a socket. The following code block is an example of the `bind()` call that assigns port 5001 to the local end point:

```
struct sockaddr_in6 sin6;
int s;

s = socket(AF_INET6, SOCK_STREAM, IPPROTO_TCP);

memset(&sin6, 0, sizeof(sin6));
sin6.sin6_family = AF_INET6;
sin6.sin6_len = sizeof(sin6);
sin6.sin6_port = htons(5001);
bind(s, (const struct sockaddr *)&sin6, sizeof(sin6));
```

Note that in this example there is no explicit address binding to the local end point. If this code block belongs to a client application, then the address binding is delayed until the `connect()` time when the destination address is known, which will then allow for the proper source address selection. If this code block is part of a server application, then the server can accept connection requests that are destined to TCP port 5001 on any of the server's IPv6 addresses.

1.8   Accepting an Incoming Connection

The `accept()` system call is used by a server application to accept and receive incoming connection requests. Multiple incoming requests may be already pending at the server socket when the `accept()` call is made. The number of allowable pending requests is specified in the `listen()` call. Any request beyond a set limit is dropped.

```
struct sockaddr_in6 sin6, sin6_accept;
socklen_t sin6_len;
int s, s2;

s = socket(AF_INET6, SOCK_STREAM, IPPROTO_TCP);

memset(&sin6, 0, sizeof(sin6));
sin6.sin6_family = AF_INET6;
sin6.sin6_len = sizeof(sin6);
sin6.sin6_port = htons(5001);
bind(s, (const struct sockaddr *)&sin6, sizeof(sin6));

listen(s, 1);

sin6_len = sizeof(sin6_accept);
s2 = accept(s, (struct sockaddr *)&sin6_accept, &sin6_len);
```

Note that the second parameter to the `listen()` call is 1, which specifies that only one connection may be pending for processing at a time. The second argument to the `accept()` can be set to NULL. In this example, `sin6_accept` is given, so on return from the `accept()` call `sin6_accept` will hold the IPv6 address of the requestor. This information can be useful for the server application to identify the request and for debugging purposes.

1.9   Transmitting Data on a UDP Socket

The `sendto()` API is called to transmit data on a UDP socket to a specified destination. The destination address is given as a function parameter. It is allowed for a UDP socket to call `connect()` and set the remote address on the socket. This is called a *connected UDP* socket. In that case, the `send()` API may be used instead of `sendto()`.

A connected UDP socket is more convenient if the UDP socket is used to communicate with only one remote node. Using an unconnected UDP socket is more flexible if that UDP socket communicates with multiple remote nodes. The following code fragment shows a UDP data transmission example:

```
struct sockaddr_in6 sin6, sin6_to;
socklen_t sin6_len;
int s, len;
unsigned char databuf[DEF_OUT_LEN];
```

```
s = socket(AF_INET6, SOCK_DGRAM, IPPROTO_UDP);

memset(&sin6, 0, sizeof(sin6));
sin6.sin6_family = AF_INET6;
sin6.sin6_len = sizeof(sin6);
sin6.sin6_port = htons(5001);

inet_pton(AF_INET6, "2001:db8::1234", &sin6.sin6_addr);

/*
 * initialize databuf with outgoing bytes
 */

len = sendto(s, databuf, len, 0
             (const struct sockaddr *)&sin6_to, sizeof(sin6_to));
```

Note that a function `inet_pton()` is shown in this example. This function converts an IPv6 address in printable string format into the binary equivalent of an IPv6 address and stores the result in the storage provided in the third function argument.

1.10 Receiving Data on a UDP Socket

The `recvfrom()` API is called to wait for and receive data on a UDP socket. The caller of `recvfrom()` may provide memory to store the peer address upon return from this API call. The retrieved peer address may then be used in a subsequent call to `sendto()` to send data to that peer. The following code fragment shows a UDP data receive example:

```
struct sockaddr_in6 sin6, sin6_from;
socklen_t sin6_len;
int s, len;
unsigned char databuf[DEF_OUT_LEN];
char buf[512];

s = socket(AF_INET6, SOCK_DGRAM, IPPROTO_UDP);

memset(&sin6, 0, sizeof(sin6));
sin6.sin6_family = AF_INET6;
sin6.sin6_len = sizeof(sin6);
sin6.sin6_port = htons(5001);
bind(s, (const struct sockaddr *)&sin6, sizeof(sin6));

len = recvfrom(s, databuf, len, 0
               (const struct sockaddr *)&sin6_from, &sin6_len);

inet_ntop(AF_INET6, &sin6_from.sin6_addr, buf, sizeof(buf));
printf("data received from: %s\n", buf);
```

The returned peer address can be given to function `inet_ntop()` and be translated into printable string for display. The `inet_ntop()` function converts an IPv6 address from its binary representation into a printable string format.

1.11 IPv4-Mapped IPv6 Address Usage

IPv4-mapped IPv6 address is designed to provide compatibility for legacy IPv4 applications that are difficult to modify to support both IPv4 and native IPv6 operations. By design, the IPv4-mapped IPv6 address does not appear on the wire. A server application can bind an IPv4-mapped IPv6 address to an IPv6 server socket to accept IPv4 connections. A server application can also bind an IPv6 socket to an unspecified address to accept both IPv4 and IPv6 connection requests. An IPv6 client application can connect to an IPv4-mapped IPv6 address over an IPv6 socket, thus allowing an IPv6 application to communicate with an IPv4 peer. When an incoming request comes from an IPv4 peer, the returned address to APIs such as `accept()` call in the IPv6 application is an IPv4-mapped IPv6 address.

Because native IPv4 listeners can coexist with IPv6 listeners that can process both IPv4 and IPv6 incoming connection, and in order to disambiguate an incoming connection among these two types of listeners, the IPv6 stack and the networking kernel must perform various search and comparison operations internally, making the implementation complex. It is difficult to handle socket options that apply only to IPv6 protocol. In addition, there is the potential of using IPv4-mapped IPv6 address to circumvent IPv6-oriented security policies. Therefore, using IPv4-mapped IPv6 address over an IPv6 socket is strongly discouraged.

The preferred practice is for an application to operate in the dual stack mode—in other words, open native IPv4 socket to communicate with an IPv4 peer while opening native IPv6 socket to communicate with native IPv6 peer.

An IPv6 socket can be marked explicitly for IPv6-only communication by setting the `IPV6_V6ONLY` socket option. Doing so will disallow any attempt to communicate over that socket using IPv4-mapped IPv6 address. The following code fragment shows how to configure this socket option:

```
int on = 1;

setsockopt (s, IPPROTO_IPV6, IPV6_V6ONLY, &on, sizeof(on));
```

1.12   Some Portability Considerations

Application developers are encouraged to use fully qualified domain name (FQDN) in programs for hosts and services when possible and to create the appropriate socket type based on the address information returned from the DNS resolution. Such a practice would aid the IPv6 transition in the infrastructure in addition to making the application portable. DNS for IPv6 is explained in detail in the reference text [LiAdv07].

Consider the example given in Figure 1-4. In this example, an inline transparent proxy is present in the network. All traffic of any kind passes through this proxy. Assume that the services offered at ipv6.google.com had been available on both IPv4 and IPv6 for a long time, but the support over the IPv4 network has recently been removed. An IPv4 Web application may have known the IPv4 address of ipv6.google.com and because this address is well established, the application hard codes this IPv4 address and works well. As soon as the services are halted for IPv4, this application fails immediately.

The job of the transparent proxy is to terminate an IPv4 connection, create another native IPv6 connection to the services at ipv6.google.com, and then splice the two connections so that content can flow through this data pipe. To accomplish what the proxy is designed to do, as a first step the proxy monitors and intercepts the DNS queries for ipv6.google.com. Once a DNS query for ipv6.google.com arrives, the proxy absorbs this query and sends back the DNS reply with its own IPv4 address as the DNS A record for ipv6.google.com. Effectively all future connections to ipv6.google.com will reach the proxy first. If an IPv4 application is written using the FQDN name for ipv6.google.com instead of hard coded IPv4 addresses, then

FIGURE 1-4

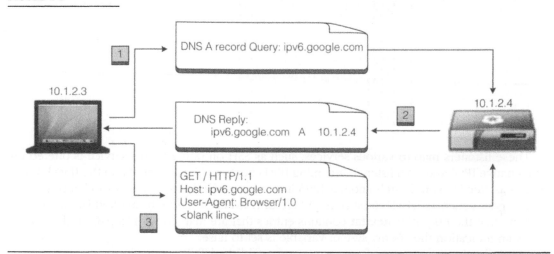

Inline transparent HTTP proxy.

this application will continue to function with the assistance of a proxy even after the service switch.

An application can be written with a good level of portability for operating in both IPv4 and IPv6 environments by taking advantage of the information offered by getaddrinfo(). getaddrinfo() returns a list of addresses for a given FQDN for a host, a service name, or a service port. The address information returned by getaddrinfo() includes the address family type and the actual address for a FQDN, and for a particular service the socket type and transport protocol type are returned. The application can then use this information to create the socket accordingly instead of hard coding to a specific type. Function getaddrinfo() is discussed in detail in Chapter 2.

1.13   Viewing and Configuration Utilities

On the FreeBSD system, the **sysctl** command can be used to set a systemwide variable that controls whether any socket created should be IPv6 only. This **sysctl** variable is net.inet6.ip6.v6only. When this variable is set to true, all sockets are created for IPv6 only operation. For example, to set this option the exact **sysctl** command is

```
sysctl net.inet6.ip.v6only = 1
```

The IPv6 connections in a running FreeBSD system can be viewed through the **netstat** and **sockstat** utilities. The following is a sample output of **netstat** command that displays the active listeners:

```
% netstat -an
Active Internet connections (including servers)
Proto Recv-Q Send-Q  Local Address         Foreign Address         (state)
tcp46      0      0   *.22                  *.*                     LISTEN
tcp4       0      0   *.22                  *.*                     LISTEN
```

```
tcp4      0    0   *.53              *.*          LISTEN
tcp46     0    0   *.53              *.*          LISTEN
tcp46     0    0   *.25              *.*          LISTEN
tcp46     0    0   *.80              *.*          LISTEN
tcp4      0    0   *.25              *.*          LISTEN
udp4      0    0   *.53              *.*
udp46     0    0   *.53              *.*
udp46     0    0   *.*               *.*
udp6      0    0   *.547             *.*
udp4      0    0   *.514             *.*
udp6      0    0   *.514             *.*
udp6      0    0   *.521             *.*
icm6      0    0   *.*               *.*
```

These listeners map to various services, such as SSH on port 22. This service is offered on both a native IPv4 and IPv6 listener. Incoming IPv4 clients will be accepted and the IPv4 listener marked as "tcp4" even though another IPv6 listener is available to accept IPv4 clients as well. Some services such as DHCPv6 on port 547 are only available on IPv6 (marked by "udp6").

Note that the output of **netstat** contains entries that are marked with "tcp46" and "udp46". This is an indication the v6only system variable is set to false.

The following is an output from **netstat** on established TCP connections:

```
% netstat -an
Active Internet connections (including servers)
Proto Recv-Q Send-Q  Local Address        Foreign Address        (state)
tcp6    0     64   2001:db8:1:200:2.22   2001:240:1:200:2.1711  ESTABLISHED
tcp6    0      0   2001:db8:1:200:2.80   2001:240:1:202:2.1055  ESTABLISHED
tcp6    0      0   2001:db9:1:200:2.80   2001:240:1:202:a.1064  ESTABLISHED
tcp6    0      0   2001:db0:1:200:2.80   2001:240:1:200:c.1058  ESTABLISHED
```

The **sockstat** command displays process information along with the active connections owned by each process. The following is a sample output:

```
% sockstat -6
USER    COMMAND    PID    FD PROTO  LOCAL ADDRESS            FOREIGN ADDRESS
root    sshd      58184   0 tcp6  2001:db8:1:200:202:b3 2001:db8:1:200:2002:b3
root    sshd      58184   1 tcp6  2001:db8:1:200:202:b3 2001:db8:1:200:2002:b3
root    sshd      58184   2 tcp6  2001:db8:1:200:202:b3 2001:db8:1:200:2002:b3
root    sshd      58184   3 tcp6  2001:db8:1:200:202:b3 2001:db8:1:200:2002:b3
root    sshd      58184   5 tcp6  2001:db8:1:200:202:b3 2001:db8:1:200:2002:b3
root    sshd      58184   6 tcp6  2001:db8:1:200:202:b3 2001:db8:1:200:2002:b3
root    sshd      58184   7 tcp6  2001:db8:1:200:202:b3 2001:db8:1:200:2002:b3
root    named      195    4 udp46 *:53                    *.*
root    named      195    5 tcp46 *:53                    *.*
root    dhcp6s     182    5 udp6  *:547                   *.*
root    dhcp6s     182    6 udp46 *:*                     *.*
root    sshd       171    3 tcp46 *:22                    *.*
root    sendmail   169    3 tcp46 *:25                    *.*
root    httpd      161    3 tcp46 *:80                    *.*
root    syslogd    126    4 udp6  *:514                   *.*
root    rtadvd     111    3 icmp6 *:*                     *.*
root    route6d    109    3 udp46 *:521                   *.*
```

1.14 Some Considerations for TCP and UDP

Although in theory transport layer protocols are independent of the network layer protocols, the TCP and UDP protocol operation has some dependencies on IPv4 and IPv6.

The TCP and UDP headers contain a checksum field for detecting packet corruption. The TCP checksum covers the entire TCP packet, and the UDP checksum covers the entire UDP packet. Both TCP and UDP checksum include a pseudo-header that contains IP header fields such as the source and destination IP addresses. The size of these addresses expands from 32 to 128 bits. UDP checksum in IPv4 is optional, but UDP checksum is mandatory in IPv6. This is mainly due to the fact that the IPv6 header does not contain a checksum field.

The increase in address size meant a reduction in maximum payload size for upper layer protocols. The minimum IPv4 header length is 20 octets, whereas the minimum IPv6 header length is 40 octets. In IPv4, options are part of the IP header, which limits the maximum size for options to 44 octets. In IPv6, the header length is fixed at 40 octets; however, options are carried in various extension headers. The size of the extension headers carried in each packet is limited only by the link MTU.

The Basic Socket API: [RFC3493]

2.1 Basic Definitions

[RFC3493] defines the in6_addr{} and the sockaddr_in6{} structures in <netinet/in.h>, though the KAME implementation actually defines them in <netinet6/in6.h> and has in.h include in6.h. This was for a historical convenience, and an application should not directly include in6.h.

    Another important data structure is sockaddr_storage{}, which has enough space to contain all possible socket address structures for various address families including AF_INET6 and AF_UNIX. Listing 2-1 shows the definition of the sockaddr_storage{} structure defined for the FreeBSD system.

Listing 2-1

```
                                                          ─ sys/socket.h
146   #define _SS_MAXSIZE    128
147   #define _SS_ALIGNSIZE  (sizeof(int64_t))
148   #define _SS_PAD1SIZE   (_SS_ALIGNSIZE - sizeof(u_char) - sizeof(sa_family_t))
149   #define _SS_PAD2SIZE   (_SS_MAXSIZE - sizeof(u_char) - sizeof(sa_family_t) - \
150                          _SS_PAD1SIZE - _SS_ALIGNSIZE)
151
152   struct sockaddr_storage {
153         u_char      ss_len;     /* address length */
154         sa_family_t ss_family;  /* address family */
155         char        __ss_pad1[_SS_PAD1SIZE];
156         int64_t     __ss_align; /* force desired structure storage alignment */
157         char        __ss_pad2[_SS_PAD2SIZE];
158   };
                                                          ─ sys/socket.h
```

As shown in Listing 2-1, the size of the structure is 128 bytes, which is defined by the _SS_MAXSIZE macro. A common usage of sockaddr_storage{} is as follows:

Listing 2-2
_____ sample code
```
    struct sockaddr_storage ss;
    struct sockaddr_in6 *sin6 = (struct sockaddr_in6 *)&ss;
```
_____ sample code

In other words, the sockaddr_storage{} structure is a placeholder structure that can be safely typecasted to any socket address structure of a specific address family type. The sockaddr_storage{} structure is particularly important for Internet Protocol version 6 (IPv6) because the sockaddr_in6{} structure is larger than the normal sockaddr{} structure on most systems. For such systems, the following bug is very likely to appear:

Listing 2-3
_____ sample code
```
    struct sockaddr sa;
    struct sockaddr_in6 *sin6 = (struct sockaddr *)&sa;

    memset(sin6, 0, sizeof(*sin6));
```
_____ sample code

In this code, the memset() operation will overwrite the memory region immediately following the space that was allocated for the sockaddr{} structure. It is therefore important to use sockaddr_storage{} as a socket address placeholder throughout the code in order to avoid introducing this kind of programming bug.

2.2   Interface Identification

[RFC3493] defines four library functions that manipulate network interface names. The function prototypes and the necessary header file for these functions are shown below.

Listing 2-4
_____ net/if.h
```
#include <net/if.h>

unsigned int  if_nametoindex(const char *ifname);

char * if_indextoname(unsigned int ifindex, char *ifname);

struct if_nameindex *if_nameindex(void);

void if_freenameindex(struct if_nameindex *ptr);
```
_____ net/if.h

if_nametoindex() returns the interface index for the given interface name ifname.

if_indextoname() performs the reverse function of if_nametoindex(), that is, it returns the interface name for the given interface index denoted as ifindex in the given buffer ifname. The return value will be the pointer to the given buffer when the function succeeds.

if_nameindex() provides an array of information on all interfaces that are available in the node. The information is stored in the if_nameindex{} structure, which is defined in <net/if.h> as follows:

Listing 2-5

——net/if.h
```
struct if_nameindex {
        u_int   if_index;       /* 1, 2, ... */
        char    *if_name;       /* null terminated name: "le0", ... */
};
```
——net/if.h

The if_nameindex() function allocates a new array, fills in the array with the if_nameindex{} structures, and returns the pointer to the newly allocated array to the caller. Each if_nameindex{} structure corresponds to a single interface. The if_index member is the interface index. The if_name member is a printable string of the interface name, such as "le0" or "fxp0."

Note that if_nameindex() does not return the length of the array. Instead, the last entry of the array is indicated by an entry with if_index being 0 and if_name being a NULL pointer.

Since the array returned from if_nameindex() is allocated within that function, a separate "destructor" function is necessary. if_freenameindex() is the corresponding destructor function. It takes a pointer to an array of if_nameindex() structures and frees all resources allocated by if_nameindex().

2.3 IPv4 Communication over AF_INET6 Socket

[RFC3493] allows an application program to perform IPv4 communication over an IPv6 (AF_INET6) socket using IPv4-mapped IPv6 addresses. For example, when an application binds IPv4-mapped IPv6 address ::ffff:192.0.2.1 to an AF_INET6 socket, those IPv4 packets with destination address of 192.0.2.1 will be delivered to that application through this AF_INET6 socket. Similarly, the application can send IPv4 packets through this socket if the destination IPv6 address is represented in the form of an IPv4-mapped IPv6 address such as ::ffff:192.0.2.9. The application data is then transmitted inside IPv4 frames and is delivered to the node whose IPv4 address is 192.0.2.9 even though the data were sent through an AF_INET6 socket.

The main purpose of this feature is to provide an easy way for application programmers to support both IPv6 and IPv4 protocols in one application and to make an IPv4-only application IPv6-aware. For example, consider the following code fragment, which is a common coding style for an IPv4 server application (error cases are omitted for brevity).

Listing 2-6

——sample code
```
int s;
unsigned short port;
struct sockaddr_in sin, sin_from;
socklen_t fromlen = sizeof(sin_from);

s = socket(AF_INET, SOCK_STREAM, IPPROTO_TCP);
```

```
     memset(&sin, 0, sizeof(sin));
     sin.sin_family = AF_INET;
     sin.sin_len = sizeof(sin);
     sin.sin_port = htons(atoi(port));
     bind(s, (struct sockaddr *)&sin, sizeof(sin));
     listen(s, 1);
     accept(s, (struct sockaddr *)&sin_from, &fromlen);
```
_____ sample code

With the usage of IPv4-mapped IPv6 addresses, we can easily convert this code to a dual-stack application as follows:

Listing 2-7
_____ sample code

```
     int s;
     unsigned short port;
     struct sockaddr_in6 sin6, sin6_from;
     socklen_t fromlen = sizeof(sin6_from);

     s = socket(AF_INET6, SOCK_STREAM, IPPROTO_TCP);
     memset(&sin, 0, sizeof(sin));
     sin6.sin6_family = AF_INET6;
     sin6.sin6_len = sizeof(sin6);
     sin6.sin6_port = htons(atoi(port));
     bind(s, (struct sockaddr *)&sin6, sizeof(sin6));
     listen(s, 1);
     accept(s, (struct sockaddr *)&sin6_from, &fromlen);
```
_____ sample code

The transport layer treats the IPv6 unspecified address `::` as a special wildcard address bound to the `AF_INET6` socket (as a result of `memset()` initialization) and accepts any IPv6 address including IPv4-mapped IPv6 addresses. This means the `AF_INET6` socket can receive both IPv4 and IPv6 packets. As such, this server application can accept both IPv4 and IPv6 connections with a single socket.

It may look useful, but some people recommend avoiding such usage of IPv4-mapped IPv6 addresses due to various technical reasons. Some of the issues are summarized as follows:

Binding ambiguity: For example, when an application binds `192.0.2.1` to an `AF_INET` socket and then binds `::ffff:192.0.2.1` to an `AF_INET6` socket, then it is impossible for the kernel to determine the right socket for delivering the incoming data. A related problem is that when an application binds `0.0.0.0` to an `AF_INET` and `::` to an `AF_INET6` socket, the kernel cannot determine the right socket for delivering IPv4 packets. There are no standards on the handling of this situation and incompatibility exists among implementations.

Socket options handling: Standardized approach on handling socket options issued over an IPv6 socket that is bound to an IPv4-mapped IPv6 address does not exist. Similarly, handling of IPv4 socket options issued on such a socket is undetermined.

Multicast ambiguity: There are no standards on the handling of multicast packets delivered over a socket bound to an IPv4-mapped IPv6 multicast address. For example, when an application specifies the outgoing interface using either the `IP_MULTICAST_IF` or the `IPV6_MULTICAST_IF` option for multicast packet transmission, the kernel behavior on the choice of the outgoing interface is undetermined.

The use of IPv4-mapped IPv6 addresses can also cause security issues [V4MAPPED]. Consider a simple subroutine shown on the next page for an example, which is supposed to be used to reject access from a set of addresses specified in the access control list, `acl` (whose definition should be straightforward and omitted in the code for brevity). The user of this function would specify `192.0.2.1` in the list if access from this IPv4 address should be denied, but it is not sufficient when the system allows IPv4 communication over an `AF_INET6` socket; `::ffff:192.0.2.1` should also be specified. The hidden dependency will increase the operational cost and may lead to insecure operation.

———————————————————————————————— sample code

```
int
access_deny(sa)
      struct sockaddr *sa;
{
      struct aclist *acl;
      struct sockaddr_in *sin, *sin_ac;
      struct sockaddr_in6 *sin6, *sin6_ac;

      for (acl = acl_top; acl != NULL; acl = acl->next) {
            if (sa->sa_family != acl->sa->sa_family)
                  continue;
            switch(sa->sa_family) {
            case AF_INET:
                  sin = (struct sockaddr_in *)sa;
                  sin_ac = (struct sockaddr_in *)acl->sa;
                  if (sin->sin_addr.s_addr == sin_ac->sin_addr.s_addr)
                        return(1);
                  break;
            case AF_INET6:
                  sin6 = (struct sockaddr_in6 *)sa;
                  sin6_ac = (struct sockaddr_in6 *)acl->sa;
                  if (IN6_ARE_ADDR_EQUAL(&sin6->sin6_addr,
                                          &sin6_ac->sin6_addr))
                        return(1);
                  break;
            }
      }

      return(0);
}
```

———————————————————————————————— sample code

In order to address these concerns, [RFC3493] defines a specific IPv6 socket option that disables the usage of IPv4-mapped IPv6 addresses. This option will be described in Section 2.5.

2.4 Address and Name Conversion Functions

One key feature of [RFC3493] is the definition of a set of functions that convert an IPv6 address to a host name.

2.4.1 `inet_pton()` and `inet_ntop()` Functions

The following two functions can convert an IPv6 address in binary form to a printable string, and vice versa.

Listing 2-8

———————————————————————————————— arpa/inet.h

```
#include <arpa/inet.h>

int inet_pton(int af, const char *src, void *dst);
const char *inet_ntop(int af, const void *src,
                      char *dst, socklen_t size);
```

———————————————————————————————— arpa/inet.h

FIGURE 2-1

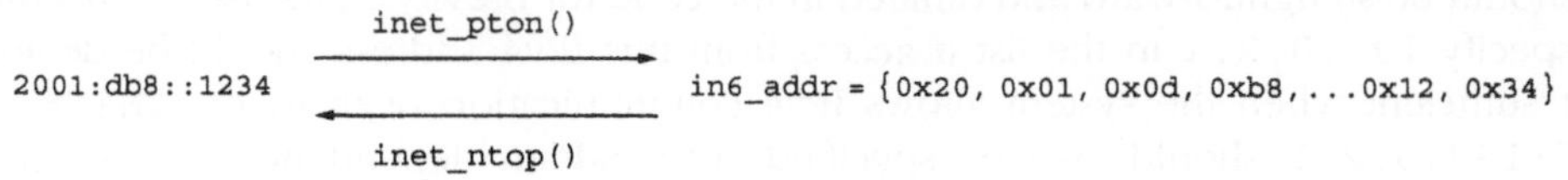

$$\text{2001:db8::1234} \xrightarrow{\text{inet\_pton()}} \xleftarrow{\text{inet\_ntop()}} \text{in6\_addr} = \{0\text{x}20, 0\text{x}01, 0\text{x}0\text{d}, 0\text{x}b8, \dots 0\text{x}12, 0\text{x}34\}$$

Address conversion by inet_pton() and inet_ntop().

inet_pton() takes an address in the printable string format (src) and converts it into a binary format (dst). inet_ntop() performs the reverse transformation of inet_pton().

As implied by the first argument af, rather than just supporting IPv6, these functions are independent of any address family. In theory, these functions can handle any address family type while all implementations known to the authors only support the AF_INET and the AF_INET6 address families.

inet_pton() returns 1 on success; it returns 0 if the given address is not parseable; it returns −1 if other system errors occur, in which case an appropriate error code will be set in errno.

inet_ntop() returns a pointer to variable dst on success; it returns NULL on failure, in which case an appropriate error code will be set in errno.

Figure 2-1 illustrates the transformations performed by inet_pton() and inet_ntop() between a printable string and the internal representation of an IPv6 address 2001:db8::1234 in the in6_addr{} structure.

Another important characteristic of these functions is that they can be thread-safe. These functions can run concurrently on different threads because the caller is responsible for allocating space to store the result. Recall that some of the IPv4-specific library functions such as inet_ntoa() cannot be easily thread-safe since these do not take a separate buffer for the output.

2.4.2 getaddrinfo() Function

[RFC3493] provides the getaddrinfo() function to convert a fully qualified domain name (FQDN) to IP addresses, described below.

Listing 2-9
netdb.h

```
#include <sys/socket.h>
#include <netdb.h>

int getaddrinfo(const char *nodename, const char *servname,
            const struct addrinfo *hints, struct addrinfo **res);
void freeaddrinfo(struct addrinfo *ai);
```
netdb.h

getaddrinfo() takes a service name like "http" or a numeric port number like "80" as well as an FQDN and returns a list of addresses along with the corresponding port number. nodename and servname are strings containing the FQDN and the service name, respectively. hints points to a structure specific to getaddrinfo(), the addrinfo{}

structure, which specifies additional information that guides the conversion process. The definition of the `addrinfo{}` structure is as follows:

Listing 2-10

_____netdb.h
```
struct addrinfo {
        int     ai_flags;       /* AI_PASSIVE, AI_CANONNAME, AI_NUMERICHOST */
        int     ai_family;      /* PF_xxx */
        int     ai_socktype;    /* SOCK_xxx */
        int     ai_protocol;    /* 0 or IPPROTO_xxx for IPv4 and IPv6 */
        size_t  ai_addrlen;     /* length of ai_addr */
        char    *ai_canonname;  /* canonical name for hostname */
        struct  sockaddr *ai_addr;      /* binary address */
        struct  addrinfo *ai_next;      /* next structure in linked list */
};
```
_____netdb.h

`ai_flags` specifies particular behavior of `getaddrinfo()`, which can be either zero (if nothing special is required) or the bitwise inclusive OR of some of the flags shown in Table 2-1.

`ai_family` specifies the address family for nodename. This is `AF_UNSPEC` if the caller does not care about the family, but can also be a specific family value (e.g. `AF_INET` or `AF_INET6` when only addresses of a particular family are required).

`ai_socktype` and `ai_protocol` specify the socket type and the transport protocol, and can be used as the second and third arguments to the `socket()` system call, respectively.

TABLE 2-1

Flag	Description
AI_PASSIVE	The caller requires addresses that are suitable for accepting incoming connections. When this flag is specified, nodename is usually NULL, and the address field of the ai_addr member is filled with the "any" address (e.g. INADDR_ANY for IPv4).
AI_CANONNAME	The caller requires a "canonical" name to be returned in the ai_canonname member of the result.
AI_NUMERICHOST	The caller specifies that the nodename should be interpreted as a numeric IP address, not a host name. In particular, this flag suppresses domain name server (DNS) name lookups.
AI_NUMERICSERV	The caller specifies that the servname should be interpreted as a numeric port number, not a service name.
AI_V4MAPPED	If no IPv6 addresses are matched, IPv4-mapped IPv6 addresses for IPv4 addresses that match nodename shall be returned. This flag is applicable only when ai_family is AF_INET6 in the hints structure.
AI_ALL	When used with the AI_V4MAPPED flag, this flag specifies that IPv4 addresses be returned in the form of IPv4-mapped IPv6 addresses with other regular IPv6 addresses.
AI_ADDRCONFIG	When specified, only addresses whose family is supported by the system will be returned.

`ai_addrlen` is the length of the `ai_addr` member, which is the socket address structure that corresponds to nodename. The value of `ai_addrlen` should be equal to the value of the `sa_len` member of `ai_addr` on systems that support the length member in the socket address structure, and thus is not so useful. However, it is important to provide the member in order to ensure portability with systems that do not have the length member in the socket address structure (e.g. Linux or Solaris, or systems derived from the 4.3 BSD socket application programming interface [API] in general).

`ai_canonname` is used to store the "canonical" name of nodename. For example, if "www" is given to getaddrinfo() as nodename in the "kame.net" domain (and the `AI_CANONNAME` is specified), then `ai_canonname` will store a string "www.kame.net". `ai_addr` stores one conversion result for nodename and servname. An address-family-dependent "address" field of the `ai_addr` member stores a binary address for nodename.

Similarly, an address-family-dependent "port" field of the `ai_addr` member stores the port number for servname. For the `AF_INET6` family, these are the `sin6_addr` and `sin6_port` members, respectively.

The result of getaddrinfo() is a list of multiple `addrinfo{}` structures because a single FQDN can often be resolved to multiple addresses of multiple address families. `ai_next` points to the next entry of such a list.

On success, the getaddrinfo() function returns 0, providing a list of addresses in the `res` argument. The list is allocated within the function and the pointer to the list is stored in the `res` argument.

The freeaddrinfo() function is a freeing function for the dynamically allocated `addrinfo{}` structure list. The function takes a pointer to the `addrinfo{}` structure, which is usually the pointer stored in the `res` argument to getaddrinfo(), and frees all of the dynamically allocated resources.

On failure, getaddrinfo() returns a nonzero error code, which can be converted to a printable string using the gai_strerror() function:

Listing 2-11

——— netdb.h

```
const char *gai_strerror(int ecode);
```

——— netdb.h

gai_strerror() is similar to the standard strerror() function, but only handles specific error codes returned from the getaddrinfo() function.

The following is a common example of code fragment that actively opens an HTTP connection to a host "www.kame.net."

Listing 2-12

——— sample code

```
1          struct addrinfo hints, *res, *res0;
2          int error;
3          int s;
4
5          memset(&hints, 0, sizeof(hints));
6          hints.ai_family = AF_UNSPEC;
7          hints.ai_socktype = SOCK_STREAM;
8          error = getaddrinfo("www.kame.net", "http", &hints, &res0);
9          if (error) {
10                 fprintf(stderr, "getaddrinfo failed: %s\n",
11                     gai_strerror(error));
```

```
12                          exit(1);
13                  }
14          s = -1;
15          for (res = res0; res; res = res->ai_next) {
16                  s = socket(res->ai_family, res->ai_socktype,
17                      res->ai_protocol);
18                  if (s < 0)
19                          continue;
20
21                  if (connect(s, res->ai_addr, res->ai_addrlen) < 0) {
22                          close(s);
23                          s = -1;
24                          continue;
25                  }
26
27                  break;   /* okay we got one */
28          }
29          if (s < 0) {
30                  fprintf(stderr, "no addresses are reachable\n");
31                  exit(1);
32          }
33
34          freeaddrinfo(res0);
```
_____ sample code

The above example illustrates the usage of getaddrinfo() and how the results from getaddrinfo() are applied in subsequent calls to socket() and to connect().

The following is an example that passively opens listening sockets to accept incoming HTTP connections.

Listing 2-13
_____ sample code

```
1           struct addrinfo hints, *res, *res0;
2           int error;
3           int s[MAXSOCK];
4           int nsock;
5           const char *cause = NULL;
6
7           memset(&hints, 0, sizeof(hints));
8           hints.ai_family = AF_UNSPEC;
9           hints.ai_socktype = SOCK_STREAM;
10          hints.ai_flags = AI_PASSIVE;
11          error = getaddrinfo(NULL, "http", &hints, &res0);
12          if (error) {
13                  fprintf(stderr, "getaddrinfo failed: %s\n",
14                      gai_strerror(error));
15                  exit(1);
16          }
17          nsock = 0;
18          for (res = res0; res && nsock < MAXSOCK; res = res->ai_next) {
19                  s[nsock] = socket(res->ai_family, res->ai_socktype,
20                      res->ai_protocol);
21                  if (s[nsock] < 0)
22                          continue;
23
24  #ifdef IPV6_V6ONLY
25                  if (res->ai_family == AF_INET6) {
26                          int on = 1;
27
28                          if (setsockopt(s[nsock], IPPROTO_IPV6, IPV6_V6ONLY,
29                              &on, sizeof(on))) {
30                                  close(s[nsock]);
31                                  continue;
32                          }
33                  }
34  #endif
```

```
35
36                    if (bind(s[nsock], res->ai_addr, res->ai_addrlen) < 0) {
37                            close(s[nsock]);
38                            continue;
39                    }
40
41                    if (listen(s[nsock], SOMAXCONN) < 0) {
42                            close(s[nsock]);
43                            continue;
44                    }
45
46                    nsock++;
47            }
48        if (nsock == 0) {
49                fprintf(stderr, "no listening socket is available\n");
50                exit(1);
51        }
52        freeaddrinfo(res0);
```
                                                                            ___ sample code

Again, the above example illustrates the usage of getaddrinfo() and how the results from getaddrinfo() are applied in subsequent calls to the socket APIs.

Note that this code explicitly enables the IPV6_V6ONLY option for each socket (lines 24–34). We describe this option in Section 2.5.

2.4.3 getnameinfo() Function

The getnameinfo() function is a reverse function of getaddrinfo(), which takes a socket address structure and converts it to printable host and service names. The function prototype is shown below.

Listing 2-14
                                                                            ___ netdb.h
```
int getnameinfo(const struct sockaddr *sa, socklen_t salen,
                char *node, socklen_t nodelen,
                char *service, socklen_t servicelen, int flags);
```
                                                                            ___ netdb.h

sa points to the socket address structure to be converted and salen specifies the length of the structure. sa and salen are the main input to the getnameinfo() function. node provides the storage to hold the resulting host name. nodelen specifies the size of the buffer referenced by node. Similarly, service is a buffer for storing the resulting service name. servicelen is the length of the buffer.

flags specifies some optional behavior for getnameinfo(). Available flags defined in [RFC3493] are shown in Table 2-2.

Note: The KAME implementation previously supported a nonstandard flag, NI_WITHSCOPEID, but it was then made obsolete. Applications should not use this flag.

getnameinfo() returns 0 on success; node and service will be filled in with the resolved host name and service name, respectively. It is possible that either node or service may be NULL, in which case only the non-NULL buffer will be filled. The function returns a nonzero error code on failure, which can be converted to a printable string by the gai_strerror() function.

TABLE 2-2

Flag	Description
NI_NOFQDN	When set, only the node name portion of the FQDN shall be returned for local hosts; though the semantics is not very clear, the expected behavior is to return the first label of an FQDN. For example, if a host name "www.kame.net" is returned by the DNS, only "www" will be returned by getnameinfo().
NI_NUMERICHOST	Specifies that a numeric address string instead of an FQDN should be returned
NI_NAMEREQD	Specifies that an FQDN-like host name is required; if getnameinfo() fails to get a name, it will return an error.
NI_NUMERICSERV	Specifies that a numeric port string instead of a service name should be returned
NI_DGRAM	Specifies that the intended service is a datagram service (SOCK_DGRAM); by default, getnameinfo() assumes a stream service (SOCK_STREAM).

The caller is responsible for memory allocation to store the results. Some systems provide the following definitions in <netdb.h> as reasonable default sizes for these buffers.

```
#define NI_MAXHOST   1025
#define NI_MAXSERV     32
```

Note: These constants were officially defined in [RFC2553], but was then removed in [RFC3493]. New portable applications should not assume these constants are always available.

In other words, the default buffer size in bytes for node is NI_MAXHOST and the default buffer size for service is NI_MAXSERV.

The following sample code illustrates the use of getnameinfo() to print out the source address of an incoming packet.

Listing 2-15

```
                                                                    sample code
        struct sockaddr_storage from0;
        struct sockaddr *from;
        socklen_t fromlen;
        char *packet;
        size_t packetlen;
        char hbuf[NI_MAXHOST], sbuf[NI_MAXSERV];
        int error, s;

        from = (struct sockaddr *)&from0;
        fromlen = sizeof(from0);
        recvfrom(s, packet, packetlen, from, &fromlen);
        error = getnameinfo(from, fromlen, hbuf, sizeof(hbuf), sbuf,
            sizeof(sbuf), 0);
        if (error != 0) {
                fprintf(stderr, "getnameinfo failed: %s\n",
                    gai_strerror(error));
        } else
                printf("host=%s, serv=%s\n", hbuf, sbuf);
                                                                    sample code
```

TABLE 2-3

Code	Description
EAI_AGAIN	The name could not be resolved at this time. Future attempts may succeed.
EAI_BADFLAGS	The flags had an invalid value.
EAI_FAIL	A nonrecoverable error occurred.
EAI_FAMILY	The address family was not recognized or the address length was invalid for the specified family.
EAI_MEMORY	There was a memory allocation failure.
EAI_NONAME	The name does not resolve for the supplied parameters. NI_NAMEREQD is set and the host's name cannot be located, or both nodename and servname were null.
EAI_OVERFLOW	An argument buffer overflowed (getnameinfo() only).
EAI_SERVICE	The service passed was not recognized for the specified socket type (getaddrinfo() only).
EAI_SOCKTYPE	The intended socket type was not recognized (getaddrinfo() only).
EAI_SYSTEM	A system error occurred. The error code can be found in errno.

Notice that this code uses a sockaddr_storage{} structure, from0, so that the recvfrom() call can store an address of any address families. Using a sockaddr{} structure is not enough because the size of the structure is usually smaller than that of the sockaddr_in6{} structure.

The getnameinfo() function returns a nonzero error code on failure, which can also be converted to a printable string by gai_strerror(). Most of the error codes are shared with getaddrinfo(). Table 2-3 summarizes the error codes defined in [RFC3493].

An implementation may define specific error codes. An application should use the codes in an opaque manner through the gai_strerror() function.

2.4.4   Important Features of getaddrinfo() and getnameinfo()

Both getaddrinfo() and getnameinfo() are designed as address-family-independent functions. In addition, these functions either receive or return the generic socket address structure and never use structures that are specific to a particular family (e.g. sockaddr_in6{} or in6_addr{}). Consequently, applications using these functions are not concerned about whether the kernel supports a particular address family. Therefore, these functions enable portable application design and allow application migration to support future network protocols without the need for source code modification.

Another important property of getaddrinfo() and getnameinfo() is that these functions are thread-safe, that is, these functions can be executed by multiple threads simultaneously. In comparison, most traditional name and address conversion functions were originally not thread-safe. Some operating systems provided special thread-safe versions of such traditional conversion functions. In general, however, a portable application cannot assume such special properties exist in the underlying OSes.

Even though by itself each of these functions is implemented in a thread-safe manner, many of the underlying libraries that each of these functions depends on are still not thread-safe. As such, the overall execution of these functions is often not thread-safe either. In fact, we will show why these functions provided by KAME lack the thread-safe feature in Chapter 6 (see Sections 6.3 and 6.7).

2.5   Basic Socket Options

RFC3493 defines several new socket options specific to the `AF_INET6` sockets. All of these options are specified at the `IPPROTO_IPV6` level when the `getsockopt()` and `setsockopt()` system calls are called and are available by including the `<netinet/in.h>` header file.

2.5.1   Unicast Option

The `IPV6_UNICAST_HOPS` option specifies the hop limit value of outgoing packets sent from the socket. If a special value of -1 is specified, the system default value will be used.

2.5.2   `IPV6_V6ONLY` Option and Code Portability

The `IPV6_V6ONLY` option specifies that when set to nonzero the socket should not send or receive IPv4 packets using IPv4-mapped IPv6 addresses (recall the discussion in Section 2.3). This option defaults to zero.

The following sample code illustrates the usage of the `IPV6_V6ONLY` option. (Note: error cases are ignored for brevity.)

Listing 2-16
—— sample code

```
#include <sys/types.h>
#include <sys/socket.h>

#include <netinet/in.h>

#include <stdio.h>
#include <netdb.h>

int
main()
{
        struct sockaddr_in6 sin6, sin6_accept;
        socklen_t sin6_len;
        int s0, s;
        int on;
        char hbuf[NI_MAXHOST];

        memset(&sin6, 0, sizeof(sin6));
        sin6.sin6_family = AF_INET6;
        sin6.sin6_len = sizeof(sin6);
        sin6.sin6_port = htons(5001);

        s0 = socket(AF_INET6, SOCK_STREAM, IPPROTO_TCP);
        on = 1;
        setsockopt(s0, SOL_SOCKET, SO_REUSEADDR, &on, sizeof(on));

#ifdef USE_IPV6_V6ONLY
```

```
        on = 1;
        setsockopt(s0, IPPROTO_IPV6, IPV6_V6ONLY, &on, sizeof(on));
#endif

        bind(s0, (const struct sockaddr *)&sin6, sizeof(sin6));
        listen(s0, 1);
        while (1) {
                sin6_len = sizeof(sin6_accept);
                s = accept(s0, (struct sockaddr *)&sin6_accept, &sin6_len);
                getnameinfo((struct sockaddr *)&sin6_accept, sin6_len,
                    hbuf, sizeof(hbuf), NULL, 0, NI_NUMERICHOST);
                printf("accept a connection from %s\n", hbuf);

                close(s);
        }

        exit(0);
}
```
── sample code

Suppose that an executable named **accept** is created from the above code and is running on a host system. If the following **telnet** commands are executed on the same host:

```
% telnet ::1 5001
% telnet 127.0.0.1 5001
```

The following output is produced if the code was built without USE_IPV6_V6ONLY and the IPv4-mapped address is supported by the system.

```
accept a connection from ::1
accept a connection from ::ffff:127.0.0.1
```

On the other hand, if the code was built with USE_IPV6_V6ONLY, the following output is produced:

```
accept a connection from ::1
```

Executing the second **telnet** command produces the following result:

```
% telnet 127.0.0.1 5001
Trying 127.0.0.1...
telnet: connect to address 127.0.0.1: Connection refused
```

As seen from this example, an AF_INET6 socket with the IPV6_V6ONLY socket option being true will only listen to and accept IPv6 connection requests.

The IPV6_V6ONLY socket option is new in [RFC3493] and some systems may not support this option. Some other systems use a different default value than the one defined in the specification. It is thus important to understand this option when attempting to write portable applications.

According to [RFC3493], an IPv6-enabled kernel should be able to send or receive IPv4 packets on an AF_INET6 socket using the IPv4-mapped IPv6 addresses as explained in Section 2.3. Real-world implementations, however, do not necessarily conform to this requirement. For example, due to concerns about the mechanism itself, some OSes such as OpenBSD refuse to implement this feature. In such a system, the only way to handle both IPv4 and IPv6 communications in a single application is to create two separate sockets (i.e. one of AF_INET for IPv4 and the other of AF_INET6 for IPv6). On the other hand, some OSes do not allow the creation of both AF_INET and AF_INET6 sockets that are bound to the wildcard address and on the same port.

The most likely approach for portability is thus to use two separate sockets and turn the IPV6_V6ONLY option on for the AF_INET6 socket. In this case, under the common interpretation of this option (even though not officially documented), both the AF_INET and the AF_INET6 sockets can coexist and be bound on the same port.

If the "default" behavior described in [RFC3493] is desired for some reason, it is advisable to set this option with the value of 0 explicitly. Even though this is the default, some systems such as NetBSD and recent versions of FreeBSD deliberately adopt a different system default based on their implementation policy.

In any case, the authors recommend the approach of two separate sockets with the IPV6_V6ONLY option set to true for the AF_INET6 socket. Now that most of the major OSes support this option, this approach will provide the most portable, most deterministic, and safest behavior.

2.5.3 Multicast Socket Options

[RFC3493] defines a set of socket options for multicast-related communication. These IPv6 multicast socket options are similar to those defined in IPv4 with one significant difference: an interface is specified by an interface index in the IPv6 multicast socket options while an interface is specified by an IPv4 address in the IPv4 options. There are two reasons for the difference. First, IPv6 explicitly allows the assignment of multiple IPv6 addresses on a single interface and thus there usually exists a one-to-many mapping between the interface and interface addresses. If we choose a particular address as the identifier of an interface, there will be an issue of ensuring consistency among multiple choices. Second, and more importantly, IPv6 link-local addresses may not be unique even within a single node, which implies that if an interface has only a link-local address, then we may not be able to uniquely identify that interface by the address. Thus, using interface index is a more appropriate identifier of an interface in the IPv6 API. This is one of the reasons that library functions such as if_nametoindex() are defined in the API specification.

The IPV6_JOIN_GROUP and IPV6_LEAVE_GROUP socket options are defined for joining and leaving a multicast group on a specified interface. Both options take the ipv6_mreq{} structure as the option argument, which is defined below.

Listing 2-17

netinet/in.h

```
struct ipv6_mreq {
        struct in6_addr    ipv6mr_multiaddr;
        unsigned int       ipv6mr_interface;
};
```

netinet/in.h

The ipv6mr_multiaddr field specifies the multicast group to join or to leave. The ipv6mr_interface field specifies the interface by its index in the host byte order.

The following code fragment illustrates a common example of joining an IPv6 multicast group. (Note: error cases are ignored for brevity.) The code opens an IPv6 UDP socket, joins an IPv6 multicast group ff02::2 on the interface "fxp0," and then waits for multicast packets sent to that group on User Datagram Protocol (UDP) port 5001.

Listing 2-18

_____ sample code

```
#include <sys/types.h>
#include <sys/socket.h>
#include <netinet/in.h>

...

        struct sockaddr_in6 sin6;
        int s;
        struct ipv6_mreq mreq;

        s = socket(AF_INET6, SOCK_DGRAM, IPPROTO_UDP);

        memset(&mreq, 0, sizeof(mreq));
        inet_pton(AF_INET6, "ff02::2", &mreq.ipv6mr_multiaddr);
        mreq.ipv6mr_interface = if_nametoindex("fxp0");
        setsockopt(s, IPPROTO_IPV6, IPV6_JOIN_GROUP, &mreq, sizeof(mreq));

        memset(&sin6, 0, sizeof(sin6));
        sin6.sin6_family = AF_INET6;
        sin6.sin6_len = sizeof(sin6);
        sin6.sin6_port = htons(5001);
        bind(s, (const struct sockaddr *)&sin6, sizeof(sin6));
```
_____ sample code

The following three socket options are also available:

The `IPV6_MULTICAST_HOPS` option specifies the hop limit value for the outgoing multicast packets on a given socket. If a special value of −1 is specified, the system default value will be used. This option is similar to the IPv4 `IP_MULTICAST_TTL` socket option but takes an integer, not a character like the IPv4 option, for specifying the hop limit. This option defaults to 1 (the minimum hop limit).

The `IPV6_MULTICAST_IF` option specifies the outgoing interface for multicast packets sent on a given socket. This option is similar to the IPv4 `IP_MULTICAST_IF` socket option but takes an interface identifier for identifying the interface.

The `IPV6_MULTICAST_LOOP` option specifies whether outgoing multicast packets on a given socket should be looped back to the sending node if there are listeners on that multicast group. When set to 0, multicast packets should not be looped back; when set to 1, multicast packets should be looped back. This option is similar to the IPv4 `IP_MULTICAST_LOOP` socket option but takes an integer, not a character like the IPv4 option, as the option value. This option defaults to 1.

Note: [RFC3678] defines further extensions to the socket API in order to support source specific multicast. These extensions are beyond the scope of this book.

2.5.4   Address Testing Macros

[RFC3493] provides convenient macros that check a given IPv6 address against a particular type of address. Table 2-4 lists the macros defined by [RFC3493]. All of these macros take a pointer to an `in6_addr{}` structure and return true (nonzero) or false (0) based on the test result.

TABLE 2-4

Macro	Description
IN6_IS_ADDR_LINKLOCAL	Checks if the given address is a unicast link-local address
IN6_IS_ADDR_SITELOCAL	Checks if the given address is a unicast site-local address (see Note 1)
IN6_IS_ADDR_MULTICAST	Checks if the given address is a multicast address
IN6_IS_ADDR_MC_NODELOCAL	Checks if the given address is an interface-local multicast address (see Note 2)
IN6_IS_ADDR_MC_LINKLOCAL	Checks if the given address is a link-local multicast address
IN6_IS_ADDR_MC_SITELOCAL	Checks if the given address is a site-local multicast address
IN6_IS_ADDR_MC_ORGLOCAL	Checks if the given address is an organization-local multicast address
IN6_IS_ADDR_MC_GLOBAL	Checks if the given address is a global multicast address

Note 1: The IETF has deprecated the syntax and usage of site-local unicast addresses [RFC3879] and is now defining a new address space for local communication [RFC4193]. However, the corresponding macro for the new space is not defined.
Note 2: According to the latest address architecture documents since [RFC3513], multicast addresses with the "scope" field being 1 are called "interface-local" multicast addresses. The API macro is based on an old architecture document [RFC2373] that defined this class of addresses as "node-local" multicast addresses.

The Advanced Socket
API: [RFC3542]

3.1 Advanced Definitions

[RFC3542] defines a large set of new definitions that includes Internet Protocol version 6 (IPv6) and the extension headers. We will show a summary of the major ones rather than showing the complete definitions. This is partly because many of the definitions are also used in the kernel as part of the IPv6 protocol stack implementation and in fact were explained in the appropriate sections in this book. In addition, the majority of applications do not care about the details because most applications do not use such advanced definitions at all. Even for those applications that need information defined in [RFC3542], the information can be accessed via higher layer functions as explained in Section 3.5.

The first set of the advanced definitions includes data structure for IPv6 and the extension headers. These definitions are available by including <netinet/ip6.h> and are summarized in Table 3-1.

The next set of definitions includes structure definitions for ICMPv6, Neighbor Discovery (ND) protocol, and Multicast Listener Discovery (MLD) protocol headers. These definitions are available by including <netinet/icmp6.h> and are summarized in Table 3-2.

[RFC3542] also defines common protocol values. Table 3-3 lists IPv6 specific protocol values defined in the RFC that can appear in the "next header" field of an IPv6 or an extension header. These definitions are available by including <netinet/in.h>.

Table 3-4 lists the ICMPv6 message type definitions that are defined in [RFC3542] and provided by including <netinet/icmp6.h>.

TABLE 3-1

Structure name	Description
ip6_hdr{}	IPv6 header
ip6_hbh{}	Hop-by-Hop Options header
ip6_dest{}	Destination Options header
ip6_rthdr{}	Routing header (in the general form)
ip6_rthdr0{}	Type-0 Routing header
ip6_frag{}	Fragment header

TABLE 3-2

Structure name	Description
icmp6_hdr{}	ICMPv6 header
nd_router_solicit{}	Neighbor Solicitation message header
nd_router_advert{}	Neighbor Advertisement message header
nd_neighbor_solicit{}	Router Solicitation message header
nd_neighbor_advert{}	Router Advertisement message header
nd_redirect{}	Redirect message header
nd_opt_hdr{}	General header of Neighbor Discovery options
nd_opt_prefix_info{}	Neighbor Discovery prefix information option
nd_opt_rd_hdr{}	Neighbor Discovery redirected header option
nd_opt_mtu{}	Neighbor Discovery MTU option
mld_hdr{}	Multicast Listener Discovery message header
icmp6_router_renum{}	Router Renumbering message header (see Note below)
rr_pco_match{}	Router Renumbering Match-Prefix part
rr_pco_use{}	Router Renumbering Use-Prefix part
rr_result{}	Router Renumbering Result message

Note: The Router Renumbering protocol is defined in [RFC2894]. This book does not cover this protocol; in fact, it is not really deployed.

3.2   IPv6 Raw Sockets

The raw socket is used in general as a mechanism to transmit and to receive data over transport protocols other than the protocols implemented in the kernel by default (e.g. Transmission Control Protocol [TCP], User Datagram Protocol [UDP], or Stream Control Transmission Protocol [SCTP] when available). Major applications of raw sockets are routing daemons that use transport protocols other than TCP or UDP, including OSPF (unicast) and PIM (multicast) routing daemons.

TABLE 3-3

Name	Value	Description
IPPROTO_HOPOPTS	0	IPv6 Hop-by-Hop Options
IPPROTO_IPV6	41	IPv6 header
IPPROTO_ROUTING	43	IPv6 Routing header
IPPROTO_FRAGMENT	44	IPv6 Fragment header
IPPROTO_ESP	50	Encapsulating security payload
IPPROTO_AH	51	Authentication header
IPPROTO_ICMPV6	58	ICMPv6
IPPROTO_NONE	59	IPv6 No Next header
IPPROTO_DSTOPTS	60	IPv6 Destination Options header

TABLE 3-4

Message type	Value	Description
ICMP6_DST_UNREACH	1	ICMPv6 destination unreachable error
ICMP6_PACKET_TOO_BIG	2	ICMPv6 packet too big error
ICMP6_TIME_EXCEEDED	3	ICMPv6 time exceeded error
ICMP6_PARAM_PROB	4	ICMPv6 parameter problem error
ICMP6_ECHO_REQUEST	128	ICMPv6 echo request
ICMP6_ECHO_REPLY	129	ICMPv6 echo reply
ND_ROUTER_SOLICIT	133	Router Solicitation
ND_ROUTER_ADVERT	134	Router Advertisement
ND_NEIGHBOR_SOLICIT	135	Neighbor Solicitation
ND_NEIGHBOR_ADVERT	136	Neighbor Advertisement
ND_REDIRECT	137	Redirect
MLD_LISTENER_QUERY	130	Multicast Listener Query
MLD_LISTENER_REPORT	131	Multicast Listener Report (version 1)
MLD_LISTENER_REDUCTION	132	Multicast Listener Done (version 1) (see Note below)
ICMP6_ROUTER_RENUMBERING	138	Router Renumbering

Note: This macro name does not match the official type name defined in [RFC2710]. The mismatch is an error in the API specification and [RFC3542] should have corrected it before publication. Unfortunately, the document was published with the confusing name.

ICMPv6 packets are also handled via a raw socket because ICMPv6 contains various functions that can be implemented in the user space, including some parts of ND and MLD.

The `type` argument to the `socket()` system call is `SOCK_RAW` when creating an IPv6 raw socket. The `protocol` argument is set to the corresponding transport protocol. For example, the following code fragment illustrates how to open an `AF_INET6` socket for ICMPv6 transport.

```
int s;
s = socket(AF_INET6, SOCK_RAW, IPPROTO_ICMPV6);
```

Unlike IPv4 raw sockets, all data sent via IPv6 raw sockets must be in the network byte order and all data received via raw sockets will be in the network byte order.

Another major difference between IPv6 and IPv4 raw sockets is that complete packets, such as IPv6 packets with extension headers, cannot be sent or received on an IPv6 raw socket. In other words, IPv6 socket API does not include an option that is equivalent to the IPv4 `IP_HDRINCL` socket option.

For outgoing packets, the majority of the header fields in both the IPv6 header and the extension headers can be set either through the *ancillary data* specified in the `sendmsg()` system call or by corresponding socket options.

For incoming packets, applications can retrieve the majority of the header fields from the IPv6 header and the extension headers through the ancillary data returned from the `recvmsg()` system call provided that the appropriate socket options have been set before issuing the `recvmsg()` system call. The details of such ancillary data and socket options will be described in Sections 7.3.3 through 7.3.5.

3.2.1 IPv6 Raw Socket Options

[RFC3542] defines two new socket options specific to IPv6 raw sockets.

The `IPV6_CHECKSUM` option specifies the offset to the checksum field, if any, in the transport layer header, assuming the use of the 16-bit one's complement of the one's complement sum as the checksum algorithm, and that the checksum field is aligned on a 16-bit boundary. The kernel will automatically add the checksum value for outgoing packets and verify the checksum value for incoming packets on the socket if the offset is given by this option. This is a useful functionality because the IPv6 checksum computation includes a pseudo IPv6 header containing the source and destination addresses that may be unknown to an application.

The `ICMP6_FILTER` option allows an application to set an inbound packet filter on an ICMPv6 socket (i.e. an `AF_INET6` raw socket with the `IPPROTO_ICMPV6` protocol). The filter is set based on the ICMPv6 message types. The `ICMP6_FILTER` option enables an application to avoid receiving uninterested ICMPv6 packets and reduces the overhead incurred by unnecessary packet processing; by default, the kernel will pass all incoming ICMPv6 messages to an ICMPv6 socket.

This option takes an `icmp6_filter{}` structure as the argument, which contains the filter rules configured with a set of macro functions. The structure and the macro functions are available by including `<netinet/icmp6.h>`.

The following code fragment is extracted from the **rtadvd** implementation, which is a network daemon that sends Router Advertisement messages. The daemon receives Router Solicitations from hosts as well as Router Advertisements from other routers, which are the only two types of ICMPv6 messages that the daemon wants to see. Therefore, the code first configures the filter with `ICMP6_FILTER_SETBLOCKALL()` so that the socket would block any ICMPv6 messages. It then specifies Router Solicitation messages and Router Advertisement messages to be passed through by calling the `ICMP6_FILTER_SETPASS()` function.

Listing 3-1

———————————————————————————————————— rtadvd/rtadvd.c

```
        struct icmp6_filter filt;
        int sock;
...

        ICMP6_FILTER_SETBLOCKALL(&filt);
        ICMP6_FILTER_SETPASS(ND_ROUTER_SOLICIT, &filt);
        ICMP6_FILTER_SETPASS(ND_ROUTER_ADVERT, &filt);
...
        if (setsockopt(sock, IPPROTO_ICMPV6, ICMP6_FILTER, &filt,
                    sizeof(filt)) < 0) {
            syslog(LOG_ERR, "<%s> IICMP6_FILTER: %s",
                    __func__, strerror(errno));
            exit(1);
        }
```

———————————————————————————————————— rtadvd/rtadvd.c

3.3 Introduction to Ancillary Data

As mentioned in the previous section, the IPv6 advanced socket application programming interface (API) employs a general framework called "ancillary data" to exchange "ancillary" information between the kernel and the application. The ancillary data are stored in the `msghdr{}` structure and is passed between the kernel and the application through the `recvmsg()` and `sendmsg()` system calls. The following is the definition of the `msghdr{}` structure:

Listing 3-2

———————————————————————————————————— sys/socket.h

```
struct msghdr {
        void        *msg_name;      /* ptr to socket address structure */
        socklen_t   msg_namelen;    /* size of socket address structure */
        struct iovec *msg_iov;      /* scatter/gather array */
        int         msg_iovlen;     /* # elements in msg_iov */
        void        *msg_control;   /* ancillary data */
        socklen_t   msg_controllen; /* ancillary data buffer length */
        int         msg_flags;      /* flags on received message */
};
```

———————————————————————————————————— sys/socket.h

As shown in the comment lines, the `msg_control` member points to a buffer containing the ancillary data, and the `msg_controllen` member specifies the length of the buffer.

The actual ancillary data are a sequence of objects, each of which begins with a header structure called `cmsghdr{}` followed by data specific to the header type. The definition of the `cmsghdr{}` structure is as follows:

Listing 3-3

———————————————————————————————————— sys/socket.h

```
struct cmsghdr {
        socklen_t   cmsg_len;    /* #bytes, including this header */
        int         cmsg_level;  /* originating protocol */
        int         cmsg_type;   /* protocol-specific type */
                /* followed by unsigned char cmsg_data[]; */
};
```

———————————————————————————————————— sys/socket.h

Padding may be necessary between the header and the data, and between the data and the next header to ensure natural pointer alignment. Whether padding is necessary and the length of the padding, when it is necessary, depend on the machine architecture. In this book, we assume the 32-bit architecture where pointers should be aligned at a 32-bit boundary.

The macros CMSG_SPACE() and CMSG_LEN() are defined to help determine the padding needed for an ancillary data object as follows:

Listing 3-4
―― sys/socket.h

```
socklen_t CMSG_SPACE(socklen_t length);
socklen_t CMSG_LEN(socklen_t length);
```
―― sys/socket.h

Given the length of an ancillary data object, CMSG_SPACE() returns an upper bound on the space required by the object and its cmsghdr{} structure, including any padding needed to satisfy alignment requirements.

Similarly, given the length of an ancillary data object, CMSG_LEN() returns the value to store in the cmsg_len member of the cmsghdr{} structure, taking into account any padding necessary to satisfy alignment requirements.

Figure 3-1 clarifies the relationship between the ancillary data-related structures and these two macros by showing the organization of two ancillary data objects. [RFC3542] defines a set of macros to parse a sequence of ancillary objects similar to the layout illustrated in Figure 3-1.

Listing 3-5
―― sys/socket.h

```
    struct cmsghdr *CMSG_FIRSTHDR(const struct msghdr *mhdr);
    struct cmsghdr *CMSG_NXTHDR(const struct msghdr *mhdr,
                               const struct cmsghdr *cmsg);
    unsigned char *CMSG_DATA(const struct cmsghdr *cmsg);
```
―― sys/socket.h

FIGURE 3-1

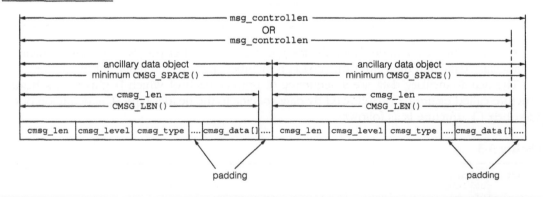

Ancillary data objects.

CMSG_FIRSTHDR() returns a pointer to the first cmsghdr{} structure in the msghdr{} structure pointed to by mhdr. The macro returns NULL if there is no ancillary data pointed to by the msghdr{} structure (i.e. if msg_control is NULL or msg_controllen is less than the size of a cmsghdr{} structure).

CMSG_NXTHDR() returns a pointer to the cmsghdr{} structure describing the next ancillary data object in the sequence. mhdr is a pointer to an msghdr{} structure and cmsg is a pointer to a cmsghdr{} structure. The return value is NULL if no additional ancillary data object exists in the sequence. A pointer to cmsghdr{} describing the first ancillary data object of the sequence is returned if the value of the cmsg pointer is NULL.

CMSG_DATA() returns a pointer to the data that immediately follows a cmsghdr{} structure, which is often called the "cmsg_data" member, even though such a member is not explicitly defined in the structure and the application cannot directly refer to it.

The following code fragment illustrates a common way of iterating through a sequence of ancillary data objects and processing each object in turn.

Listing 3-6

———————————————————————————— sample code

```
        struct msghdr    msg;
        struct cmsghdr   *cmsgptr;

...

        for (cmsgptr = CMSG_FIRSTHDR(&msg); cmsgptr != NULL;
            cmsgptr = CMSG_NXTHDR(&msg, cmsgptr)) {
                if (cmsgptr->cmsg_level == ... &&
                    cmsgptr->cmsg_type == ... ) {
                        unsigned char  *ptr;

                        ptr = CMSG_DATA(cmsgptr);
                        /* process data pointed to by ptr */
                }
        }
```

———————————————————————————— sample code

3.4 IPv6 Packet Information

As previously explained, an application does not have direct access to the IPv6 header and any extension headers of any packet. Instead, [RFC3542] defines a higher level interface to access this packet information using ancillary data objects, which are as follows:

(1) The send and receive interface, the source and destination addresses

(2) The Hop Limit

(3) The Traffic Class

(4) Routing header

(5) Hop-by-Hop options header

(6) Destination options header

(7) Next Hop address

TABLE 3-5

Type of information	*optlevel/cmsg_level*	*optname/cmsg_type*	*optval/cmsg_data[]*
1	IPPROTO_IPV6	IPV6_PKTINFO	in6_pktinfo{}
2	IPPROTO_IPV6	IPV6_HOPLIMIT	int
3	IPPROTO_IPV6	IPV6_TCLASS	int
4	IPPROTO_IPV6	IPV6_RTHDR	ip6_rthdr{}
5	IPPROTO_IPV6	IPV6_HOPOPTS	ip6_hbh{}
6	IPPROTO_IPV6	IPV6_DSTOPTS	ip6_dest{}
6	IPPROTO_IPV6	IPV6_RTHDRDSTOPTS	ip6_dest{}
7	IPPROTO_IPV6	IPV6_NEXTHOP	sockaddr{}

3.4.1   Send Information

An application takes one or both of the following approaches when providing information for the outgoing packet:

- Specify the value via a socket option
- Specify the value as an ancillary data object

Packet information specified via the first approach is called the *"sticky options"* because these options affect all outgoing packets sent on the corresponding socket. On the other hand, packet information specified via the ancillary data objects affect only the packet to which the ancillary data objects are attached.

Table 3-5 lists the synopsis of these options and objects corresponding to the information above. Note that the same constant for the cmsg_level member is used as the second argument to the getsockopt() and setsockopt() functions, which is called the socket "option level." Similarly, the same constant for the cmsg_type member is used as the third argument to getsockopt() and setsockopt(), which is called the socket "option name."

It should be noted that two separate options or object types are assigned the same information type 6 (i.e. the Destination options header). This assignment reflects the fact that there are two types of Destination options headers in the standard ordering of extension headers. IPV6_DSTOPTS refers to the common type of Destination options header that is addressed to the final recipient of the packet while IPV6_RTHDRDSTOPTS is only effective when the Routing header is also present. The Destination options header specified by IPV6_RTHDRDSTOPTS must be placed before the Routing header.

Another note is that IPV6_HOPLIMIT can be specified only through an ancillary data object because the basic API defines more fine-grained socket options: the IPV6_UNICAST_HOPS and the IPV6_MULTICAST_HOPS options.

A new structure, in6_pktinfo{}, is introduced for specifying or retrieving values of the IPV6_PKTINFO option. in6_pktinfo{} is defined in <netinet/in.h> and its definition is as follows:

Listing 3-7

netinet/in.h

```
struct in6_pktinfo {
        struct in6_addr    ipi6_addr;      /* src/dst IPv6 address */
        unsigned int       ipi6_ifindex;   /* send/recv interface index */
};
```

netinet/in.h

The `in6_pktinfo{}` structure can be used as an option value with the `IPV6_PKTINFO` socket option or as an ancillary data object. For incoming packets, `ipi6_addr` and `ipi6_ifindex` contain the destination address of the packets and the index of the receiving interface, respectively. For outgoing packets, `ipi6_addr` specifies the source address of the packets and `ipi6_ifindex` specifies the index of the outgoing interface. In the latter case, the source address is not specified when the `ipi6_addr` member is the unspecified address; the outgoing interface is not specified if the `ipi6_ifindex` member is 0.

3.4.2 Receive Information

An application can retrieve the desired information from received packets by indicating to the kernel one or more of the following options:

- `IPV6_RECVPKTINFO`
- `IPV6_RECVHOPLIMIT`
- `IPV6_RECVTCLASS`
- `IPV6_RECVRTHDR`
- `IPV6_RECVHOPOPTS`
- `IPV6_RECVDSTOPTS`

These options generally correspond to the options listed in Table 3-5 except `IPV6_RTHDRDSTOPTS` and `IPV6_NEXTHOP`. A receiving application should expect any ordering of extension headers. Thus, it is meaningless to try to classify Destination options headers based on a particular ordering. The `IPV6_NEXTHOP` option is only applicable to packet transmissions.

An application informs the kernel of its interested information by setting the corresponding option to a nonzero value (the default is zero). The kernel automatically creates an ancillary data object and attaches that object to the received data when the kernel receives a packet that contains the desired information. The application can access the information through the `msg_control` member of the `msghdr{}` structure when the application calls `recvmsg()` to receive the packet. For example, the following code fragment is found in an application that wants to retrieve the hop limit value from the incoming packets.

Listing 3-8

sample code

```
    int on;

    on = 1;
    setsockopt(s, IPPROTO_IPV6, IPV6_RECVHOPLIMIT, &on, sizeof(on));
```

sample code

3.4.3   Transport Layer Considerations

An application communicating over either UDP or raw sockets can use the ancillary data objects and the socket options mechanisms described so far to either specify packet information for outgoing packets or receive packet information from incoming packets. However, an application communicating over TCP sockets can only specify the packet information for outgoing packets through socket options. The limitation is due to the fact that the TCP protocol offers data stream service that does not map user data to TCP segment (or packet) boundaries (Recall that ancillary data objects work per packet basis).

3.5   Manipulation of IPv6 Extension Headers

The advanced socket API provides a set of higher-level interfaces that allows the manipulation of some of the IPv6 extension headers in the application space. Using these interfaces, an application can either construct or parse the extension headers without the need to know the detailed header formats.

3.5.1   Manipulation of a Routing Header

The following six library functions are provided to manipulate the IPv6 Routing headers.

Listing 3-9

netinet/in.h

```
#include <netinet/in.h>

socklen_t inet6_rth_space(int type, int segments);
void *inet6_rth_init(void *bp, socklen_t bp_len, int type,
                     int segments);
int inet6_rth_add(void *bp, const struct in6_addr *addr);
int inet6_rth_reverse(const void *in, void *out);
int inet6_rth_segments(const void *bp);
struct in6_addr *inet6_rth_getaddr(const void *bp, int index);
```

netinet/in.h

The first three functions are for constructing a Routing header. `inet6_rth_space()` returns the number of bytes required to build a Routing header based on the given information. `inet6_rth_init()` initializes buffer data for a Routing header. `inet6_rth_add()` adds an IPv6 address to the Routing header being constructed.

The next three functions are for examining a received Routing header. `inet6_rth_reverse()` reverses the addresses stored in a Routing header. `inet6_rth_segments()` returns the number of segments that are in a Routing header. `inet6_rth_getaddr()` fetches the address at the given index from a Routing header.

We omit the detailed description of these functions (see [RFC3542] for details).

3.5.2   Manipulation of Hop-by-Hop and Destination Options Headers

A set of library functions are provided to manipulate the Hop-by-Hop and the Destination options headers. These functions are generic and can be used for both types of options. The following four functions are for constructing an options header.

Listing 3-10

```
#include <netinet/in.h>

int inet6_opt_init(void *extbuf, socklen_t extlen);
int inet6_opt_append(void *extbuf, socklen_t extlen, int offset,
                     uint8_t type, socklen_t len, uint_t align,
                     void **databufp);
int inet6_opt_finish(void *extbuf, socklen_t extlen, int offset);
int inet6_opt_set_val(void *databuf, int offset, void *val,
                      socklen_t vallen);
```

`inet6_opt_init()` initializes the buffer data for an options header. `inet6_opt_append()` adds one Type-Length-Value (TLV) option to a list of options. `inet6_opt_finish()` completes the insertion of a TLV option to a list of options headers. `inet6_opt_set_val()` sets the value of an option.

The following three functions are for examining a received options header.

Listing 3-11

```
#include <netinet/in.h>

int inet6_opt_next(void *extbuf, socklen_t extlen, int offset,
                   uint8_t *typep, socklen_t *lenp,
                   void **databufp);
int inet6_opt_find(void *extbuf, socklen_t extlen, int offset,
                   uint8_t type, socklen_t *lenp,
                   void **databufp);
int inet6_opt_get_val(void *databuf, int offset, void *val,
                      socklen_t vallen);
```

`inet6_opt_next()` extracts the next option from the options header pointed by `extbuf`. `inet6_opt_find()` extracts an option of a specified type from the header. `inet6_opt_get_val()` retrieves the value of an option.

We omit the detailed description of these functions. Instead, we show a usage example using the **pim6sd** daemon, which is the KAME implementation of an IPv6 multicast routing daemon. The **pim6sd** daemon needs to send MLD query packets, which contain a Router Alert Hop-by-Hop option. The **pim6sd** daemon also specifies the source address and the outgoing interface using the `IPV6_PKTINFO` ancillary data object.

Listing 3-12 illustrates the function `make_mld6_msg()`, which is the function used in **pim6sd** to construct ancillary data objects including the one for Router Alert option (omitting unnecessary parts for the discussion here).

Listing 3-12

```
440    static void
441    make_mld6_msg(type, code, src, dst, group, ifindex, delay, datalen, alert)
442        int type, code, ifindex, delay, datalen, alert;
443        struct sockaddr_in6 *src, *dst;
444        struct in6_addr *group;
445    {
446        struct mld_hdr *mhp = (struct mld_hdr *)mld6_send_buf;
447        int ctllen, hbhlen = 0;
448
       ....
478
```

```
479            /* estimate total ancillary data length */
480            ctllen = 0;
481            if (ifindex != -1 || src)
482                    ctllen += CMSG_SPACE(sizeof(struct in6_pktinfo));
483            if (alert) {
484     #ifdef USE_RFC2292BIS
485                    if ((hbhlen = inet6_opt_init(NULL, 0)) == -1)
486                            log(LOG_ERR, 0, "inet6_opt_init(0) failed");
487                    if ((hbhlen = inet6_opt_append(NULL, 0, hbhlen, IP6OPT_ROUTER_ALERT, 2,
488                                            2, NULL)) == -1)
489                            log(LOG_ERR, 0, "inet6_opt_append(0) failed");
490                    if ((hbhlen = inet6_opt_finish(NULL, 0, hbhlen)) == -1)
491                            log(LOG_ERR, 0, "inet6_opt_finish(0) failed");
492                    ctllen += CMSG_SPACE(hbhlen);
493     #else   /* old advanced API */
494                    hbhlen = inet6_option_space(sizeof(raopt));
495                    ctllen += hbhlen;
496     #endif
497            }
498            /* extend ancillary data space (if necessary) */
499            if (ctlbuflen < ctllen) {
500                    if (sndcmsgbuf)
501                            free(sndcmsgbuf);
502                    if ((sndcmsgbuf = malloc(ctllen)) == NULL)
503                            log(LOG_ERR, 0, "make_mld6_msg: malloc failed");
                                                     /* assert */
504                    ctlbuflen = ctllen;
505            }
506            /* store ancillary data */
507            if ((sndmh.msg_controllen = ctllen) > 0) {
508                    struct cmsghdr *cmsgp;
509
510                    sndmh.msg_control = sndcmsgbuf;
511                    cmsgp = CMSG_FIRSTHDR(&sndmh);
512
513                    if (ifindex != -1 || src) {
514                            struct in6_pktinfo *pktinfo;
515
516                            cmsgp->cmsg_len = CMSG_LEN(sizeof(struct in6_pktinfo));
517                            cmsgp->cmsg_level = IPPROTO_IPV6;
518                            cmsgp->cmsg_type = IPV6_PKTINFO;
519                            pktinfo = (struct in6_pktinfo *)CMSG_DATA(cmsgp);
520                            memset((caddr_t)pktinfo, 0, sizeof(*pktinfo));
521                            if (ifindex != -1)
522                                    pktinfo->ipi6_ifindex = ifindex;
523                            if (src)
524                                    pktinfo->ipi6_addr = src->sin6_addr;
525                            cmsgp = CMSG_NXTHDR(&sndmh, cmsgp);
526                    }
527                    if (alert) {
528     #ifdef USE_RFC2292BIS
529                            int currentlen;
530                            void *hbhbuf, *optp = NULL;
531
532                            cmsgp->cmsg_len = CMSG_LEN(hbhlen);
533                            cmsgp->cmsg_level = IPPROTO_IPV6;
534                            cmsgp->cmsg_type = IPV6_HOPOPTS;
535                            hbhbuf = CMSG_DATA(cmsgp);
536
537                            if ((currentlen = inet6_opt_init(hbhbuf, hbhlen)) == -1)
538                                    log(LOG_ERR, 0, "inet6_opt_init(len = %d) failed",
539                                        hbhlen);
540                            if ((currentlen = inet6_opt_append(hbhbuf, hbhlen,
541                                                            currentlen,
542                                                            IP6OPT_ROUTER_ALERT, 2,
543                                                            2, &optp)) == -1)
544                                    log(LOG_ERR, 0,
545                                        "inet6_opt_append(len = %d/%d) failed",
```

```
546                                         currentlen, hbhlen);
547                     (void)inet6_opt_set_val(optp, 0, &rtalert_code,
548                                    sizeof(rtalert_code));
549                     if (inet6_opt_finish(hbhbuf, hbhlen, currentlen) == -1)
550                         log(LOG_ERR, 0, "inet6_opt_finish(buf) failed");
551     #else  /* old advanced API */
552                     if (inet6_option_init((void *)cmsgp, &cmsgp, IPV6_HOPOPTS))
553                         log(LOG_ERR, 0, /* assert */
554                             "make_mld6_msg: inet6_option_init failed");
555                     if (inet6_option_append(cmsgp, raopt, 4, 0))
556                         log(LOG_ERR, 0, /* assert */
557                             "make_mld6_msg: inet6_option_append failed");
558     #endif
559                     cmsgp = CMSG_NXTHDR(&sndmh, cmsgp);
560             }
561         }
562         else
563             sndmh.msg_control = NULL; /* clear for safety */
564     }
```
———————————————————————————————————— ${KAME}/kame/kame/pim6sd/mld6.c

Buffer size estimation

479–482 For MLD query messages, `ifindex` is always a nonzero positive integer specifying the outgoing interface. `src` specifies an IPv6 link-local address to be used as the packet source address. `CMSG_SPACE()` gives the length of the space necessary for storing the `IPV6_PKTINFO` object including any trailing padding if required.

483–497 Similarly, `alert` is always nonzero for MLD query packets. The `inet6_opt_xxx()` functions are used here just for calculating the length of the required space for storing the information in the context in which they are called (e.g. the base Hop-by-Hop options header, the Router Alert option, or the necessary paddings), when the first argument to these functions is a NULL pointer. `inet6_opt_init()` would return 2 that include the Next Header and the Header Length fields of the Hop-by-Hop options header. `inet6_opt_append()` then calculates the length needed to store the Router Alert option, taking into account paddings when necessary. In this case, this function would return 4, the length of the Router Alert option including its type and length fields. Finally, `inet6_opt_finish()` provides the length of trailing padding bytes or simply 0 if no padding is necessary. In this particular case, the function would return 2 because trailing padding bytes are necessary to make the entire length of the Hop-by-Hop options header a multiple of 8 bytes. As a result, `hbhlen` would be 8. `CMSG_SPACE()` gives the necessary length of the space to store the header, including padding.

Allocate buffer

498–505 `ctlbuflen` is a static variable that remembers the length of an already allocated buffer. If `ctlbuflen` is shorter than the length just calculated, which is always the case when this function is called for the first time, the previously allocated buffer (if any) is freed and a new buffer of the required length is allocated.

Build ancillary data objects

507–511 `sndmh` is the `msghdr{}` structure for this packet. Its `msg_control` member is set to the allocated buffer for the ancillary data objects. `CMSG_FIRSTHDR()` gives the head of the buffer as a pointer to a `cmsghdr{}` structure.

FIGURE 3-2

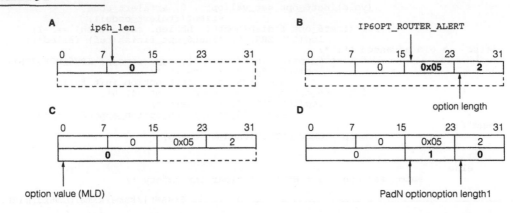

Building a Hop-by-Hop options header containing a Router Alert option.

513–526 The first ancillary data are an `IPV6_PKTINFO` object containing the source address and the outgoing interface. `cmsg_level` and `cmsg_type` are set to `IPPROTO_IPV6` and `IPV6_PKTINFO`, respectively, as shown in Table 3-5. `CMSG_DATA()` is an `in6_pktinfo{}` structure that is pointed to by the variable `pktinfo`. Both the `ipi6_ifindex` and `ipi6_addr` structure members are initialized with the given parameters. `CMSG_NXTHDR()` then advances the pointer to the next `cmsghdr{}`.

527–561 Similarly, the `cmsg_level` and `cmsg_type` members for the second ancillary data object are set for the `IPV6_HOPOPTS` object. This time, `inet6_opt_init()` initializes the Header Length field of the data, assuming it is an `ip6_hbh{}` structure, as shown in part A of Figure 3-2. `inet6_opt_append()` sets the option type and length fields for the Router Alert option as shown in part B of Figure 3-2. `inet6_opt_set_val()` copies the Router Alert code to the data field of the option in part C of Figure 3-2. Finally, `inet6_opt_finish()` fills in the rest of the buffer with a PadN option that contains only a one-byte length field as shown in part D of Figure 3-2.

Figure 3-3 depicts the complete form of the `msghdr{}` structure and ancillary data objects after the building process. As shown in this figure, there is no need for padding in this example. Therefore, `CMSG_SPACE()` and `CMSG_LEN()` give the same length for both objects. In fact, this is the common case because the requirement alignment is a multiple of 4 bytes for the main target architecture of KAME's implementation, and both the `cmsghdr{}` structure and many ancillary objects are aligned on a 4-byte boundary.

3.6   Path MTU APIs

The advanced API defines a set of interfaces that deal with path MTU information. All these interfaces work as socket option while some also work as ancillary data objects. The socket option level or the `cmsg` level is always set to `IPPROTO_IPV6`.

Table 3-6 summarizes these options.

FIGURE 3-3

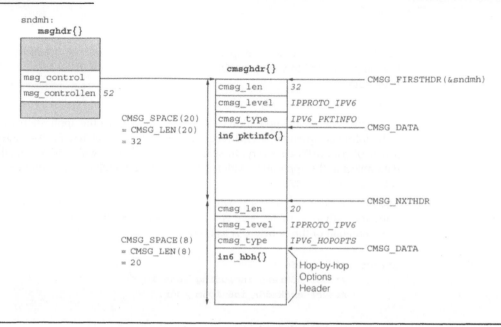

Complete form of the msghdr *and ancillary data objects.*

TABLE 3-6

Option	Description
IPV6_USE_MIN_MTU	This option controls whether path MTU discovery should be performed for outgoing packet(s) or the packet(s) should simply be fragmented at the IPv6 minimum MTU (1280 bytes). Its parameter takes one of the following integer values:
	−1 perform path MTU discovery for unicast destinations but do not perform it for multicast destinations. Packets to multicast destinations are therefore sent with the minimum MTU.
	0 always perform path MTU discovery.
	1 always disable path MTU discovery and send packets at the minimum MTU.
	The default value is −1.
	IPV6_USE_MIN_MTU can also be specified as an ancillary data object.
IPV6_DONTFRAG	This option specifies whether IPv6 fragmentation should be performed for outgoing packet(s). It takes an integer parameter, which if set to a nonzero value indicates that fragmentation should be disabled.
	IPV6_DONTFRAG can also be specified as an ancillary data object. Additionally, it is only expected to work for UDP and raw sockets. Its effect on a TCP socket is undefined.

(Continued)

TABLE 3-6 *(Continued)*

Option	Description
	IPV6_DONTFRAG can also be specified as an ancillary data object. Additionally, it is only expected to work for UDP and raw sockets. Its effect on a TCP socket is undefined.
IPV6_RECVPATHMTU	IPV6_RECVPATHMTU only works as a socket option.
	This option allows an application to inform the kernel that the application wants to be informed when the kernel receives an ICMPv6 Packet Too Big Message as a part of path MTU discovery. In such a case, the kernel will send an ancillary data object to the application with the level set to IPPROTO_IPV6 and the type set to IPV6_PATHMTU.
	The first byte of cmsg_data[] will point to an ip6_mtuinfo{} structure carrying the path MTU value together with the associated IPv6 destination address. The definition of this structure is as follows:

```
struct ip6_mtuinfo {
        /* dst address including zone ID */
        struct sockaddr_in6 ip6m_addr;

        /* path MTU in host byte order */
        uint32_t            ip6m_mtu;
};
```

Option	Description
	The ip6m_addr member specifies the destination address of the corresponding path while the ip6m_mtu member specifies the path MTU value in the host byte order.
IPV6_PATHMTU	IPV6_PATHMTU only works as a socket option and is only applicable to the getsockopt() operation on a connected socket. Its argument is an ip6_mtuinfo{} structure just described above, storing the known path MTU to the destination of the socket.

3.7   Socket Extensions for the "r" Commands

[RFC3542] defines the following three functions to support the "r" (remote) commands, for example, **rlogin**.

- rresvport_af() – a multiprotocol version of rresvport()
- rcmd_af()   – a multiprotocol version of rcmd()
- rexec_af()   – a multiprotocol version of rexec()

The reason separate functions are introduced is that the original functions hide details of the underlying socket and the original implementations may not be prepared to handle IPv6 addresses via, for example, the getpeername() system call. Defining new functions while keeping the old ones intact assures backward compatibility for the traditional applications.

Since "r" commands are rarely used these days, we simply list the new function names here and do not go into the details. Consult [RFC3542] for the complete information including function prototypes of these functions.

3.8 Summary Tables of Socket Options

Socket options at the `IPPROTO_IPV6` level for `SOCK_RAW`, `SOCK_DGRAM`, or `SOCK_STREAM` sockets are summarized in this section. For each option, the kernel function that processes that particular option is specified. These kernel functions will be described in Chapter 4.

Table 3-7 lists multicast-related options. These options are processed by `ip6_setmoptions()` and `ip6_getmoptions()`.

TABLE 3-7

optname	optval type	Description
IPV6_JOIN_GROUP	struct ipv6_mreq	Join a multicast group on a specified interface (set only).
IPV6_LEAVE_GROUP	struct ipv6_mreq	Leave from a multicast group on a specified interface (set only).
IPV6_MULTICAST_HOPS	int	Set or get the hop limit for outgoing multicast packets.
IPV6_MULTICAST_IF	u_int	Set or get the outgoing interface for multicast packets.
IPV6_MULTICAST_LOOP	u_int	Set or get a Boolean value of whether outgoing multicast packets are looped back to local listeners.

Table 3-8 lists other basic API socket options.

TABLE 3-8

optname	optval type	Kernel function	Description
IPV6_UNICAST_HOPS	int	ip6_ctloutput()	Set or get the hop limit for outgoing unicast packets.
IPV6_V6ONLY	int	ip6_ctloutput()	Set or get a Boolean value of whether IPv4 packets can be sent to or received on an AF_INET6 socket.

Table 3-9 lists socket options related to raw IPv6 sockets.

TABLE 3-9

optname	optval type	Kernel function	Description
IPV6_CHECKSUM	int	ip6_raw_ctloutput()	Set or get the offset to the checksum field.
ICMP6_FILTER	struct icmp6_filter	icmp6_ctloutput()	Set or get filter configuration based on ICMPv6 types (ICMPv6 only).

TABLE 3-10

optname	optval type	Kernel function	Description
IPV6_RECVPKTINFO	int	ip6_ctloutput()	Enable or disable receiving inbound packet information (the receiving interface and the packet's destination address).
IPV6_RECVHOPLIMIT	int	ip6_ctloutput()	Enable or disable receiving the hop limit of inbound packets.
IPV6_RECVRTHDR	int	ip6_ctloutput()	Enable or disable receiving the Routing header(s) (if any) of inbound packets.
IPV6_RECVHOPOPTS	int	ip6_ctloutput()	Enable or disable receiving the Hop-by-Hop options header (if any) of inbound packets (superuser privilege required*).
IPV6_RECVDSTOPTS	int	ip6_ctloutput()	Enable or disable receiving the Destination options header(s) (if any) of inbound packets (superuser privilege required*).
IPV6_RECVTCLASS	int	ip6_ctloutput()	Enable or disable receiving the Traffic Class value of inbound packets.
IPV6_RECVRTHDRDSTOPTS	int	ip6_ctloutput()	(obsolete)

* The privilege requirement is not given in the API specification, but is given by KAME specific. See the discussion for Listing 3.8.

Table 3-10 lists options for retrieving information from incoming packets.

Table 3-11 lists options that specify attributes for outbound packets. Most of these options can also be specified as ancillary data types to manipulate a particular behavior for a single output operation. Note that IPV6_HOPLIMIT cannot be used as a socket option.

TABLE 3-11

optname	optval type	Kernel function	Description
IPV6_PKTINFO	struct in6_pktinfo	ip6_setpktoption()	Set or get outgoing packet information (the outgoing interface and the packet's source address).
IPV6_HOPLIMIT	int	ip6_setpktoption()	Set or get the hop limit of outgoing packets (ancillary data only).
IPV6_NEXTHOP	struct sockaddr	ip6_setpktoption()	Set or get the next hop address.
IPV6_RTHDR	struct ip6_rthdr	ip6_setpktoption()	Set or get the Routing header included in outgoing packets.
IPV6_HOPOPTS	struct ip6_hbh	ip6_setpktoption()	Set or get the Hop-by-Hop options header included in outgoing packets (superuser privilege required*).
IPV6_DSTOPTS	struct ip6_dest	ip6_setpktoption()	Set or get the Destination options header included in outgoing packets (superuser privilege required*).
IPV6_RTHDRDSTOPTS	struct ip6_dest	ip6_setpktoption()	Set or get the Destination options header before a Routing header (when specified) included in outgoing packets (superuser privilege required*).
IPV6_TCLASS	int	ip6_setpktoption()	Set or get the Traffic Class value of outgoing packets.
IPV6_PREFER_TEMPADDR	int	ip6_setpktoption()	Enable or disable whether temporary addresses (for privacy extension to address autoconfiguration) should be preferred in source address selection (not defined in standard document).

The privilege requirement is not in the API specification, but is KAME specific. See the discussion for Listing 3-8.

Table 3-12 lists path MTU-related options. The first two options can also be specified as ancillary data types.

TABLE 3-12

optname	*optval type*	*Kernel function*	*Description.*
IPV6_USE_MIN_MTU	int	ip6_setpktoption()	Set or get the control value to specify whether outgoing packets should be fragmented at the minimum MTU.
IPV6_DONTFRAG	int	ip6_setpktoption()	Set or get a Boolean value of whether IPv6 fragmentation should be prohibited.
IPV6_RECVPATHMTU	int	ip6_ctloutput()	Enable or disable receiving path MTU information for the path of outgoing packets (non-TCP socket only).
IPV6_PATHMTU	struct ip6_mtuinfo	ip6_ctloutput()	Get the path MTU information for the current destination (connected socket only).

Kernel Implementation of IPv6 Socket APIs

In this chapter, we describe the KAME kernel implementation of the application programming interface (API) specifications shown so far. We particularly focus on how the IPv6 socket options and ancillary data objects are specified and work in the kernel implementation.

4.1 Code Introduction

Table 4-1 summarizes the source files containing the kernel implementation of the various Internet Protocol version 6 (IPv6) APIs that are described in this chapter.

In general, the kernel implementation is categorized into the following three sections.

The IPv6 socket option processing section handles the `setsockopt()` and `getsockopt()` system calls through the corresponding transport layer. Figure 4-1 shows function call graphs of this section.

TABLE 4-1

File	Description
`${KAME}/kame/sys/netinet6/ip6_var.h`	Kernel internal structures for the API implementation
`${KAME}/kame/sys/netinet6/ip6_output.c`	Handling socket options and the outgoing path of ancillary data objects
`${KAME}/kame/sys/netinet6/icmp6.c`	Handling ICMPv6 socket options
`${KAME}/kame/sys/netinet6/ip6_input.c`	Handling the incoming path of ancillary data objects

FIGURE 4-1

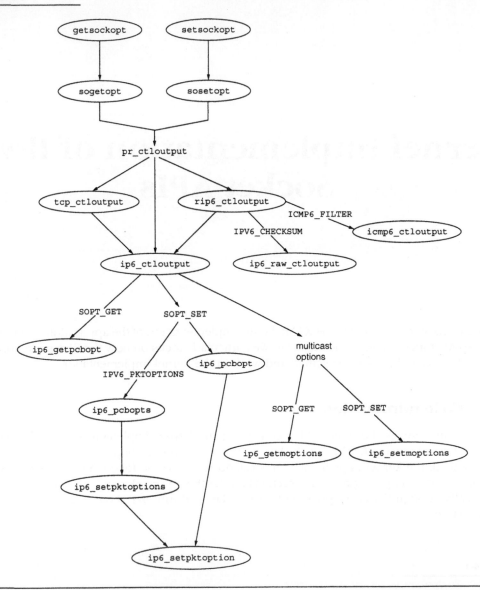

IPv6 Socket Option processing.

The outgoing path of the ancillary data objects section deals with ancillary data objects specified for a particular outgoing packet. Figure 4-2 shows the function call graphs for this part. Notice that some parts of Figure 4-2 are shared with Figure 4-1.

In the inbound path, ancillary data objects that correspond to an incoming packet are constructed in the `ip6_savecontrol()` function and are handed to the receiving socket. Figure 4-3 shows function call graphs of this part.

FIGURE 4-2

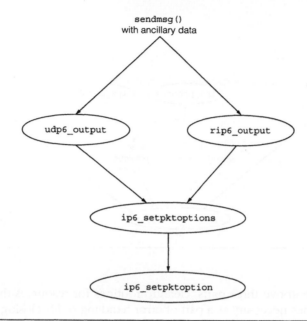

Outgoing path of ancillary data objects.

FIGURE 4-3

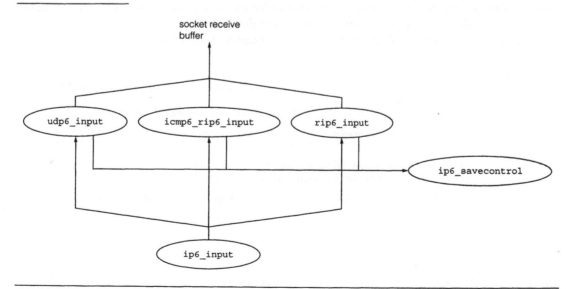

Incoming path of ancillary data objects.

FIGURE 4-4

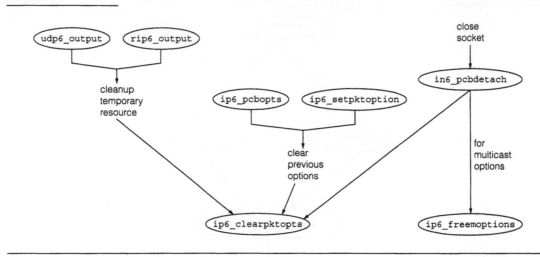

Cleanup process.

In addition to the above three parts, cleanup routines for resources that were temporarily allocated are sometimes necessary as a part of error handling or for closing a socket. Figure 4-4 shows the procedure for such cleanup.

4.2 `ip6_pktopts{}` Structure

The `ip6_pktopts{}` structure contains packet option information for outgoing packets. This structure can be specified for an outgoing packet or for a socket to specify the option information that applies to all outgoing packets transmitted over that socket.

Listing 4-1 shows the definition of the `ip6_pktopts{}` structure.

Listing 4-1

—— ip6_var.h

```
148    struct      ip6_pktopts {
149           int    ip6po_hlim;          /* Hoplimit for outgoing packets */
150
151           /* Outgoing IF/address information */
152           struct  in6_pktinfo *ip6po_pktinfo;
153
154           /* Next-hop address information */
155           struct  ip6po_nhinfo ip6po_nhinfo;
156
157           struct  ip6_hbh *ip6po_hbh; /* Hop-by-Hop options header */
158
159           /* Destination options header (before a routing header) */
160           struct  ip6_dest *ip6po_dest1;
161
162           /* Routing header related info. */
163           struct  ip6po_rhinfo ip6po_rhinfo;
164
165           /* Mobile IPv6 type 2 Routing header. */
166           struct  ip6po_rhinfo ip6po_rhinfo2;
167
```

```
168             /* Destination options header (after a routing header) */
169             struct  ip6_dest *ip6po_dest2;
170
171             /* Mobility header (just before an upper layer header) */
172             struct  ip6_mobility *ip6po_mobility;
173
174             int     ip6po_tclass;          /* traffic class */
175
176             int     ip6po_minmtu;  /* fragment vs PMTU discovery policy */
177 #define IP6PO_MINMTU_MCASTONLY  -1 /* default; send at min MTU for multicast*/
178 #define IP6PO_MINMTU_DISABLE     0 /* always perform pmtu disc */
179 #define IP6PO_MINMTU_ALL         1 /* always send at min MTU */
180
181             int     ip6po_prefer_tempaddr;  /* whether temporary addresses are
182                                              preferred as source address */
183 #define IP6PO_TEMPADDR_SYSTEM    -1 /* follow the system default */
184 #define IP6PO_TEMPADDR_NOTPREFER 0 /* not prefer temporary address */
185 #define IP6PO_TEMPADDR_PREFER    1 /* prefer temporary address */
186
187             int ip6po_flags;
188 #define IP6PO_REACHCONF 0x01            /* upper-layer reachability confirmation */
192 #define IP6PO_DONTFRAG  0x04            /* disable fragmentation (IPV6_DONTFRAG) */
193 #define IP6PO_USECOA    0x08            /* use care of address */
194
195             int     needfree;       /* members dynamically allocated */
196 };
```
—— ip6_var.h

148–196 The structure members ip6po_hlim, ip6po_pktinfo, ip6po_nhinfo, and
ip6po_tclass specify nondefault attributes for the outgoing packet(s). ip6po_hlim
specifies the hop limit to be inserted in the Hop Limit field of the IPv6 header.
ip6po_pktinfo specifies both the outgoing interface and the packet's source address.
ip6po_tclass specifies the Traffic Class value. The ip6po_nhinfo member specifies a
nondefault next hop address that is often a router. Listing 4-2 below gives the definition
of the ip6po_nhinfo{} structure. The ip6_rhinfo member stores Routing header-
related information. It will be described in Listing 4-3.

The structure members ip6po_hbh through ip6po_dest2 specify IPv6 extension headers that are to be inserted in the outgoing packet(s). Note that there are two
types of Destination options header: the one before a Routing header (if any) and the one
after a Routing header. ip6po_dest1 and ip6po_dest2 correspond to a Destination
options header before and after a Routing header, respectively.

ip6po_rhinfo2 and ip6po_mobility are header information related to
Mobile IPv6. These are out of scope of this book.

ip6po_minmtu controls the policy on how path MTU discovery should be
applied for the corresponding outgoing packets.

ip6po_prefer_tempaddr is taken into consideration in source address selection for outgoing packets in terms of whether temporary addresses that are generated for
privacy extension, which is defined in [RFC3041], should be preferred.

ip6po_flags controls several additional parameters which indicate whether
confirmation about a neighbor's reachability provided by an upper layer should be used,
whether to disable IPv6 fragmentation (mainly for debugging purposes), and whether
a care-of-address should be preferred over a home address for a source address on a
mobile node.

needfree is a member for internal use to control memory management of this
structure.

The following two listings show internal structures used in the `ip6_pktopts{}` structure.

Listing 4-2

```
136     /* Nexthop related info */
137     struct   ip6po_nhinfo {
138             struct      sockaddr *ip6po_nhi_nexthop;
140             struct      route ip6po_nhi_route; /* Route to the nexthop */
144     };
145     #define ip6po_nexthop       ip6po_nhinfo.ip6po_nhi_nexthop
146     #define ip6po_nextroute     ip6po_nhinfo.ip6po_nhi_route
```

136–144 `ip6po_nhi_nexthop` is a socket address structure that contains the address of the next hop. `ip6po_nhi_route` stores a cached route for this next hop address.

145–146 Two shortcut macros are defined to get access to the structure members from the `ip6_pktopts{}` structure.

Listing 4-3

```
122     /* Routing header related info */
123     struct   ip6po_rhinfo {
124             struct   ip6_rthdr *ip6po_rhi_rthdr; /* Routing header */
126             struct   route ip6po_rhi_route; /* Route to the 1st hop */
130     };
131     #define ip6po_rthdr        ip6po_rhinfo.ip6po_rhi_rthdr
132     #define ip6po_route        ip6po_rhinfo.ip6po_rhi_route
```

122–130 `ip6po_rhi_rthdr` points to the actual routing header. `ip6po_rhi_route` stores a cached route for the first hop specified in the Routing header.

131–132 Two shortcut macros are defined to get access to the structure members from the `ip6_pktopts{}` structure.

A couple of utility functions that handle the `ip6_pktopts{}` structure are defined, which will be described below.

4.2.1 `init_ip6pktopts()` Functions

The `init_ip6pktopts()` function simply initializes the content of the `ip6_pktopts{}` structure with system default parameters.

Listing 4-4

```
3269    void
3270    init_ip6pktopts(opt)
3271            struct ip6_pktopts *opt;
3272    {
3273
3274            bzero(opt, sizeof(*opt));
3275            opt->ip6po_hlim = -1;          /* -1 means default hop limit */
3276            opt->ip6po_tclass = -1;         /* -1 means default traffic class */
3277            opt->ip6po_minmtu = IP6PO_MINMTU_MCASTONLY;
3278            opt->ip6po_prefer_tempaddr = IP6PO_TEMPADDR_SYSTEM;
3279    }
```

4.2.2 `ip6_clearpktopts()` Function

The `ip6_clearpktopts()` function initializes the option data freeing the values that were set by a previous operation with the default value if applicable.

Listing 4-5

```
                                                              ip6_output.c
3426    void
3427    ip6_clearpktopts(pktopt, optname)
3428            struct ip6_pktopts *pktopt;
3429            int optname;
3430    {
3431            int needfree;
3432
3433            if (pktopt == NULL)
3434                    return;
3435
3436            needfree = pktopt->needfree;
3437
3438            if (optname == -1 || optname == IPV6_PKTINFO) {
3439                    if (needfree && pktopt->ip6po_pktinfo)
3440                            free(pktopt->ip6po_pktinfo, M_IP6OPT);
3441                    pktopt->ip6po_pktinfo = NULL;
3442            }
3443            if (optname == -1 || optname == IPV6_HOPLIMIT)
3444                    pktopt->ip6po_hlim = -1;
3445            if (optname == -1 || optname == IPV6_TCLASS)
3446                    pktopt->ip6po_tclass = -1;
3447            if (optname == -1 || optname == IPV6_NEXTHOP) {
3448                    if (pktopt->ip6po_nextroute.ro_rt) {
3449                            RTFREE(pktopt->ip6po_nextroute.ro_rt);
3450                            pktopt->ip6po_nextroute.ro_rt = NULL;
3451                    }
3452                    if (needfree && pktopt->ip6po_nexthop)
3453                            free(pktopt->ip6po_nexthop, M_IP6OPT);
3454                    pktopt->ip6po_nexthop = NULL;
3455            }
3456            if (optname == -1 || optname == IPV6_HOPOPTS) {
3457                    if (needfree && pktopt->ip6po_hbh)
3458                            free(pktopt->ip6po_hbh, M_IP6OPT);
3459                    pktopt->ip6po_hbh = NULL;
3460            }
3461            if (optname == -1 || optname == IPV6_RTHDRDSTOPTS) {
3462                    if (needfree && pktopt->ip6po_dest1)
3463                            free(pktopt->ip6po_dest1, M_IP6OPT);
3464                    pktopt->ip6po_dest1 = NULL;
3465            }
3466            if (optname == -1 || optname == IPV6_RTHDR) {
3467                    if (needfree && pktopt->ip6po_rhinfo.ip6po_rhi_rthdr)
3468                            free(pktopt->ip6po_rhinfo.ip6po_rhi_rthdr, M_IP6OPT);
3469                    pktopt->ip6po_rhinfo.ip6po_rhi_rthdr = NULL;
3470                    if (pktopt->ip6po_route.ro_rt) {
3471                            RTFREE(pktopt->ip6po_route.ro_rt);
3472                            pktopt->ip6po_route.ro_rt = NULL;
3473                    }
3474            }
3475            if (optname == -1 || optname == IPV6_DSTOPTS) {
3476                    if (needfree && pktopt->ip6po_dest2)
3477                            free(pktopt->ip6po_dest2, M_IP6OPT);
3478                    pktopt->ip6po_dest2 = NULL;
3479            }
3480    }
                                                              ip6_output.c
```

3426–3434 optname specifies the option name for which function `ip6_clearpktopts()` will clear and initialize the data. All options are cleared if optname is −1. `ip6_clearpktopts()` does not perform any action if pktopt is NULL.

3436 The `needfree` member of the `pktopt` structure is set if the corresponding options were used as sticky options that are stored in dynamically allocated memory.

3438–3479 The rest of the function just reinitializes the specified field(s) of the `pktopt` structure. The memory space is freed here if the option content was dynamically allocated. In addition, if a routing entry is associated with a particular option, which is the case for the `IPV6_NEXTHOP` and the `IPV6_RTHDR` options, then the `RTFREE()` macro is invoked to release the reference count on that route entry.

4.3　IPv6 Socket Option Processing—`ip6_ctloutput()` Function

The `ip6_ctloutput()` function is a common routine for most IPv6-related socket options that is called from upper layer `ctloutput` functions (see Figure 4-1). It is a large function containing more than 1000 lines, but its organization is pretty straightforward. The function essentially consists of one big `switch` statement for the operation types: `SOPT_SET` which corresponds to the `setsockopt()` system call and `SOPT_GET` which corresponds to the `getsockopt()` system call. In the following subsections, we see the function based on this big picture.

4.3.1　Initialization

Listing 4-6

── ip6_output.c

```
1937    /*
1938     * IP6 socket option processing.
1939     */
1941    int
1942    ip6_ctloutput(so, sopt)
1943            struct socket *so;
1944            struct sockopt *sopt;
1953    {
1954            int privileged, optdatalen, uproto;
1955            void *optdata;
1956            struct ip6_recvpktopts *rcvopts;
1964            struct inpcb *in6p = sotoinpcb(so);
1965            int error, optval;
1966            int level, op, optname;
1967            int optlen;
1971            struct proc *p;
1973
1974            if (sopt) {
1975                    level = sopt->sopt_level;
1976                    op = sopt->sopt_dir;
1977                    optname = sopt->sopt_name;
1978                    optlen = sopt->sopt_valsize;
1982                    p = sopt->sopt_p;
1984            } else {
1985                    panic("ip6_ctloutput: arg soopt is NULL");
1986            }
2007            error = optval = 0;
2008
2012            privileged = (p == 0 || suser(p)) ? 0 : 1;
2016            uproto = (int)so->so_proto->pr_protocol;
2017            rcvopts = in6p->in6p_inputopts;
```

── ip6_output.c

1974–2007 `sopt` is a generic structure defined in FreeBSD for identifying a particular socket option. The `ip6_ctloutput()` function first decodes some part of the structure. Since the `getsockopt()` and the `setsockopt()` system calls always pass a valid `sopt` structure and because the `ip6_ctloutput()` function is only called from a socket option context, this function assumes `sopt` is non-NULL.

2012–2017 `privileged` is set to 1 when the superuser calls the operation. `uproto` is the upper layer protocol associated with the socket, such as `IPPROTO_TCP` or `IPPROTO_UDP`. `rcvopts` is actually not used in this function.

4.3.2 Set Operations

We then show the `setsockopt()` operations for IPv6 socket options.

Listing 4-7

```
                                                              ip6_output.c
2019          if (level == IPPROTO_IPV6) {
2020                  switch (op) {
2021
2023                  case SOPT_SET:
2027                          switch (optname) {
2028                          case IPV6_2292PKTOPTIONS:
2029  #ifdef IPV6_PKTOPTIONS
2030                          case IPV6_PKTOPTIONS:
2031  #endif
2032                          {
2034                                  struct mbuf *m;
2035
2036                                  error = soopt_getm(sopt, &m); /* XXX */
2037                                  if (error != NULL)
2038                                          break;
2039                                  error = soopt_mcopyin(sopt, m); /* XXX */
2040                                  if (error != NULL)
2041                                          break;
2042                                  error = ip6_pcbopts(&in6p->in6p_outputopts,
2043                                                     m, so, sopt);
2044                                  m_freem(m); /* XXX */
2049                                  break;
2050                          }
                                                              ip6_output.c
```

2028–2050 The `IPV6_PKTOPTIONS` socket option allows the application to specify a set of option information that applies to outgoing packets transmitted over a particular socket. This feature was once specified in [RFC2292] but was removed from [RFC3542]. The kernel code still keeps the `case` statement just for maintaining binary backward compatibility.

Listing 4-8

```
                                                              ip6_output.c
2052                          /*
2053                           * Use of some Hop-by-Hop options or some
2054                           * Destination options, might require special
2055                           * privilege.  That is, normal applications
2056                           * (without special privilege) might be forbidden
2057                           * from setting certain options in outgoing packets,
2058                           * and might never see certain options in received
2059                           * packets. [RFC 2292 Section 6]
2060                           * KAME specific note:
2061                           *  KAME prevents non-privileged users from sending or
2062                           *  receiving ANY hbh/dst options in order to avoid
```

```
2063                           *  overhead of parsing options in the kernel.
2064                           */
2065                          case IPV6_RECVHOPOPTS:
2066                          case IPV6_RECVDSTOPTS:
2067                          case IPV6_RECVRTHDRDSTOPTS:
2068                                  if (!privileged) {
2069                                          error = EPERM;
2070                                          break;
2071                                  }
2072                                  /* FALLTHROUGH */
```
—— ip6_output.c

2052–2072 KAME implementation requires the application to have the superuser privilege in order to receive the Hop-by-Hop or the Destination options headers. This is too restrictive since [RFC3542] only states that a nonprivileged application may not see some options. However, KAME's restriction is intentional and helps to avoid expensive packet parsing for determining whether or not the incoming options can be passed to the application.

Listing 4-9
—— ip6_output.c

```
2073                          case IPV6_UNICAST_HOPS:
2074                          case IPV6_HOPLIMIT:
2075                          case IPV6_FAITH:
2076
2077                          case IPV6_RECVPKTINFO:
2078                          case IPV6_RECVHOPLIMIT:
2079                          case IPV6_RECVRTHDR:
2080                          case IPV6_RECVPATHMTU:
2081                          case IPV6_RECVTCLASS:
2082                          case IPV6_V6ONLY:
2083                          case IPV6_AUTOFLOWLABEL:
2084                                  if (optlen != sizeof(int)) {
2085                                          error = EINVAL;
2086                                          break;
2087                                  }
```
—— ip6_output.c

2073–2087 All these options take a fixed size (i.e. an integer) argument. Other data types are rejected here.

Listing 4-10
—— ip6_output.c

```
2089                              error = sooptcopyin(sopt, &optval,
2090                                      sizeof optval, sizeof optval);
2091                          if (error)
2092                                  break;
```
—— ip6_output.c

2089–2092 The `sooptcopyin()` function copies the socket option data passed from the application to a memory space internal to the kernel.

Listing 4-11
—— ip6_output.c

```
2096                          switch (optname) {
2097
2098                          case IPV6_UNICAST_HOPS:
2099                                  if (optval < -1 || optval >= 256)
```

```
2100                                                    error = EINVAL;
2101                                      else {
2102                                              /* -1 = kernel default */
2103                                              in6p->in6p_hops = optval;
2105                                              if ((in6p->in6p_vflag &
2106                                                  INP_IPV4) != 0)
2107                                                      in6p->inp_ip_ttl = optval;
2109                                      }
2110                                      break;
```
_____ ip6_output.c

2098–2110 The `IPV6_UNICAST_HOPS` socket option specifies the hop limit of outgoing unicast packets. A valid value is copied into the corresponding PCB entry. The given hop
limit value is also used as the TTL value in IPv4 packets if the socket is used for both IPv4
and IPv6 communication using IPv4-mapped IPv6 addresses. This behavior is a FreeBSD-
specific extension and is not defined in the specification.

Listing 4-12
_____ ip6_output.c
```
2111    #define OPTSET(bit) \
2112    do { \
2113            if (optval) \
2114                    in6p->in6p_flags |= (bit); \
2115            else \
2116                    in6p->in6p_flags &= ~(bit); \
2117    } while (/*CONSTCOND*/ 0)
```
_____ ip6_output.c

2111–2117 Socket options are often used to turn on or off a particular behavior that can be represented by a Boolean value. The `OPTSET()` macro is a shortcut to support the common
operation.

Listing 4-13
_____ ip6_output.c
```
2118    #define OPTSET2292(bit) \
2119    do { \
2120            in6p->in6p_flags |= IN6P_RFC2292; \
2121            if (optval) \
2122                    in6p->in6p_flags |= (bit); \
2123            else \
2124                    in6p->in6p_flags &= ~(bit); \
2125    } while (/*CONSTCOND*/ 0)
2126    #define OPTBIT(bit) (in6p->in6p_flags & (bit) ? 1 : 0)
```
_____ ip6_output.c

2118–2125 [RFC2292] and [RFC3542] define incompatible advanced APIs, and the usage when
these two specifications are mixed is not defined. For example, if the `IPV6_PKTOPTIONS`
socket option (only available in [RFC2292]) specifies a Hop-by-Hop options header to be
included in outbound packets while the [RFC3542] version of the `IPV6_HOPOPTS` socket
option is specified for the same socket, it is not clear which option should be preferred.
While this kernel implementation tries to support both specifications as much as possible,
it is inadvisable to mix the different specifications. In order to detect and reject the mixed
usage, the `OPTSET2292()` macro is used to turn the `IN6P_RFC2292` flag in the PCB
on or off, which controls whether the associated socket will only accept options that are
defined in [RFC2292].

2126 The `OPTBIT()` macro is a shortcut for checking if a particular option is turned on.

Listing 4-14

_____ ip6_output.c

```
2128                    case IPV6_RECVPKTINFO:
2129                            /* cannot mix with RFC2292 */
2130                            if (OPTBIT(IN6P_RFC2292)) {
2131                                    error = EINVAL;
2132                                    break;
2133                            }
2134                            OPTSET(IN6P_PKTINFO);
2135                            break;
2136
2137                    case IPV6_HOPLIMIT:
2138                    {
2139                            struct ip6_pktopts **optp;
2140
2141                            /* cannot mix with RFC2292 */
2142                            if (OPTBIT(IN6P_RFC2292)) {
2143                                    error = EINVAL;
2144                                    break;
2145                            }
2146                            optp = &in6p->in6p_outputopts;
2147                            error = ip6_pcbopt(IPV6_HOPLIMIT,
2148                                               (u_char *)&optval,
2149                                               sizeof(optval),
2150                                               optp,
2151                                               privileged, uproto);
2152                            break;
2153                    }
2154
2155                    case IPV6_RECVHOPLIMIT:
2156                            /* cannot mix with RFC2292 */
2157                            if (OPTBIT(IN6P_RFC2292)) {
2158                                    error = EINVAL;
2159                                    break;
2160                            }
2161                            OPTSET(IN6P_HOPLIMIT);
2162                            break;
2163
2164                    case IPV6_RECVHOPOPTS:
2165                            /* cannot mix with RFC2292 */
2166                            if (OPTBIT(IN6P_RFC2292)) {
2167                                    error = EINVAL;
2168                                    break;
2169                            }
2170                            OPTSET(IN6P_HOPOPTS);
2171                            break;
2172
2173                    case IPV6_RECVDSTOPTS:
2174                            /* cannot mix with RFC2292 */
2175                            if (OPTBIT(IN6P_RFC2292)) {
2176                                    error = EINVAL;
2177                                    break;
2178                            }
2179                            OPTSET(IN6P_DSTOPTS);
2180                            break;
2181
2182                    case IPV6_RECVRTHDRDSTOPTS:
2183                            /* cannot mix with RFC2292 */
2184                            if (OPTBIT(IN6P_RFC2292)) {
2185                                    error = EINVAL;
2186                                    break;
2187                            }
2188                            OPTSET(IN6P_RTHDRDSTOPTS);
2189                            break;
```

```
2190
2191                        case IPV6_RECVRTHDR:
2192                                /* cannot mix with RFC2292 */
2193                                if (OPTBIT(IN6P_RFC2292)) {
2194                                        error = EINVAL;
2195                                        break;
2196                                }
2197                                OPTSET(IN6P_RTHDR);
2198                                break;
2199
2200                        case IPV6_FAITH:
2201                                OPTSET(IN6P_FAITH);
2202                                break;
2203
2204                        case IPV6_RECVPATHMTU:
2205                                /*
2206                                 * We ignore this option for TCP
2207                                 * sockets.
2208                                 * (rfc2292bis leaves this case
2209                                 * unspecified.)
2210                                 */
2211                                if (uproto != IPPROTO_TCP)
2212                                        OPTSET(IN6P_MTU);
2213                                break;
2214
2215                        case IPV6_V6ONLY:
2216                                /*
2217                                 * make setsockopt(IPV6_V6ONLY)
2218                                 * available only prior to bind(2).
2219                                 * see ipng mailing list, Jun 22 2001.
2220                                 */
2221                                if (in6p->in6p_lport ||
2222                                    !SA6_IS_ADDR_UNSPECIFIED(&in6p->in6p_lsa)) {
2223                                        error = EINVAL;
2224                                        break;
2225                                }
2234                                OPTSET(IN6P_IPV6_V6ONLY);
2236                                if (optval)
2237                                        in6p->in6p_vflag &= ~INP_IPV4;
2238                                else
2239                                        in6p->in6p_vflag |= INP_IPV4;
2248                                break;
2249                        case IPV6_RECVTCLASS:
2250                                /* cannot mix with RFC2292 XXX */
2251                                if (OPTBIT(IN6P_RFC2292)) {
2252                                        error = EINVAL;
2253                                        break;
2254                                }
2255                                OPTSET(IN6P_TCLASS);
2256                                break;
2257                        case IPV6_AUTOFLOWLABEL:
2258                                OPTSET(IN6P_AUTOFLOWLABEL);
2259                                break;
2260
2261                        }
2262                        break;
```
—— ip6_output.c

2128–2262 These cases are almost based on the same logic, that is, set or clear the flag bit associated with a particular option in the corresponding socket. An error of EINVAL is returned if an [RFC3542] option is being specified while an [RFC2292] option has already been set.

IPV6_HOPLIMIT is an exception. The option value is an actual hop limit value, not a flag bit. The ip6_pcbopt() function will handle the actual procedure later.

Since [RFC3542] intentionally leaves, it open how the `IPV6_RECVPATHMTU` option can be used for Transmission Control Protocol (TCP) sockets, this option is ignored on TCP sockets.

The `IPV6_V6ONLY` option disables the usage of IPv4-mapped IPv6 addresses on an `AF_INET6` socket for IPv4 communication. This option can be set only when the socket is not bound to any specific address. Otherwise, an error of `EINVAL` is returned.

This restriction was introduced to avoid the following scenario:

- An `AF_INET6` socket is created and the `IPV6_V6ONLY` option is turned on.

- The `AF_INET6` socket is then bound to a specific TCP port (e.g. 80).

- An `AF_INET` socket is created and bound to the same TCP port. This should succeed since these two sockets do not conflict with each other.

- The `IPV6_V6ONLY` option is then turned off on the `AF_INET6` socket. Without the restriction, this would also succeed.

- Now the two sockets effectively conflict, and it will be unclear which socket accepts incoming TCP/IPv4 connections to port 80.

While this restriction should make sense, it was not incorporated in [RFC3493], unfortunately. Even if it is not prohibited, an application should not set this option on a bound socket.

It should also be noted that the `setsockopt()` operation simply sets the `IN6P_IPV6_V6ONLY` flag in the PCB flags field. It does not yet clear the `INP_IPV4` flag of the `inp_vflag`, and in this sense, the socket is not really "IPv6-only" at the moment. The `INP_IPV4` flag will be cleared when other socket operations such as the `bind()` system call are performed.

Listing 4-15

_____ ip6_output.c

```
2264                        case IPV6_OTCLASS:
2265                        {
2266                                struct ip6_pktopts **optp;
2267                                u_int8_t tclass;
2268
2269                                if (optlen != sizeof(tclass)) {
2270                                        error = EINVAL;
2271                                        break;
2272                                }
2274                                error = sooptcopyin(sopt, &tclass,
2275                                        sizeof tclass, sizeof tclass);
2276                                if (error)
2277                                        break;
2281                                optp = &in6p->in6p_outputopts;
2282                                error = ip6_pcbopt(optname,
2283                                                (u_char *)&tclass,
2284                                                sizeof(tclass),
2285                                                optp,
2286                                                privileged, uproto);
2287                                break;
2288                        }
```
_____ ip6_output.c

2264–2288 This `case` statement handles an old definition of a socket option for specifying the value of the IPv6 Traffic Class field of an outgoing packet. Formerly, the option value was defined as an unsigned 8-bit integer, but it was later changed to a generic integer in [RFC3542]. The `case` statement for `IPV6_OTCLASS` provides binary backward compatibility for old applications that still use the previous definition. For this reason, `IPV6_OTCLASS` is a kernel-only definition and is hidden from applications. We will only describe the new option, `IPV6_TCLASS`, in this book.

Listing 4-16

─── *ip6_output.c*

```
2290                    case IPV6_TCLASS:
2291                    case IPV6_DONTFRAG:
2292                    case IPV6_USE_MIN_MTU:
2293                    case IPV6_PREFER_TEMPADDR:
2294                            if (optlen != sizeof(optval)) {
2295                                    error = EINVAL;
2296                                    break;
2297                            }
2299                            error = sooptcopyin(sopt, &optval,
2300                                    sizeof optval, sizeof optval);
2301                            if (error)
2302                                    break;
2306                            {
2307                                    struct ip6_pktopts **optp;
2308                                    optp = &in6p->in6p_outputopts;
2309                                    error = ip6_pcbopt(optname,
2310                                                    (u_char *)&optval,
2311                                                    sizeof(optval),
2312                                                    optp,
2313                                                    privileged, uproto);
2314                            break;
2315                            }
```

─── *ip6_output.c*

2290–2315 These options take integer values and are not subject to compatibility issues that exist between the two versions of the advanced API specification. The `sooptcopyin()` function copies the option value after length validation. The `ip6_pcbopt()` function completes the process.

Listing 4-17

─── *ip6_output.c*

```
2317                    case IPV6_2292PKTINFO:
2318                    case IPV6_2292HOPLIMIT:
2319                    case IPV6_2292HOPOPTS:
2320                    case IPV6_2292DSTOPTS:
2321                    case IPV6_2292RTHDR:
2322                            /* RFC 2292 */
2323                            if (optlen != sizeof(int)) {
2324                                    error = EINVAL;
2325                                    break;
2326                            }
2328                            error = sooptcopyin(sopt, &optval,
2329                                    sizeof optval, sizeof optval);
2330                            if (error)
2331                                    break;
2335                            switch (optname) {
2336                            case IPV6_2292PKTINFO:
2337                                    OPTSET2292(IN6P_PKTINFO);
2338                                    break;
2339                            case IPV6_2292HOPLIMIT:
2340                                    OPTSET2292(IN6P_HOPLIMIT);
2341                                    break;
2342                            case IPV6_2292HOPOPTS:
```

```
2343                                        /*
2344                                         * Check super-user privilege.
2345                                         * See comments for IPV6_RECVHOPOPTS.
2346                                         */
2347                                        if (!privileged)
2348                                                return (EPERM);
2349                                        OPTSET2292(IN6P_HOPOPTS);
2350                                        break;
2351                                    case IPV6_2292DSTOPTS:
2352                                        if (!privileged)
2353                                                return (EPERM);
2354                                        OPTSET2292(IN6P_DSTOPTS|IN6P_RTHDRDSTOPTS);
      /* XXX */
2355                                        break;
2356                                    case IPV6_2292RTHDR:
2357                                        OPTSET2292(IN6P_RTHDR);
2358                                        break;
2359                                    }
2360                                    break;
```
_____ ip6_output.c

Line 2354 is broken here for layout reasons. However, it is a single line of code.

2317–2360 These case statements provide backward compatibility to [RFC2292]-specific
options. The OPTSET2292() macro is used to mark the socket so that it processes only
[RFC2292] options. For Hop-by-Hop and Destination options headers, a superuser privilege
is required for the same reason described earlier.

Since [RFC3542] differentiates the two possible positions of Destination options
headers and the kernel implementation supports the specification, the code in the case
statement for IPV6_2292DSTOPTS sets two flag bits in the socket: one flag bit for the
Destination options header that appears before the Routing header, and one flag bit for the
Destination options header that appears after the Routing header (if any Routing header
exists).

Listing 4-18
_____ ip6_output.c

```
2361                            case IPV6_PKTINFO:
2362                            case IPV6_HOPOPTS:
2363                            case IPV6_RTHDR:
2364                            case IPV6_DSTOPTS:
2365                            case IPV6_RTHDRDSTOPTS:
2366                            case IPV6_NEXTHOP:
2367                            {
2368                                    /* new advanced API (2292bis) */
2369                                    u_char *optbuf;
2370                                    int optlen;
2371                                    struct ip6_pktopts **optp;
2372
2373                                    /* cannot mix with RFC2292 */
2374                                    if (OPTBIT(IN6P_RFC2292)) {
2375                                            error = EINVAL;
2376                                            break;
2377                                    }
2378
2380                                    optbuf = sopt->sopt_val;
2381                                    optlen = sopt->sopt_valsize;
2395                                    optp = &in6p->in6p_outputopts;
2396                                    error = ip6_pcbopt(optname,
2397                                                    optbuf, optlen,
2398                                                    optp, privileged, uproto);
2399                                    break;
2400                            }
```
_____ ip6_output.c

2361–2400 These option types were defined in [RFC2292] but are currently used only in the context of [RFC3542]. So the `case` statements first check for the presence of the `IN6P_RFC2292` flag to reject a mixed usage, and then call function `ip6_pcbopt()` for the actual processing.

Note: This code has a bug. Since `sopt_val` points to an address in the user space, the value must be verified and copied to the kernel space using `copyin()` via `sooptcopyin()`. Although the direct reference to `sopt_val` as is done in this code does not cause a problem for valid values, invalid input can make the kernel panic. This bug has been fixed in later versions of the kernel.

Listing 4-19

```
                                                              ip6_output.c
2401    #undef OPTSET
2402
2403                        case IPV6_MULTICAST_IF:
2404                        case IPV6_MULTICAST_HOPS:
2405                        case IPV6_MULTICAST_LOOP:
2406                        case IPV6_JOIN_GROUP:
2407                        case IPV6_LEAVE_GROUP:
2409                        {
2410                                if (sopt->sopt_valsize > MLEN) {
2411                                        error = EMSGSIZE;
2412                                        break;
2413                                }
2414                                /* XXX */
2415                        }

2438                                MGET(m, sopt->sopt_p ? M_WAIT : M_DONTWAIT,
    MT_HEADER);
2440                                if (m == 0) {
2441                                        error = ENOBUFS;
2442                                        break;
2443                                }
2456                                m->m_len = sopt->sopt_valsize;
                                                              ip6_output.c
```
Line 2438 is broken here for layout reasons. However, it is a single line of code.

2403–2456 Since the `ip6_setmoptions()` function expects an `mbuf` to store option value, the value passed from the application should be copied into an `mbuf`. This allocation is actually redundant but is done here for portability with other BSD variants.

Listing 4-20

```
                                                              ip6_output.c
2457                                error = sooptcopyin(sopt, mtod(m, char *),
2458                                                    m->m_len, m->m_len);
2459                                error = ip6_setmoptions(sopt->sopt_name,
2460                                                        &in6p->in6p_moptions,
2461                                                        m);
2462                                (void)m_free(m);
2463                        }
        (cases for other OSes)

2473                                break;
                                                              ip6_output.c
```

2457–2463 The `sooptcopyin()` function copies the option value into the kernel. The `ip6_setmoptions()` function processes the options (Note: There is a small bug here. An error from `sooptcopyin()` should be handled correctly). The temporarily allocated `mbuf` is not necessary and is freed.

Listing 4-21

_____ ip6_output.c
```
2476                        case IPV6_PORTRANGE:
2478                            error = sooptcopyin(sopt, &optval,
2479                                sizeof optval, sizeof optval);
2480                        if (error)
2481                            break;
2485
2486                        switch (optval) {
2487                        case IPV6_PORTRANGE_DEFAULT:
2488                                in6p->in6p_flags &= ~(IN6P_LOWPORT);
2489                                in6p->in6p_flags &= ~(IN6P_HIGHPORT);
2490                                break;
2491
2492                        case IPV6_PORTRANGE_HIGH:
2493                                in6p->in6p_flags &= ~(IN6P_LOWPORT);
2494                                in6p->in6p_flags |= IN6P_HIGHPORT;
2495                                break;
2496
2497                        case IPV6_PORTRANGE_LOW:
2498                                in6p->in6p_flags &= ~(IN6P_HIGHPORT);
2499                                in6p->in6p_flags |= IN6P_LOWPORT;
2500                                break;
2501
2502                        default:
2503                                error = EINVAL;
2504                                break;
2505                        }
2506                        break;
```
_____ ip6_output.c

2476–2506 The `IPV6_PORTRANGE` option is specific to some BSD variants, which specifies the port range for a TCP or User Datagram Protocol (UDP) socket with an unspecified (zero) port number. The code simply sets or clears some flag bits in the socket.

Listing 4-22

_____ ip6_output.c
```
2652                        default:
2653                            error = ENOPROTOOPT;
2654                            break;
2655                        }
2660                        break;
```
_____ ip6_output.c

2652–2655 An error of `ENOPROTOOPT` is returned if an unknown option type is encountered.

4.3.3   Get Operations

In this part, we show the `getsockopt()` operations for IPv6 socket options. Most options are handled within this function. Some others, especially the multicast-related options and options defined in [RFC3542], need additional subroutines.

Listing 4-23

ip6_output.c
```
2663                         case SOPT_GET:
2667                             switch (optname) {
2668
2669                             case IPV6_2292PKTOPTIONS:
2670    #ifdef IPV6_PKTOPTIONS
2671                             case IPV6_PKTOPTIONS:
2672    #endif
2674                                     if (in6p->in6p_inputopts &&
2675                                         in6p->in6p_inputopts->head) {
2676                                             struct mbuf *m;
2677                                             m = m_copym(in6p->in6p_inputopts->head,
2678                                                 0, M_COPYALL, M_WAIT);
2679                                             error = soopt_mcopyout(sopt, m);
2680                                             if (error == 0)
2681                                                     m_freem(m);
2682                                     } else
2683                                             sopt->sopt_valsize = 0;
2694                                     break;
```
ip6_output.c

2669–2694 The getsockopt() operation for the IPV6_PKTOPTIONS socket option retrieves
option information, such as IPv6 extension headers that are stored in the socket. [RFC3542]
deprecated this and the kernel no longer stores any information on the socket. The code simply provides backward compatibility to older applications by always returning empty data.

Listing 4-24

ip6_output.c
```
2696                         case IPV6_RECVHOPOPTS:
2697                         case IPV6_RECVDSTOPTS:
2698                         case IPV6_RECVRTHDRDSTOPTS:
2699                         case IPV6_UNICAST_HOPS:
2700                         case IPV6_RECVPKTINFO:
2701                         case IPV6_RECVHOPLIMIT:
2702                         case IPV6_RECVRTHDR:
2703                         case IPV6_RECVPATHMTU:
2704
2705                         case IPV6_FAITH:
2706                         case IPV6_V6ONLY:
2708                         case IPV6_PORTRANGE:
2710                         case IPV6_RECVTCLASS:
2711                         case IPV6_AUTOFLOWLABEL:
2712                             switch (optname) {
2713
2714                             case IPV6_RECVHOPOPTS:
2715                                     optval = OPTBIT(IN6P_HOPOPTS);
2716                                     break;
2717
2718                             case IPV6_RECVDSTOPTS:
2719                                     optval = OPTBIT(IN6P_DSTOPTS);
2720                                     break;
2721
2722                             case IPV6_RECVRTHDRDSTOPTS:
2723                                     optval = OPTBIT(IN6P_RTHDRDSTOPTS);
2724                                     break;
2725
2726                             case IPV6_UNICAST_HOPS:
2727                                     optval = in6p->in6p_hops;
2728                                     break;
2729
2730                             case IPV6_RECVPKTINFO:
2731                                     optval = OPTBIT(IN6P_PKTINFO);
2732                                     break;
```

```
2733
2734                                    case IPV6_RECVHOPLIMIT:
2735                                            optval = OPTBIT(IN6P_HOPLIMIT);
2736                                            break;
2737
2738                                    case IPV6_RECVRTHDR:
2739                                            optval = OPTBIT(IN6P_RTHDR);
2740                                            break;
2741
2742                                    case IPV6_RECVPATHMTU:
2743                                            optval = OPTBIT(IN6P_MTU);
2744                                            break;
2745
2746                                    case IPV6_FAITH:
2747                                            optval = OPTBIT(IN6P_FAITH);
2748                                            break;
2749
2750                                    case IPV6_V6ONLY:
2752                                            optval = OPTBIT(IN6P_IPV6_V6ONLY);
2756                                            break;
2757
2759                                    case IPV6_PORTRANGE:
2760                                        {
2761                                            int flags;
2762                                            flags = in6p->in6p_flags;
2763                                            if (flags & IN6P_HIGHPORT)
2764                                                    optval = IPV6_PORTRANGE_HIGH;
2765                                            else if (flags & IN6P_LOWPORT)
2766                                                    optval = IPV6_PORTRANGE_LOW;
2767                                            else
2768                                                    optval = 0;
2769                                            break;
2770                                        }
2772                                    case IPV6_RECVTCLASS:
2773                                            optval = OPTBIT(IN6P_TCLASS);
2774                                            break;
2775
2776                                    case IPV6_AUTOFLOWLABEL:
2777                                            optval = OPTBIT(IN6P_AUTOFLOWLABEL);
2778                                            break;
2779
2783                                    }
2784                                    if (error)
2785                                            break;
2787                                    error = sooptcopyout(sopt, &optval,
2788                                            sizeof optval);
2794                                    break;
```
                                                                         ip6_output.c

2696–2794 These case statements return an integer value to the application, which indicates whether a particular option is enabled or not. The OPTBIT() macro returns 1 if the given option is enabled and the macro returns 0 otherwise. IPV6_UNICAST_HOPS is an exception where the actual hop limit value is returned. The other exception is IPV6_PORTRANGE, which returns the range identifier, that is, either IPV6_PORTRANGE_HIGH or IPV6_PORTRANGE_LOW.

The sooptcopyout() function copies the option value into the application memory space.

Listing 4-25
                                                                         ip6_output.c
```
2796                            case IPV6_PATHMTU:
2797                                {
2798                                    u_long pmtu = 0;
2799                                    struct ip6_mtuinfoxo mtuinfo;
```

```
....
2801                                        struct route *ro = &in6p->in6p_route;
....
2805
2806                                        if (!(so->so_state & SS_ISCONNECTED))
2807                                                return (ENOTCONN);
2808                                        /*
2809                                         * XXX: we dot not consider the case of source
2810                                         * routing, nor optional information to specify
2811                                         * the outgoing interface.
2812                                         */
2813                                        error = ip6_getpmtu(ro, NULL, NULL,
2814                                            &in6p->in6p_fsa, &pmtu, NULL);
2815                                        if (error)
2816                                                break;
2817                                        if (pmtu > IPV6_MAXPACKET)
2818                                                pmtu = IPV6_MAXPACKET;
2819
2820                                        bzero(&mtuinfo, sizeof(mtuinfo));
2821                                        mtuinfo.ip6m_mtu = (u_int32_t)pmtu;
2822                                        optdata = (void *)&mtuinfo;
2823                                        optdatalen = sizeof(mtuinfo);
2825                                        error = sooptcopyout(sopt, optdata,
2826                                            optdatalen);
2836                                        break;
2837                        }
```
── ip6_output.c

2796–2837 IPV6_PATHMTU is a read-only socket option that returns the path MTU value obtained for the remote address of a given connected socket. An ENOTCONN error is returned if the socket is not connected. The `ip6_getpmtu()` function stores the path MTU value in variable `pmtu`. The code states that the path MTU value may be inaccurate if the application uses source routing or if the application explicitly specifies the outgoing interface. In such cases, the outgoing interface may differ from that stored in the cached route `ro`, and the link MTU of the interface can be smaller than the stored path MTU.

Listing 4-26
── ip6_output.c

```
2839                        case IPV6_2292PKTINFO:
2840                        case IPV6_2292HOPLIMIT:
2841                        case IPV6_2292HOPOPTS:
2842                        case IPV6_2292RTHDR:
2843                        case IPV6_2292DSTOPTS:
2844                                if (optname == IPV6_2292HOPOPTS ||
2845                                    optname == IPV6_2292DSTOPTS ||
2846                                    !privileged)
2847                                        return (EPERM);
2848                                switch (optname) {
2849                                case IPV6_2292PKTINFO:
2850                                        optval = OPTBIT(IN6P_PKTINFO);
2851                                        break;
2852                                case IPV6_2292HOPLIMIT:
2853                                        optval = OPTBIT(IN6P_HOPLIMIT);
2854                                        break;
2855                                case IPV6_2292HOPOPTS:
2856                                        if (!privileged)
2857                                                return (EPERM);
2858                                        optval = OPTBIT(IN6P_HOPOPTS);
2859                                        break;
2860                                case IPV6_2292RTHDR:
2861                                        optval = OPTBIT(IN6P_RTHDR);
2862                                        break;
2863                                case IPV6_2292DSTOPTS:
2864                                        if (!privileged)
```

```
2865                                              return (EPERM);
2866                               optval = OPTBIT(IN6P_DSTOPTS|
    IN6P_RTHDRDSTOPTS);
2867                               break;
2868                       }
2870                       error = sooptcopyout(sopt, &optval,
2871                           sizeof optval);
2877                       break;
                                                          ip6_output.c
```

Line 2866 is broken here for layout reasons. However, it is a single line of code.

2839–2877 These cases are provided for backward compatibility to [RFC2292]. Each of the cases returns if the corresponding option is enabled on the socket. A superuser privilege is required for `IPV6_2292HOPOPTS` and `IPV6_2292DSTOPTS`, which is actually too restrictive. Since these operations just provide the fact if the corresponding bit is set, there is no reason to prohibit those. In fact, `getsockopt()` for similar options in [RFC3542] (such as `IPV6_RECVHOPLIMIT`) does not require the privilege.

Listing 4-27
```
                                                          ip6_output.c
2878                       case IPV6_PKTINFO:
2879                       case IPV6_HOPOPTS:
2880                       case IPV6_RTHDR:
2881                       case IPV6_DSTOPTS:
2882                       case IPV6_RTHDRDSTOPTS:
2883                       case IPV6_NEXTHOP:
2884                       case IPV6_OTCLASS:
2885                       case IPV6_TCLASS:
2886                       case IPV6_DONTFRAG:
2887                       case IPV6_USE_MIN_MTU:
2888                       case IPV6_PREFER_TEMPADDR:
2890                               error = ip6_getpcbopt(in6p->in6p_outputopts,
2891                                   optname, sopt);
2896                               break;
                                                          ip6_output.c
```

2878–2896 These options have either a large or variable length option value and are processed in `ip6_getpcbopt()`. `ip6_getpcbopt()` is described in Section 4.4.

Listing 4-28
```
                                                          ip6_output.c
2898                       case IPV6_MULTICAST_IF:
2899                       case IPV6_MULTICAST_HOPS:
2900                       case IPV6_MULTICAST_LOOP:
2901                       case IPV6_JOIN_GROUP:
2902                       case IPV6_LEAVE_GROUP:
2904                           {
2905                               struct mbuf *m;
2906                               error = ip6_getmoptions(sopt->sopt_name,
2907                                   in6p->in6p_moptions, &m);
2908                               if (error == 0)
2909                                       error = sooptcopyout(sopt,
2910                                           mtod(m, char *), m->m_len);
2911                               m_freem(m);
2912                           }
2917                               break;
                                                          ip6_output.c
```

2898–2917 The `getsockopt()` operation for multicast-related options are handled in `ip6_getmoptions()`. For portability reasons, the function internally allocates a new

mbuf and stores the option values to it. Since FreeBSD does not use an mbuf for
getsockopt(), the sooptcopyout() function copies the stored value to the application space here and frees the mbuf.

Listing 4-29
_____ ip6_output.c
```
3035                            default:
3036                                    error = ENOPROTOOPT;
3037                                    break;
3038                            }
3039                            break;
3040                    }
```
_____ ip6_output.c

3035–3038 An ENOPROTOOPT error is returned if an unknown option type is encountered.

Listing 4-30
_____ ip6_output.c
```
3041            } else {                    /* level != IPPROTO_IPV6 */
3042                    error = EINVAL;
3047            }
3048            return (error);
3049    }
```
_____ ip6_output.c

3041–3049 This else statement corresponds to the if clause at line 2019 (Listing 4-7), which
means the option level is not IPv6. An EINVAL error is returned in this case.

4.4 Getting Socket Options: `ip6_getpcbopt()` Function

The ip6_getpcbopt() function, shown in Listing 4-31, is a subroutine of ip6_ctloutput(),
which performs the actual socket option processing for the getsockopt() operation.

Listing 4-31
_____ ip6_output.c
```
3303    static int
3304    ip6_getpcbopt(pktopt, optname, sopt)
3305            struct ip6_pktopts *pktopt;
3306            struct sockopt *sopt;
3307            int optname;
3315    {
3316            void *optdata = NULL;
3317            int optdatalen = 0;
3318            struct ip6_ext *ip6e;
3319            int error = 0;
3320            struct in6_pktinfo null_pktinfo;
3321            int deftclass = 0, on;
3322            int defminmtu = IP6PO_MINMTU_MCASTONLY;
3323            int defpreftemp = IP6PO_TEMPADDR_SYSTEM;
3327
3328            switch (optname) {
3329            case IPV6_PKTINFO:
3330                    if (pktopt && pktopt->ip6po_pktinfo)
3331                            optdata = (void *)pktopt->ip6po_pktinfo;
3332                    else {
3333                            /* XXX: we don't have to do this every time... */
3334                            bzero(&null_pktinfo, sizeof(null_pktinfo));
3335                            optdata = (void *)&null_pktinfo;
```

```
3336                    }
3337                    optdatalen = sizeof(struct in6_pktinfo);
3338                    break;
3339            case IPV6_OTCLASS:
3340                    /* XXX */
3341                    return (EINVAL);
3342            case IPV6_TCLASS:
3343                    if (pktopt && pktopt->ip6po_tclass >= 0)
3344                            optdata = (void *)&pktopt->ip6po_tclass;
3345                    else
3346                            optdata = (void *)&deftclass;
3347                    optdatalen = sizeof(int);
3348                    break;
3349            case IPV6_HOPOPTS:
3350                    if (pktopt && pktopt->ip6po_hbh) {
3351                            optdata = (void *)pktopt->ip6po_hbh;
3352                            ip6e = (struct ip6_ext *)pktopt->ip6po_hbh;
3353                            optdatalen = (ip6e->ip6e_len + 1) << 3;
3354                    }
3355                    break;
3356            case IPV6_RTHDR:
3357                    if (pktopt && pktopt->ip6po_rthdr) {
3358                            optdata = (void *)pktopt->ip6po_rthdr;
3359                            ip6e = (struct ip6_ext *)pktopt->ip6po_rthdr;
3360                            optdatalen = (ip6e->ip6e_len + 1) << 3;
3361                    }
3362                    break;
3363            case IPV6_RTHDRDSTOPTS:
3364                    if (pktopt && pktopt->ip6po_dest1) {
3365                            optdata = (void *)pktopt->ip6po_dest1;
3366                            ip6e = (struct ip6_ext *)pktopt->ip6po_dest1;
3367                            optdatalen = (ip6e->ip6e_len + 1) << 3;
3368                    }
3369                    break;
3370            case IPV6_DSTOPTS:
3371                    if (pktopt && pktopt->ip6po_dest2) {
3372                            optdata = (void *)pktopt->ip6po_dest2;
3373                            ip6e = (struct ip6_ext *)pktopt->ip6po_dest2;
3374                            optdatalen = (ip6e->ip6e_len + 1) << 3;
3375                    }
3376                    break;
3377            case IPV6_NEXTHOP:
3378                    if (pktopt && pktopt->ip6po_nexthop) {
3379                            optdata = (void *)pktopt->ip6po_nexthop;
3380                            optdatalen = pktopt->ip6po_nexthop->sa_len;
3381                    }
3382                    break;
3383            case IPV6_USE_MIN_MTU:
3384                    if (pktopt)
3385                            optdata = (void *)&pktopt->ip6po_minmtu;
3386                    else
3387                            optdata = (void *)&defminmtu;
3388                    optdatalen = sizeof(int);
3389                    break;
3390            case IPV6_DONTFRAG:
3391                    if (pktopt && ((pktopt->ip6po_flags) & IP6PO_DONTFRAG))
3392                            on = 1;
3393                    else
3394                            on = 0;
3395                    optdata = (void *)&on;
3396                    optdatalen = sizeof(on);
3397                    break;
3398            case IPV6_PREFER_TEMPADDR:
3399                    if (pktopt)
3400                            optdata = (void *)&pktopt->ip6po_prefer_tempaddr;
3401                    else
3402                            optdata = (void *)&defpreftemp;
3403                    optdatalen = sizeof(int);
```

```
3404                    break;
3405            default:                    /* should not happen */
3406                    printf("ip6_getpcbopt: unexpected option: %d\n", optname);
3407                    return (ENOPROTOOPT);
3408            }
3409
3411            error = sooptcopyout(sopt, optdata, optdatalen);
3422
3423            return (error);
3424    }
```
——— ip6_output.c

3303–3323 The option values to be returned to the application will be copied to `sopt.ptdata` and `optdatalen` specify the address of option value and its length, respectively, which will be used at the end of this function as generic parameters.

3328–3404 The corresponding member in the `ip6_pktopts{}` structure is examined depending on the option name. If the option is present and succeeds validation, then `optdata` is set to point to the option data, and `optdatalen` is set to the size of the option. Otherwise, either that particular option has been unset or no option has ever been set (in which case `pktopt` is NULL), and `optdata` and `optdatalen` are set as specified in [RFC3542]. For example, if no option value has been set for the `IPV6_PKTINFO` option, `optdata` points to `null_pktinfo`, a zero-cleared `in6_pktinfo{}` structure.

3405–3408 Since `ip6_ctloutput()` calls this function only when a supported option is specified, the default case should not occur. Otherwise, it means a bug in the kernel code, and an `ENOPROTOOPT` error is returned.

3411–3423 `sooptcopyout()` copies the identified data into `sopt`, and the return value of that function, which is usually 0, will be returned to the application.

4.5   Setting Socket Options and Ancillary Data

In this Section, we describe the processing of socket options and ancillary data objects for outgoing packets. It covers the following four functions:

- `ip6_pcbopts()`
- `ip6_pcbopt()`
- `ip6_setpktoptions()`
- `ip6_setpktoption()`

The first two are for socket options and act as a subroutine of `ip6_ctloutput()`. The last two are common routines for socket options and ancillary data objects. For the latter usage, an upper layer output function calls `ip6_setpktoptions()`, which then calls `ip6_setpktoption()`.

4.5.1 `ip6_pcbopts()` Function

The `ip6_pcbopts()` function is a dedicated processing function for handling the `setsockopt()` operation on the `IPV6_PKTOPTIONS` socket option.

Listing 4-32

―――ip6_output.c

```
3193    /*
3194     * Set up IP6 options in pcb for insertion in output packets or
3195     * specifying behavior of outgoing packets.
3196     */
3197    static int
3199    ip6_pcbopts(pktopt, m, so, sopt)
3203            struct ip6_pktopts **pktopt;
3204            struct mbuf *m;
3205            struct socket *so;
3207            struct sockopt *sopt;
3209    {
3210            struct ip6_pktopts *opt = *pktopt;
3211            int error = 0;
3216            struct proc *p = sopt->sopt_p;
3223            int priv = 0;
3224
3225            /* turn off any old options. */
3226            if (opt) {
3227    #ifdef DIAGNOSTIC
3228                    if (opt->ip6po_pktinfo || opt->ip6po_nexthop ||
3229                        opt->ip6po_hbh || opt->ip6po_dest1 || opt->ip6po_dest2 ||
3230                        opt->ip6po_rhinfo.ip6po_rhi_rthdr)
3231                            printf("ip6_pcbopts: all specified options are cleared.\n");
3232    #endif
3233                    ip6_clearpktopts(opt, -1);
3234            } else
3235                    opt = malloc(sizeof(*opt), M_IP6OPT, M_WAITOK);
3236            *pktopt = NULL;
```

―――ip6_output.c

3225–3233 opt points to the pktopt variable containing the existing option structure if pktopt is a valid pointer. Since IPV6_PKTOPTIONS controls all possible options in a single operation, the side effect is that all the options will be turned off at once. This inconvenience is in fact one of the motivations for revising this API. The already allocated space is reused for the new set of options.

3235   A new ip6_pktopts{} structure is allocated if there have been no options set for the socket.

3236   The pointer stored in pktopt is cleared for possible error or clearing cases below.

Listing 4-33

―――ip6_output.c

```
3238            if (!m || m->m_len == 0) {
3239                    /*
3240                     * Only turning off any previous options, regardless of
3241                     * whether the opt is just created or given.
3242                     */
3243                    free(opt, M_IP6OPT);
3244                    return (0);
3245            }
```

―――ip6_output.c

3238–3245 The existing options are cleared if either no actual data is given or the given data are empty.

Listing 4-34

―――ip6_output.c

```
3247            /* set options specified by user. */
3249            if (p && !suser(p))
```

```
3250                     priv = 1;
3255           if ((error = ip6_setpktoptions(m, opt, NULL, priv, 1,
3256               so->so_proto->pr_protocol)) != 0) {
3257                     ip6_clearpktopts(opt, -1); /* XXX: discard all options */
3258                     free(opt, M_IP6OPT);
3259                     return (error);
3260           }
```
—— ip6_output.c

3249–3260 Function `ip6_setpktoptions()` performs the actual operation. `ip6_clearpktopts()` frees all intermediate structures if `ip6_setpktoptions()` returns a failure code. In that case, the option structure itself is also freed and the corresponding error code is returned.

Listing 4-35
—— ip6_output.c
```
3261           *pktopt = opt;
3262           return (0);
3263   }
```
—— ip6_output.c

3261–3262 The setsockopt operation succeeded. The new or updated option structure is stored in the socket.

4.5.2 `ip6_pcbopt()` Function

`ip6_pcbopt()` is a wrapper function for `ip6_setpktoption()` that handles the set operations for [RFC3542] socket options. Only `ip6_ctloutput()` calls this function.

Listing 4-36
—— ip6_output.c
```
3282   static int
3283   ip6_pcbopt(optname, buf, len, pktopt, priv, uproto)
3284           int optname, len, priv;
3285           u_char *buf;
3286           struct ip6_pktopts **pktopt;
3287           int uproto;
3288   {
3289           struct ip6_pktopts *opt;
3290
3291           if (*pktopt == NULL) {
3292                   *pktopt = malloc(sizeof(struct ip6_pktopts), M_IP6OPT,
3293                       M_WAITOK);
3294                   init_ip6pktopts(*pktopt);
3295                   (*pktopt)->needfree = 1;
3296           }
3297           opt = *pktopt;
3298
3299           return (ip6_setpktoption(optname, buf, len, opt, priv, 1, 0, uproto));
3300   }
```
—— ip6_output.c

3282–3300 `pktopt` points to the address of the pointer to the socket options of a given socket. A new structure is allocated and is initialized if the socket options pointer is NULL. The `needfree` member is set to 1 to indicate that the structure is dynamically allocated and needs to be freed later in function `ip6_clearpktopts()`. After preparing `pktopt`, it is then passed to `ip6_setpktoption()` along with other parameters for processing.

4.5.3 `ip6_setpktoptions()` Function

The `ip6_setpktoptions()` function is called within two different code paths. The first code path comes from the `ip6_pcbopts()` function, which sets [RFC2292] style socket options. The other code path is from the transport layer output functions for configuring per-packet ancillary data object.

Listing 4-37
_____ ip6_output.c

```
4366    /*
4367     * Set IPv6 outgoing packet options based on advanced API.
4368     */
4369    int
4370    ip6_setpktoptions(control, opt, stickyopt, priv, needcopy, uproto)
4371            struct mbuf *control;
4372            struct ip6_pktopts *opt, *stickyopt;
4373            int priv, needcopy, uproto;
```
_____ ip6_output.c

4366–4373 A nonzero value of `needcopy` implies that the first code path is taken. `opt` points to the option data structure to be configured while `stickyopt` is the same structure that is already set on the socket as sticky options. The `stickyopt` variable is only necessary for the configuration of ancillary data. Variable `control` is an mbuf that stores user-supplied options.

Listing 4-38
_____ ip6_output.c

```
4374    {
4375            struct cmsghdr *cm = 0;
4376
4377            if (control == 0 || opt == 0)
4378                    return (EINVAL);
```
_____ ip6_output.c

4377–4378 In general, `control` contains the socket option requested by the application, and the result is returned in `opt`. Both varibles must be non-NULL.

Listing 4-39
_____ ip6_output.c

```
4380            if (stickyopt) {
4381                    /*
4382                     * If stickyopt is provided, make a local copy of the options
4383                     * for this particular packet, then override them by ancillary
4384                     * objects.
4385                     * XXX: need to gain a reference for the cached route of the
4386                     * next hop in case of the overriding.
4387                     */
4388                    *opt = *stickyopt;
4389                    if (opt->ip6po_nextroute.ro_rt)
4390                            opt->ip6po_nextroute.ro_rt->rt_refcnt++;
4391            } else
4392                    init_ip6pktopts(opt);
4393            opt->needfree = needcopy;
4394
4395            /*
```

```
4396                    * XXX: Currently, we assume all the optional information is stored
4397                    * in a single mbuf.
4398                    */
4399                   if (control->m_next)
4400                           return (EINVAL);
4401
4402                   for (; control->m_len; control->m_data += CMSG_ALIGN(cm->cmsg_len),
4403                       control->m_len -= CMSG_ALIGN(cm->cmsg_len)) {
4404                           int error;
4405
4406                           if (control->m_len < CMSG_LEN(0))
4407                                   return (EINVAL);
4408
4409                           cm = mtod(control, struct cmsghdr *);
4410                           if (cm->cmsg_len == 0 || cm->cmsg_len > control->m_len)
4411                                   return (EINVAL);
4412                           if (cm->cmsg_level != IPPROTO_IPV6)
4413                                   continue;
4414
4415                           error = ip6_setpktoption(cm->cmsg_type, CMSG_DATA(cm),
4416                               cm->cmsg_len - CMSG_LEN(0), opt, priv, needcopy, 1, uproto);
4417                           if (error)
4418                                   return (error);
4419                   }
4420
4421                   return (0);
4422           }
```
—— ip6_output.c

4380–4392 A non-NULL `stickyopt` prompts the creation of a merged structure that contains both the existing sticky option and the per-packet objects. The content of `stickyopt` is copied into `opt`. If a route to a particular next hop is cached, the reference counter to the route is incremented, since the copy implicitly requests a new reference.

The `init_ip6pktopts()` function prepares a clean set of option structure if the sticky option is missing.

4393 The `needfree` member controls if the internal data of the `opt` structure should be dynamically allocated and freed.

4399–4400 As indicated by the comment, the current implementation requires all the option data to be stored in a single mbuf. This requirement is just for simplicity but is probably sufficient in practical usage.

4402–4422 The `for` loop iterates through all the options specified in the control variable. Each option must be at least `CMSG_LEN(0)` bytes to ensure the `cmsg_len` and the `cmsg_level` members can be safely referenced. `cmsg_len` must not be 0 or else it would cause an infinite loop. This routine is only interested in IPv6-related options, and thus options other than those at the `IPPROTO_IPV6` level are ignored. Function `ip6_setpktoption()` processes one given option at a time. `ip6_setpktoptions()` terminates the process and returns the error if any invocation of `ip6_setpktoption()` indicates an error condition.

4.5.4 `ip6_setpktoption()` Function

The `ip6_setpktoption()` function processes a given socket option or ancillary data object, most of which are defined as advanced API options.

TABLE 4-2

Sticky	Cmsg	Meaning
0	0	An impossible case
0	1	An ancillary data object (for [RFC2292] and [RFC3542])
1	0	An [RFC3542] socket option
1	1	An [RFC2292] socket option

Listing 4-40

ip6_output.c

```
4424    /*
4425     * Set a particular packet option, as a sticky option or an ancillary data
4426     * item.  "len" can be 0 only when it's a sticky option.
4427     * We have 4 cases of combination of "sticky" and "cmsg":
4428     * "sticky=0, cmsg=0": impossible
4429     * "sticky=0, cmsg=1": RFC2292 or rfc2292bis ancillary data
4430     * "sticky=1, cmsg=0": rfc2292bis socket option
4431     * "sticky=1, cmsg=1": RFC2292 socket option
4432     */
4433    static int
4434    ip6_setpktoption(optname, buf, len, opt, priv, sticky, cmsg, uproto)
4435            int optname, len, priv, sticky, cmsg, uproto;
4436            u_char *buf;
4437            struct ip6_pktopts *opt;
```

ip6_output.c

4433–4437 Whether the function operates on a socket option or an ancillary data object depends on the values of `sticky` and `cmsg`. The semantics of each combination is summarized in Table 4-2.

Listing 4-41

ip6_output.c

```
4438    {
4439            int minmtupolicy, preftemp;
4440
4441            if (!sticky && !cmsg) {
4442    #ifdef DIAGNOSTIC
4443                    printf("ip6_setpktoption: impossible case\n");
4444    #endif
4445                    return (EINVAL);
4446            }
4447
4448            /*
4449             * IPV6_2292xxx is for backward compatibility to RFC2292, and should
4450             * not be specified in the context of rfc2292bis.  Conversely,
4451             * rfc2292bis types should not be specified in the context of RFC2292.
4452             *
4453             */
4454            if (!cmsg) {
4455                    switch (optname) {
4456                    case IPV6_2292PKTINFO:
4457                    case IPV6_2292HOPLIMIT:
4458                    case IPV6_2292NEXTHOP:
4459                    case IPV6_2292HOPOPTS:
4460                    case IPV6_2292DSTOPTS:
4461                    case IPV6_2292RTHDR:
4462                    case IPV6_2292PKTOPTIONS:
```

```
4463                               return (ENOPROTOOPT);
4464                     }
4465            }
4466            if (sticky && cmsg) {
4467                     switch (optname) {
4468                     case IPV6_PKTINFO:
4469                     case IPV6_HOPLIMIT:
4470                     case IPV6_NEXTHOP:
4471                     case IPV6_HOPOPTS:
4472                     case IPV6_DSTOPTS:
4473                     case IPV6_RTHDRDSTOPTS:
4474                     case IPV6_RTHDR:
4475                     case IPV6_REACHCONF:
4476                     case IPV6_USE_MIN_MTU:
4477                     case IPV6_DONTFRAG:
4478                     case IPV6_OTCLASS:
4479                     case IPV6_TCLASS:
4480                     case IPV6_PREFER_TEMPADDR: /* XXX: not an rfc2292bis option */
4481                               return (ENOPROTOOPT);
4482                     }
4483            }
```
——— ip6_output.c

4441–4446 The impossible combination of sticky and cmsg is explicitly rejected for safety.

4454–4462 The option must be an [RFC3542] socket option if cmsg is 0, and thus [RFC2292] option names are invalid.

4466–4483 The option must be an [RFC2292] socket option if both sticky and cmsg are true. In this case, option names that are only valid in the context of [RFC3542] are rejected. IPV6_PREFER_TEMPADDR is rejected here because it is an experimental option for source address selection and is not defined in either [RFC2292] or [RFC3542].

The following part of the function processes the given option identified by optname.

4.5.5   Set Packet Information

Listing 4-42
——— ip6_output.c
```
4484
4485            switch (optname) {
4486            case IPV6_2292PKTINFO:
4487            case IPV6_PKTINFO:
4488            {
4489                     struct ifnet *ifp = NULL;
4490                     struct in6_pktinfo *pktinfo;
4491
4492                     if (len != sizeof(struct in6_pktinfo))
4493                               return (EINVAL);
4494
4495                     pktinfo = (struct in6_pktinfo *)buf;
4496
4497                     /*
4498                      * An application can clear any sticky IPV6_PKTINFO option by
4499                      * doing a "regular" setsockopt with ipi6_addr being
4500                      * in6addr_any and ipi6_ifindex being zero.
4501                      * [rfc2292bis-02, Section 6]
4502                      */
4503                     if (optname == IPV6_PKTINFO && opt->ip6po_pktinfo) {
4504                               if (pktinfo->ipi6_ifindex == 0 &&
4505                                    IN6_IS_ADDR_UNSPECIFIED(&pktinfo->ipi6_addr)) {
```

```
4506                                ip6_clearpktopts(opt, optname);
4507                                break;
4508                        }
4509                }
4510
4511            if (uproto == IPPROTO_TCP && optname == IPV6_PKTINFO &&
4512                sticky && !IN6_IS_ADDR_UNSPECIFIED(&pktinfo->ipi6_addr)) {
4513                    return (EINVAL);
4514            }
4515
4516            /* validate the interface index if specified. */
4517            if (pktinfo->ipi6_ifindex > if_index ||
4518                pktinfo->ipi6_ifindex < 0) {
4519                    return (ENXIO);
4520            }
4521            if (pktinfo->ipi6_ifindex) {
4523                    ifp = ifnet_byindex(pktinfo->ipi6_ifindex);
4527                    if (ifp == NULL)
4528                            return (ENXIO);
4529            }
4530
4531            /*
4532             * We store the address anyway, and let in6_selectsrc()
4533             * validate the specified address.  This is because ipi6_addr
4534             * may not have enough information about its scope zone, and
4535             * we may need additional information (such as outgoing
4536             * interface or the scope zone of a destination address) to
4537             * disambiguate the scope.
4538             * XXX: the delay of the validation may confuse the
4539             * application when it is used as a sticky option.
4540             */
4541            if (sticky) {
4542                    if (opt->ip6po_pktinfo == NULL) {
4543                            opt->ip6po_pktinfo = malloc(sizeof(*pktinfo),
4544                                M_IP6OPT, M_WAITOK);
4545                    }
4546                    bcopy(pktinfo, opt->ip6po_pktinfo, sizeof(*pktinfo));
4547            } else
4548                    opt->ip6po_pktinfo = pktinfo;
4549            break;
4550        }
```
——— ip6_output.c

4486–4493 The `IPV6_PKTINFO` option can specify both the source address and the outgoing interface for packets transmitted over the given socket.

The option argument is a fixed size of the `in6_pktinfo{}` structure. An `EINVAL` error is returned if the given data size does not match the expected value.

4498–4509 In the context of [RFC3542], if the given `pktinfo` structure is empty and the `pktinfo` structure is already set for the socket, then the operation clears the previous `pktinfo` structure.

4511–4514 An `EINVAL` error is returned if a nonzero address is being set as an [RFC3542] socket option on a TCP socket. The reason is that the source address of a TCP connection cannot be changed dynamically once the connection is established. In fact, an application can specify the source address for a TCP socket using the `bind()` system call.

4516–4529 The interface index is checked against a valid range of interface indices if the outgoing interface is specified. This interface index must also correspond to a valid `ifnet{}` structure. The second condition is usually satisfied but is not always the case if interfaces have been dynamically destroyed and recreated.

4531–4550 The given option is stored for either the socket or the packet. Although both [RFC2292] and [RFC3542] require that the specified address be a valid unicast address of the sending node, address validation is postponed because the address itself may not have sufficient information for scope zone validation. As the code comment indicates, this behavior may confuse the application when this is used as a socket option because an invalid address may not be detected until packet transmission occurs. An application should therefore `bind()` the address to a socket first if the application wants that address to be the source address for subsequent outgoing packets rather than taking the `IPV6_PKTINFO` socket option approach.

4.5.6 Set Hop Limit

Listing 4-43

——— ip6_output.c
```
4552            case IPV6_2292HOPLIMIT:
4553            case IPV6_HOPLIMIT:
4554            {
4555                    int *hlimp;
4556
4557                    /*
4558                     * rfc2292bis-03 obsoleted the usage of sticky IPV6_HOPLIMIT
4559                     * to simplify the ordering among hoplimit options.
4560                     */
4561                    if (optname == IPV6_HOPLIMIT && sticky)
4562                            return (ENOPROTOOPT);
4563
4564                    if (len != sizeof(int))
4565                            return (EINVAL);
4566                    hlimp = (int *)buf;
4567                    if (*hlimp < -1 || *hlimp > 255)
4568                            return (EINVAL);
4569
4570                    opt->ip6po_hlim = *hlimp;
4571                    break;
4572            }
```
——— ip6_output.c

4557–4562 Since the basic API defines options to manipulate the hop limit for both unicast and multicast packets, [RFC3542] deprecated the usage of `IPV6_HOPLIMIT` as a socket option.

4564–4570 This option has a fixed-length argument that specifies the hop limit value. If the length is correct and the value is within range, the hop limit value is set in the corresponding field of the option structure. A value of −1 has a special meaning that the system's default hop limit will be used.

4.5.7 Set Traffic Class (Old Style)

Listing 4-44

——— ip6_output.c
```
4574            case IPV6_OTCLASS:
4575                    if (len != sizeof(u_int8_t))
4576                            return (EINVAL);
4577
4578                    opt->ip6po_tclass = *(u_int8_t *)buf;
4579                    break;
```
——— ip6_output.c

4574–4579 IPV6_OTCLASS is only provided for binary backward compatibility to an old specification of the Traffic Class API.

Listing 4-45

-- ip6_output.c
```
4581          case IPV6_TCLASS:
4582          {
4583                  int tclass;
4584
4585                  if (len != sizeof(int))
4586                          return (EINVAL);
4587                  tclass = *(int *)buf;
4588                  if (tclass < -1 || tclass > 255)
4589                          return (EINVAL);
4590
4591                  opt->ip6po_tclass = tclass;
4592                  break;
4593          }
```
-- ip6_output.c

4581–4593 This option specifies the value for the Traffic Class field for outgoing packets. Since the field length is 8 bits, a nonnegative option argument must be between 0 and 255. A value of −1 has a special meaning that the system's default value will be used.

4.5.8 Specify the Next Hop Address

Listing 4-46

-- ip6_output.c
```
4595          case IPV6_2292NEXTHOP:
4596          case IPV6_NEXTHOP:
4597                  if (!priv)
4598                          return (EPERM);
4599
4600                  if (len == 0) {          /* just remove the option */
4601                          ip6_clearpktopts(opt, IPV6_NEXTHOP);
4602                          break;
4603                  }
4604
4605                  /* check if cmsg_len is large enough for sa_len */
4606                  if (len < sizeof(struct sockaddr) || len < *buf)
4607                          return (EINVAL);
4608
4609                  switch (((struct sockaddr *)buf)->sa_family) {
4610                  case AF_INET6:
4611                  {
4612                          struct sockaddr_in6 *sa6 = (struct sockaddr_in6 *)buf;
4613                          int error;
4614
4615                          if (sa6->sin6_len != sizeof(struct sockaddr_in6))
4616                                  return (EINVAL);
4617
4618                          if (SA6_IS_ADDR_UNSPECIFIED(sa6) ||
4619                              IN6_IS_ADDR_MULTICAST(&sa6->sin6_addr)) {
4620                                  return (EINVAL);
4621                          }
4622                          if ((error = scope6_check_id(sa6, ip6_use_defzone))
4623                              != 0) {
4624                                  return (error);
4625                          }
4627                          sa6->sin6_scope_id = 0; /* XXX */
4629                          break;
4630                  }
```

```
4631                    case AF_LINK:          /* should eventually be supported */
4632                    default:
4633                            return (EAFNOSUPPORT);
4634                    }
4635
4636                    /* turn off the previous option, then set the new option. */
4637                    ip6_clearpktopts(opt, IPV6_NEXTHOP);
4638                    if (sticky) {
4639                            opt->ip6po_nexthop = malloc(*buf, M_IP6OPT, M_WAITOK);
4640                            bcopy(buf, opt->ip6po_nexthop, *buf);
4641                    } else
4642                            opt->ip6po_nexthop = (struct sockaddr *)buf;
4643                    break;
```
—— ip6_output.c

4597–4598 [RFC2292] and [RFC3542] require the application to have the superuser privilege to specify the next hop.

4600–4603 The current next hop value is cleared if the application gives an empty argument.

4605–4607 The option argument must be at least as large as the generic socket address structure. Note that the first byte of a socket address structure on FreeBSD stores its length.

4609–4610 This implementation only supports IPv6 next hop addresses that are stored in sockaddr_in6{} structures. In fact, [RFC3542] clearly concentrates on the case of IPv6 next hop.

4618–4621 Semantically, invalid next hop addresses are rejected here.

4622–4630 The scope6_check_id() function validates the address with respect to the scope zone ID stored in the sockaddr_in6{} structure. If the application does not specify a zone ID when the zone information is required and the system allows the use of the default zone ID, then the function sets the sin6_scope_id field to the default zone. Note, however, that line 4627 then clears the zone ID value. The reason is that the current kernel implementation does not honor the zone ID for routing unless an experimental kernel option is defined.

4636–4637 The ip6_clearpktopts() function once clears the previously specified next hop information if any.

4638–4642 If this is specified as a socket option, new memory space is allocated to store the address, and the socket address structure is copied to the allocated space. Otherwise, ip6po_nexthop simply points to the address structure.

Listing 4-47
—— ip6_output.c
```
4645            case IPV6_2292HOPOPTS:
4646            case IPV6_HOPOPTS:
4647            {
4648                    struct ip6_hbh *hbh;
4649                    int hbhlen;
4650
4651                    /*
4652                     * XXX: We don't allow a non-privileged user to set ANY HbH
4653                     * options, since per-option restriction has too much
4654                     * overhead.
4655                     */
4656                    if (!priv)
4657                            return (EPERM);
```

```
4658
4659                      if (len == 0) {
4660                              ip6_clearpktopts(opt, IPV6_HOPOPTS);
4661                              break;           /* just remove the option */
4662                      }
4663
4664                      /* message length validation */
4665                      if (len < sizeof(struct ip6_hbh))
4666                              return (EINVAL);
4667                      hbh = (struct ip6_hbh *)buf;
4668                      hbhlen = (hbh->ip6h_len + 1) << 3;
4669                      if (len != hbhlen)
4670                              return (EINVAL);
4671
4672                      /* turn off the previous option, then set the new option. */
4673                      ip6_clearpktopts(opt, IPV6_HOPOPTS);
4674                      if (sticky) {
4675                              opt->ip6po_hbh = malloc(hbhlen, M_IP6OPT, M_WAITOK);
4676                              bcopy(hbh, opt->ip6po_hbh, hbhlen);
4677                      } else
4678                              opt->ip6po_hbh = hbh;
4679
4680                      break;
4681              }
```
――― ip6_output.c

4651–4657 [RFC2292] and [RFC3542] conditionally require the application to have the superuser privilege in order to set a Hop-by-Hop options header. This current implementation only supports per-header control even though the RFCs describe per-option control. The reason is that parsing the options can incur performance penalty, especially when parsing ancillary data objects.

4659–4662 The option data that was set previously is cleared when presented with empty data.

4664–4670 The option argument must contain a valid Hop-by-Hop options header. The length validation against the size of the `ip6_hbh{}` structure ensures safe access to the length field in the header.

4672–4681 The code logic here is the same as that of `IPV6_NEXTHOP`: clear the previous option data, allocate new space if necessary, and copy the new data.

4.5.9   Specify Destination Options Headers

According to [RFC2460], a Destination options header can appear before and after the Routing header. In order to deal with the different positions, the code to specify the Destination options headers becomes a bit complicated.

Listing 4-48
――― ip6_output.c

```
4683         case IPV6_2292DSTOPTS:
4684         case IPV6_DSTOPTS:
4685         case IPV6_RTHDRDSTOPTS:
4686         {
4687                 struct ip6_dest *dest, **newdest = NULL;
4688                 int destlen;
4689
4690                 if (!priv)          /* XXX: see the comment for IPV6_HOPOPTS */
4691                         return (EPERM);
4692
```

```
4693                    if (len == 0) {
4694                            ip6_clearpktopts(opt, optname);
4695                            break;          /* just remove the option */
4696                    }
4697
4698                    /* message length validation */
4699                    if (len < sizeof(struct ip6_dest))
4700                            return (EINVAL);
4701                    dest = (struct ip6_dest *)buf;
4702                    destlen = (dest->ip6d_len + 1) << 3;
4703                    if (len != destlen)
4704                            return (EINVAL);
4705
4706                    /*
4707                     * Determine the position that the destination options header
4708                     * should be inserted; before or after the routing header.
4709                     */
4710                    switch (optname) {
4711                    case IPV6_2292DSTOPTS:
4712                            /*
4713                             * The old advacned API is ambiguous on this point.
4714                             * Our approach is to determine the position based
4715                             * according to the existence of a routing header.
4716                             * Note, however, that this depends on the order of the
4717                             * extension headers in the ancillary data; the 1st
4718                             * part of the destination options header must appear
4719                             * before the routing header in the ancillary data,
4720                             * too.
4721                             * RFC2292bis solved the ambiguity by introducing
4722                             * separate ancillary data or option types.
4723                             */
4724                            if (opt->ip6po_rthdr == NULL)
4725                                    newdest = &opt->ip6po_dest1;
4726                            else
4727                                    newdest = &opt->ip6po_dest2;
4728                            break;
4729                    case IPV6_RTHDRDSTOPTS:
4730                            newdest = &opt->ip6po_dest1;
4731                            break;
4732                    case IPV6_DSTOPTS:
4733                            newdest = &opt->ip6po_dest2;
4734                            break;
4735                    }
4736
4737                    /* turn off the previous option, then set the new option. */
4738                    ip6_clearpktopts(opt, optname);
4739                    if (sticky) {
4740                            *newdest = malloc(destlen, M_IP6OPT, M_WAITOK);
4741                            bcopy(dest, *newdest, destlen);
4742                    } else
4743                            *newdest = dest;
4744
4745                    break;
4746            }
```
                                                              ─── ip6_output.c

4683–4691 Similar to the requirement for setting the Hop-by-Hop options header, an application must have the superuser privilege in order to set the Destination options header.

4693–4704 The option data that was set previously is cleared when presented with empty data.

4711–4728 In [RFC2292], the location for the Destination options header can be specified ambignously, regardless of the presence of a Routing header. This behavior is confusing to say the least and thus has been revised in [RFC3542].

4728–4731 [RFC3542] introduces a separate option name, IPV6_RTHDRDSTOPTS, to specify the location before a Routing header. This position is used only when a Routing header is actually specified.

4732–4735 In [RFC3542], IPV6_DSTOPTS means the location after a Routing header. This position is used regardless of the existence of a Routing header.

4737–4745 The code logic here is the same as that of IPV6_NEXTHOP (Listing 4-46).

4.5.10   Specify Routing Header

Listing 4-49

—— ip6_output.c
```
4748          case IPV6_2292RTHDR:
4749          case IPV6_RTHDR:
4750          {
4751                  struct ip6_rthdr *rth;
4752                  int rthlen;
4753
4754                  if (len == 0) {
4755                          ip6_clearpktopts(opt, IPV6_RTHDR);
4756                          break;            /* just remove the option */
4757                  }
4758
4759                  /* message length validation */
4760                  if (len < sizeof(struct ip6_rthdr))
4761                          return (EINVAL);
4762                  rth = (struct ip6_rthdr *)buf;
4763                  rthlen = (rth->ip6r_len + 1) << 3;
4764                  if (len != rthlen)
4765                          return (EINVAL);
4766
4767                  switch (rth->ip6r_type) {
4768                  case IPV6_RTHDR_TYPE_0:
4769                          if (rth->ip6r_len == 0)      /* must contain one addr */
4770                                  return (EINVAL);
4771                          if (rth->ip6r_len % 2)  /* length must be even */
4772                                  return (EINVAL);
4773                          if (rth->ip6r_len / 2 != rth->ip6r_segleft)
4774                                  return (EINVAL);
4775                          break;
4776                  default:
4777                          return (EINVAL);         /* not supported */
4778                  }
4779
4780                  /* turn off the previous option */
4781                  ip6_clearpktopts(opt, IPV6_RTHDR);
4782                  if (sticky) {
4783                          opt->ip6po_rthdr = malloc(rthlen, M_IP6OPT, M_WAITOK);
4784                          bcopy(rth, opt->ip6po_rthdr, rthlen);
4785                  } else
4786                          opt->ip6po_rthdr = rth;
4787
4788                  break;
4789          }
```
—— ip6_output.c

4748–4757 The option data that was set previously is cleared when presented with empty data.

4759–4765 At a minimum, the option must contain the fixed part of the Routing header (i.e. the size of the ip6_rthdr{} structure). The header length as specified by the ip6r_len field must be consistent with the data length.

4767–4778 The API implementation supports only the type 0 Routing header, that is, it does not consider the type 2 Routing header for Mobile IPv6. At least one intermediate address must be given for the type 0 header. `ip6r_len` must be an even integer as specified in [RFC2460] and must be consistent with the number of segments left that is given in the `ip6r_segleft` field.

4780–4788 The option data is stored in the socket at the completion of all the necessary validations.

4.5.11 Specify Reachability Confirmation

Listing 4-50

ip6_output.c

```
4790
4791            case IPV6_REACHCONF:
4792                    if (!cmsg)
4793                            return (ENOPROTOOPT);
4794
4795    #if 0
4796                    /*
4797                     * it looks dangerous to allow IPV6_REACHCONF to
4798                     * normal user.  it affects the ND state (system state)
4799                     * and can affect communication by others - jinmei
4800                     */
4801                    if (!priv)
4802                            return (EPERM);
4803    #else
4804                    /*
4805                     * we limit max # of subsequent userland reachability
4806                     * conformation by using ln->ln_byhint.
4807                     */
4808    #endif
4809                    if (len)
4810                            return (EINVAL);
4811                    opt->ip6po_flags |= IP6PO_REACHCONF;
4812                    break;
```

ip6_output.c

4791–4812 The `IPV6_REACHCONF` option was introduced briefly in the revision of the advanced API but has finally been removed in [RFC3542] due to lack of practical usage scenarios. This code is thus experimental and may not appear in future implementations that conform to [RFC3542].

4.5.12 Specify Sending Packets with the Minimum MTU

Listing 4-51

ip6_output.c

```
4814            case IPV6_USE_MIN_MTU:
4815                    if (len != sizeof(int))
4816                            return (EINVAL);
4817                    minmtupolicy = *(int *)buf;
4818                    if (minmtupolicy != IP6PO_MINMTU_MCASTONLY &&
4819                        minmtupolicy != IP6PO_MINMTU_DISABLE &&
4820                        minmtupolicy != IP6PO_MINMTU_ALL) {
4821                            return (EINVAL);
4822                    }
4823                    opt->ip6po_minmtu = minmtupolicy;
4824                    break;
```

ip6_output.c

4814–4824 The `IPV6_USE_MIN_MTU` option takes an integer argument and its effect on path MTU discovery and fragmentation is described in Table 3-6 (Section 3.6). The option value is saved in the socket after successful validation.

4.5.13 Specify Sending Packets without Fragmentation

Listing 4-52

```
                                                              ip6_output.c
4826           case IPV6_DONTFRAG:
4827                   if (len != sizeof(int))
4828                           return (EINVAL);
4829
4830                   if (uproto == IPPROTO_TCP || *(int *)buf == 0) {
4831                           /*
4832                            * we ignore this option for TCP sockets.
4833                            * (rfc2292bis leaves this case unspecified.)
4834                            */
4835                           opt->ip6po_flags &= ~IP6PO_DONTFRAG;
4836                   } else
4837                           opt->ip6po_flags |= IP6PO_DONTFRAG;
4838                   break;
                                                              ip6_output.c
```

4826–4838 The `IPV6_DONTFRAG` option instructs the kernel to avoid fragmentation even when packets do not fit in the path MTU. This option is usually set for debugging purposes. The option data is a Boolean value and must be an integer. [RFC3542] does not specify the expected behavior of this option when applied to a TCP socket. The KAME implementation ignores any attempts to set this option on TCP sockets.

4.5.14 Specify Preferring Temporary Addresses

Listing 4-53

```
                                                              ip6_output.c
4840           case IPV6_PREFER_TEMPADDR:
4841                   if (len != sizeof(int))
4842                           return (EINVAL);
4843                   preftemp = *(int *)buf;
4844                   if (preftemp != IP6PO_TEMPADDR_SYSTEM &&
4845                       preftemp != IP6PO_TEMPADDR_NOTPREFER &&
4846                       preftemp != IP6PO_TEMPADDR_PREFER) {
4847                           return (EINVAL);
4848                   }
4849                   opt->ip6po_prefer_tempaddr = preftemp;
4850                   break;
4851
4852           default:
4853                   return (ENOPROTOOPT);
4854           } /* end of switch */
4855
4856           return (0);
4857   }
                                                              ip6_output.c
```

4840–4849 The `IPV6_PREFER_TEMPADDR` option specifies that IPv6 temporary addresses for privacy extension should be preferred as the source address of packets sent over the given socket. This option is not defined in any standard documents and is experimental. The option data must be an integer that indicates the preference.

4852–4856 An `ENOPROTOOPT` error is returned if an unknown option type is encountered.

4.6 Cleaning Up: `ip6_freepcbopts()` Function

The `ip6_freepcbopts()` function, shown below, is called to free all sticky options when a socket is closed. Its behavior is trivial: releasing all internal resources by `ip6_clearpktopts()` and freeing the options structure.

Listing 4-54

_____ ip6_output.c
```
3547    void
3548    ip6_freepcbopts(pktopt)
3549            struct ip6_pktopts *pktopt;
3550    {
3551            if (pktopt == NULL)
3552                    return;
3553
3554            ip6_clearpktopts(pktopt, -1);
3555
3556            free(pktopt, M_IP6OPT);
3557    }
```
_____ ip6_output.c

4.7 IPv6 Multicast Socket Options

In this Section, we describe the processing of multicast-related socket options. It covers three functions for setting, getting, and freeing these options.

4.7.1 `ip6_setmoptions()` Function

The `ip6_setmoptions()` function is a subroutine of `ip6_ctloutput()` that handles the multicast-related socket options for the `setsockopt()` system call.

These socket options are maintained in the `in6p_moptions` member of the corresponding PCB, which points to an `ip6_moptions{}` structure. We first examine this structure, shown in Listing 4-55.

Listing 4-55

_____ ip6_var.h
```
111    struct  ip6_moptions {
112            struct          ifnet *im6o_multicast_ifp; /* ifp for outgoing multicasts */
113            u_char          im6o_multicast_hlim; /* hoplimit for outgoing multicasts */
114            u_char          im6o_multicast_loop; /* 1 >= hear sends if a member */
115            LIST_HEAD(, in6_multi_mship) im6o_memberships;
116    };
```
_____ ip6_var.h

`im6o_multicast_ifp` holds a pointer to the outgoing interface for multicast packet transmission. `im6o_multicast_hlim` defines the hop limit value to be placed in the Hop Limit field of the IPv6 header of the outgoing multicast packets. `im6o_multicast_loop` specifies whether the transmitting node should receive its own transmissions if the node is a member of the destination multicast group on the outgoing interface. The `im6o_memberships` member is a list of membership information about multicast groups that the application joins on this socket. Each entry of the list is an `in6_multi_mship{}` structure.

Through the following listings, we see the details of `ip6_setmoptions()`. The calling function, `ip6_ctloutput()`, passes a pointer to the PCB's `ip6_moptions{}` structure and socket option parameters stored in an mbuf.

Listing 4-56

ip6_output.c

```
3559     /*
3560      * Set the IP6 multicast options in response to user setsockopt().
3561      */
3562     static int
3563     ip6_setmoptions(optname, im6op, m)
3564             int optname;
3565             struct ip6_moptions **im6op;
3566             struct mbuf *m;
3567     {
3568             int error = 0;
3569             u_int loop, ifindex;
3570             struct ipv6_mreq *mreq;
3571             struct ifnet *ifp;
3572             struct ip6_moptions *im6o = *im6op;
3573             struct sockaddr_in6 sa6_mc;
3575             struct route ro;
3579             struct in6_multi_mship *imm;
3585             struct proc *p = curproc;          /* XXX */
3596
3597             if (im6o == NULL) {
3598                     /*
3599                      * No multicast option buffer attached to the pcb;
3600                      * allocate one and initialize to default values.
3601                      */
3602                     im6o = (struct ip6_moptions *)
3603                             malloc(sizeof(*im6o), M_IPMOPTS, M_WAITOK);
3604                     *im6op = im6o;
3605                     im6o->im6o_multicast_ifp = NULL;
3606                     im6o->im6o_multicast_hlim = ip6_defmcasthlim;
3607                     im6o->im6o_multicast_loop = IPV6_DEFAULT_MULTICAST_LOOP;
3608                     LIST_INIT(&im6o->im6o_memberships);
3609             }
```

ip6_output.c

3532–3585 im6op is a pointer to the address of the `inp6_moptions` member of a PCB. Its value is NULL unless a multicast-related socket option has been set for that PCB. curproc is a global variable that identifies the process that issued the socket option, which will be used to determine whether the process has sufficient privilege to perform such socket operations.

3357–3608 If there has been no multicast socket option set for the socket (i.e. PCB), inp6_moptions is NULL, and so is im6o. Then a new object is allocated and initialized with the system's default values.

Listing 4-57

ip6_output.c

```
3611             switch (optname) {
3612
3613             case IPV6_MULTICAST_IF:
3614                     /*
3615                      * Select the interface for outgoing multicast packets.
3616                      */
3617                     if (m == NULL || m->m_len != sizeof(u_int)) {
3618                             error = EINVAL;
3619                             break;
3620                     }
```

```
3621                    bcopy(mtod(m, u_int *), &ifindex, sizeof(ifindex));
3622                    if (ifindex < 0 || if_index < ifindex) {
3623                            error = ENXIO;          /* XXX EINVAL? */
3624                            break;
3625                    }
3629                    ifp = ifindex2ifnet[ifindex];
3631                    if (ifp == NULL || (ifp->if_flags & IFF_MULTICAST) == 0) {
3632                            error = EADDRNOTAVAIL;
3633                            break;
3634                    }
3635                    im6o->im6o_multicast_ifp = ifp;
3636                    break;
```
── ip6_output.c

3613–3620 The `IPV6_MULTICAST_IF` socket option takes an integer argument that is the interface index of the outgoing interface of multicast packets sent over the given socket. An `EINVAL` error is returned if an argument is missing or if the argument has an invalid length.

3621–3625 The argument value is copied to variable `ifindex`. An `ENXIO` error is returned if the value is outside the valid range.

3629–3634 An `EADDRNOTAVAIL` error is returned if either the specified interface has been dynamically detached or the interface does not have multicast capability. Note the error code is derived from the IPv4 multicast API, which identifies the interface by an IPv4 address. In fact, since the IPv6 API uses an interface index for identifying an interface (see Section 2.5), the error code is misleading in its name.

3635–3636 The specified interface is set in the `im6o_multicast_ifp` member at the completion of successful validation.

Listing 4-58
── ip6_output.c

```
3638            case IPV6_MULTICAST_HOPS:
3639                {
3640                    /*
3641                     * Set the IP6 hoplimit for outgoing multicast packets.
3642                     */
3643                    int optval;
3644                    if (m == NULL || m->m_len != sizeof(int)) {
3645                            error = EINVAL;
3646                            break;
3647                    }
3648                    bcopy(mtod(m, u_int *), &optval, sizeof(optval));
3649                    if (optval < -1 || optval >= 256)
3650                            error = EINVAL;
3651                    else if (optval == -1)
3652                            im6o->im6o_multicast_hlim = ip6_defmcasthlim;
3653                    else
3654                            im6o->im6o_multicast_hlim = optval;
3655                    break;
3656                }
```
── ip6_output.c

3638–3650 The `IPV6_MULTICAST_HOPS` option takes an integer value that is between −1 and 255 (inclusive) as an argument. An `EINVAL` error is returned if the argument is missing, has an invalid length, or is out of scope.

3652–3655 The option value −1 implies reinitializing `im6o_multicast_hlim` with the system default value. Any other option value will be set as the Hop Limit for outgoing multicast packets.

Listing 4-59

```
                                                                    ip6_output.c
3658            case IPV6_MULTICAST_LOOP:
3659                    /*
3660                     * Set the loopback flag for outgoing multicast packets.
3661                     * Must be zero or one.
3662                     */
3663                    if (m == NULL || m->m_len != sizeof(u_int)) {
3664                            error = EINVAL;
3665                            break;
3666                    }
3667                    bcopy(mtod(m, u_int *), &loop, sizeof(loop));
3668                    if (loop > 1) {
3669                            error = EINVAL;
3670                            break;
3671                    }
3672                    im6o->im6o_multicast_loop = loop;
3673                    break;
                                                                    ip6_output.c
```

3658–3673 `IPV6_MULTICAST_LOOP` takes an unsigned integer Boolean as an argument. A valid option value will be stored in `im6o_multicast_loop`.

Listing 4-60

```
                                                                    ip6_output.c
3675            case IPV6_JOIN_GROUP:
3676                    /*
3677                     * Add a multicast group membership.
3678                     * Group must be a valid IP6 multicast address.
3679                     */
3680                    if (m == NULL || m->m_len != sizeof(struct ipv6_mreq)) {
3681                            error = EINVAL;
3682                            break;
3683                    }
                                                                    ip6_output.c
```

3675–3683 The argument to the `IPV6_JOIN_GROUP` option must be an `ipv6_mreq{}` structure. An `EINVAL` error is returned if the argument is not provided or has an invalid length.

Listing 4-61

```
                                                                    ip6_output.c
3684                    mreq = mtod(m, struct ipv6_mreq *);
3685                    if (IN6_IS_ADDR_UNSPECIFIED(&mreq->ipv6mr_multiaddr)) {
3686                            /*
3687                             * We use the unspecified address to specify to accept
3688                             * all multicast addresses. Only super user is allowed
3689                             * to do this.
3690                             */
3692                            if (suser(p))
3696                            {
3697                                    error = EACCES;
3698                                    break;
3699                            }
3700                    } else if (!IN6_IS_ADDR_MULTICAST(&mreq->ipv6mr_multiaddr)) {
3701                            error = EINVAL;
3702                            break;
3703                    }
                                                                    ip6_output.c
```

3684–3699 `ipv6mr_multiaddr` field must hold a valid IPv6 multicast address. The KAME implementation allows a privileged application to specify the IPv6 unspecified address. While the intention may be to allow the socket to accept packets from any multicast address, the system does not actually behave that way. First, the `IN6_LOOKUP_MULTI()` macro does not have a special matching rule for the unspecified address. Secondly, in order to accept any multicast addresses on an interface, it is necessary to specify the promiscuous mode for the interface's multicast filter, which will not actually be done in this case. Later versions of the KAME implementation removed this code and similar code that exists for `IPV6_LEAVE_GROUP`.

3700–3703 An `EINVAL` error is returned if the given address is neither the unspecified address nor a multicast address.

Listing 4-62
_____ ip6_output.c
```
3705                    bzero(&sa6_mc, sizeof(sa6_mc));
3706                    sa6_mc.sin6_family = AF_INET6;
3707                    sa6_mc.sin6_len = sizeof(sa6_mc);
3708                    sa6_mc.sin6_addr = mreq->ipv6mr_multiaddr;
3709
3710                    /*
3711                     * If the interface is specified, validate it.
3712                     */
3713                    if (mreq->ipv6mr_interface < 0
3714                     || if_index < mreq->ipv6mr_interface) {
3715                            error = ENXIO;          /* XXX EINVAL? */
3716                            break;
3717                    }
3718                    /*
3719                     * If no interface was explicitly specified, choose an
3720                     * appropriate one according to the given multicast address.
3721                     */
3722                    if (mreq->ipv6mr_interface == 0) {
3723                            struct sockaddr_in6 *dst;
3724
3725                            /*
3726                             * Look up the routing table for the
3727                             * address, and choose the outgoing interface.
3728                             *    XXX: is it a good approach?
3729                             */
3730                            ro.ro_rt = NULL;
3731                            dst = (struct sockaddr_in6 *)&ro.ro_dst;
3732                            *dst = sa6_mc;
3733  #ifndef SCOPEDROUTING       /* XXX this is actually unnecessary here */
3734                            dst->sin6_scope_id = 0;
3735  #endif
3736                            rtalloc((struct route *)&ro);
3737                            if (ro.ro_rt == NULL) {
3738                                    error = EADDRNOTAVAIL;
3739                                    break;
3740                            }
3741                            ifp = ro.ro_rt->rt_ifp;
3742                            rtfree(ro.ro_rt);
3743                    } else {
3747                            ifp = ifindex2ifnet[mreq->ipv6mr_interface];
3749                    }
3750
3751                    /*
3752                     * See if we found an interface, and confirm that it
3753                     * supports multicast
3754                     */
```

```
3755              if (ifp == NULL || (ifp->if_flags & IFF_MULTICAST) == 0) {
3756                  error = EADDRNOTAVAIL;
3757                  break;
3758              }
```
── ip6_output.c

3705–3708 Variable sa6_mc is a sockaddr_in6{} structure that is initialized for later use. The supplied multicast address is saved in the sin6_addr field.

3713–3717 An EINVAL error is returned if the given interface index is out of range. Note that index 0 is explicitly allowed.

3722–3743 The application sets ipv6mr_interface to 0 when the application wants the kernel to automatically choose an appropriate interface for transmission. The KAME implementation simply follows the traditional IPv4 implementation logic in this case (i.e. calling rtalloc() to search the routing table for the specified destination multicast address and use the interface returned in the route entry as the outgoing interface). Variable ro holds the returned route. An EADDRNOTAVAIL error is returned if rtalloc() fails. The route entry is detached because it is not used anymore. Note that if the node cuts through a scope zone boundary of a multicast address, the routing table lookup approach is not applicable because the destination multicast address is ambiguous without the corresponding interface. Such is usually the case for interface-local and link-local multicast addresses, and thus the application must explicitly specify the interface index.

3743–3747 ifp is set to point to the corresponding interface structure by calling ifindex2ifnet() if the application provides an interface index.

3755–3758 ifp can be NULL if the specified interface has been dynamically detached. Even if the interface is valid, it may not support multicast. In either case an EADDRNOTAVAIL error is returned.

Note: As discussed in the case of IPV6_MULTICAST_IF (Listing 4-57), this error code is not really appropriate for the IPv6 multicast API, which does not use an IP address to specify an interface.

Listing 4-63

── ip6_output.c
```
3760              /* Fill in the scope zone ID */
3761              if (in6_addr2zoneid(ifp, &sa6_mc.sin6_addr,
3762                                  &sa6_mc.sin6_scope_id)) {
3763                  error = EADDRNOTAVAIL; /* XXX: should not happen */
3764                  break;
3765              }
3766              in6_embedscope(&sa6_mc.sin6_addr, &sa6_mc); /* XXX */
3767
3768              /*
3769               * See if the membership already exists.
3770               */
3771              for (imm = im6o->im6o_memberships.lh_first;
3772                  imm != NULL; imm = imm->i6mm_chain.le_next)
3773                  if (imm->i6mm_maddr->in6m_ifp == ifp &&
3774                      SA6_ARE_ADDR_EQUAL(&imm->i6mm_maddr->in6m_sa,
3775                                         &sa6_mc))
3776                          break;
3777              if (imm != NULL) {
3778                  error = EADDRINUSE;
3779                  break;
```

```
3780                    }
3781                    /*
3782                     * Everything looks good; add a new record to the multicast
3783                     * address list for the given interface.
3784                     */
3789                    imm = in6_joingroup(ifp, &sa6_mc, &error);
3790                    if (imm == NULL)
3791                            break;
3796                    LIST_INSERT_HEAD(&im6o->im6o_memberships, imm, i6mm_chain);
3797                    break;
```
                                                                        ————— ip6_output.c

3760–3766 `in6_addr2zoneid()` is called to set an appropriate multicast scope zone identifier in the `sin6_scope_id` member of `sa6_mc` once the interface is identified. This
operation should not fail because both the address and the interface are known to be valid,
but the error cases are considered for safety. `in6_embedscope()` then embeds the zone
ID (if necessary) into the 128-bit `sin6_addr` field. In theory such a step is unnecessary
because `sa6_mc` has complete information to disambiguate the address in terms of scopes.
Unfortunately, however, the kernel code still needs to compare the addresses only by the
`sin6_addr` field. This is the reason that `in6_embedscope()` must be called here.

3771–3780 An EADDRINUSE error is returned if the specified group address is already present
in the `im6o_memberships` over the given interface.

3781–3797 Finally, function `in6_joingroup()` completes the join process. On failure,
`in6_joingroup()` returns a NULL pointer and sets the appropriate error. On success,
`imm` points to a valid multicast group membership structure and then `imm` is inserted into
the `im6o_memberships` list.

Listing 4-64
                                                                        ————— ip6_output.c

```
3799            case IPV6_LEAVE_GROUP:
3800                    /*
3801                     * Drop a multicast group membership.
3802                     * Group must be a valid IP6 multicast address.
3803                     */
3804                    if (m == NULL || m->m_len != sizeof(struct ipv6_mreq)) {
3805                            error = EINVAL;
3806                            break;
3807                    }
3808                    mreq = mtod(m, struct ipv6_mreq *);
3809                    if (IN6_IS_ADDR_UNSPECIFIED(&mreq->ipv6mr_multiaddr)) {
3811                            if (suser(p))
3815                            {
3816                                    error = EACCES;
3817                                    break;
3818                            }
3819                    } else if (!IN6_IS_ADDR_MULTICAST(&mreq->ipv6mr_multiaddr)) {
3820                            error = EINVAL;
3821                            break;
3822                    }
```
                                                                        ————— ip6_output.c

3799–3807 Similar to IPV6_JOIN_GROUP, the IPV6_LEAVE_GROUP socket option takes an
`ipv6_mreq{}` structure as the option argument. An EINVAL error is returned if the
argument is not provided or if it has an invalid length.

3808–3822 Similarly, the `ipv6mr_multiaddr` field must be either the unspecified address or
a valid IPv6 multicast address.

Listing 4-65
_____ ip6_output.c
```
3824                    bzero(&sa6_mc, sizeof(sa6_mc));
3825                    sa6_mc.sin6_family = AF_INET6;
3826                    sa6_mc.sin6_len = sizeof(sa6_mc);
3827                    sa6_mc.sin6_addr = mreq->ipv6mr_multiaddr;
3828
3829                    /*
3830                     * If an interface address was specified, get a pointer
3831                     * to its ifnet structure.
3832                     */
3833                    if (mreq->ipv6mr_interface < 0
3834                     || if_index < mreq->ipv6mr_interface) {
3835                            error = ENXIO;          /* XXX EINVAL? */
3836                            break;
3837                    }
3841                    ifp = ifindex2ifnet[mreq->ipv6mr_interface];
3843
3844                    /* Fill in the scope zone ID */
3845                    if (ifp) {
3846                            if (in6_addr2zoneid(ifp, &sa6_mc.sin6_addr,
3847                                &sa6_mc.sin6_scope_id)) {
3848                                    /* XXX: should not happen */
3849                                    error = EADDRNOTAVAIL;
3850                                    break;
3851                            }
3852                            in6_embedscope(&sa6_mc.sin6_addr, &sa6_mc); /* XXX */
3853                    } else {
3854                            /*
3855                             * The API spec says as follows:
3856                             *  If the interface index is specified as 0, the
3857                             *  system may choose a multicast group membership to
3858                             *  drop by matching the multicast address only.
3859                             * On the other hand, we cannot disambiguate the scope
3860                             * zone unless an interface is provided.  Thus, we
3861                             * check if there's ambiguity with the default scope
3862                             * zone as the last resort.
3863                             */
3864                            if ((error = scope6_check_id(&sa6_mc,
3865                                ip6_use_defzone)) != 0) {
3866                                    break;
3867                            }
3868                    }
```
_____ ip6_output.c

3824–3827 sa6_mc is a sockaddr_in6{} structure containing the specified multicast address.

3829–3841 An ENXIO error is returned if the given interface index stored in ipv6mr_interface is out of range. Otherwise, ifp points to the corresponding ifnet{} structure. ifp may still be NULL if ipv6mr_interface is 0 or if the interface has been dynamically detached. The latter case should be caught separately and an appropriate error should be returned, but the current code ignores this condition, which is a bug but is effectively hidden (see below).

3845–3853 The corresponding scope zone identifier is set in the sin6_scope_id member of sa6_mc if ifp points to a valid ifnet{} structure. Similar to the implementation for IPV6_JOIN_GROUP, in6_embedscope() is called so that the sin6_addr member contains enough information to disambiguate the address.

3853–3858 As explained earlier, ifp is NULL if the application does not specify the interface index. The API specification allows the 0-valued interface index, but the given address may be ambiguous without the actual interface information, especially for interface-local and link-local addresses. As a last resort, the implementation tries to disambiguate the address using the default scope zone if the use of the default zone is permitted. Any failure will cause the process to be terminated, and the error from `scope6_check_id()` will be returned to the application.

In any event, applications should not rely on this feature; it must always specify the corresponding interface to avoid ambiguity (see also Listing 4-62).

Listing 4-66

```
                                                                  ip6_output.c
3870                    /*
3871                     * Find the membership in the membership list.
3872                     */
3873                    for (imm = im6o->im6o_memberships.lh_first;
3874                         imm != NULL; imm = imm->i6mm_chain.le_next) {
3875                            if ((ifp == NULL || imm->i6mm_maddr->in6m_ifp == ifp) &&
3876                                    SA6_ARE_ADDR_EQUAL(&imm->i6mm_maddr->in6m_sa,
3877                                    &sa6_mc))
3878                                            break;
3879                    }
3880                    if (imm == NULL) {
3881                            /* Unable to resolve interface */
3882                            error = EADDRNOTAVAIL;
3883                            break;
3884                    }
3885                    /*
3886                     * Give up the multicast address record to which the
3887                     * membership points.
3888                     */
3889                    LIST_REMOVE(imm, i6mm_chain);
3890                    in6_leavegroup(imm);
3891                    break;
```

(MLDv2 specific code, omitted)

```
4277            default:
4278                    error = EOPNOTSUPP;
4279                    break;
4280            }
                                                                  ip6_output.c
```

3870–3884 An `EADDRNOTAVAIL` error is returned if the given multicast address over the given interface is not found in the multicast membership list stored in `im6o_memberships`.

3885–3891 The multicast address is removed from the group membership list. Function `in6_leavegroup()` will complete the process by sending an Multicast Listener Discovery (MLD) Done message if necessary and reset the interface accordingly.

4277–4280 An `EOPNOTSUPP` error would be returned if an unsupported option type were encountered. However, this error condition should not occur here because this function is called only for the supported options.

Listing 4-67

```
                                                                  ip6_output.c
4282                    /*
4283                     * If all options have default values, no need to keep the mbuf.
4284                     */
4285                    if (im6o->im6o_multicast_ifp == NULL &&
4286                            im6o->im6o_multicast_hlim == ip6_defmcasthlim &&
4287                            im6o->im6o_multicast_loop == IPV6_DEFAULT_MULTICAST_LOOP &&
```

```
4288                  im6o->im6o_memberships.lh_first == NULL) {
4289                  free(*im6op, M_IPMOPTS);
4290                  *im6op = NULL;
4291          }
4292
4293          return (error);
4294  }
```
——— ip6_output.c

4282–4291 In some cases, im6o results in its default status after the process of the option. In those cases, the allocated option structure is freed to save memory.

4.7.2 `ip6_getmoptions()` Function

The `ip6_getmoptions()` function handles the `getsockopt()` system call for three IPv6 multicast options: `IPV6_MULTICAST_IF`, `IPV6_MULTICAST_HOPS`, and `IPV6_MULTICAST_LOOP`. Like `ip6_setmoptions()`, it is a subroutine of `ip6_ctloutput()` and takes the PCB's `ip6_moptions{}` structure.

Listing 4-68
——— ip6_output.c

```
4296  /*
4297   * Return the IP6 multicast options in response to user getsockopt().
4298   */
4299  static int
4300  ip6_getmoptions(optname, im6o, mp)
4301          int optname;
4302          struct ip6_moptions *im6o;
4303          struct mbuf **mp;
4304  {
4305          u_int *hlim, *loop, *ifindex;
4306
4308          *mp = m_get(M_WAIT, MT_HEADER);                /* XXX */
4312
4313          switch (optname) {
4314
4315          case IPV6_MULTICAST_IF:
4316                  ifindex = mtod(*mp, u_int *);
4317                  (*mp)->m_len = sizeof(u_int);
4318                  if (im6o == NULL || im6o->im6o_multicast_ifp == NULL)
4319                          *ifindex = 0;
4320                  else
4321                          *ifindex = im6o->im6o_multicast_ifp->if_index;
4322                  return (0);
4323
4324          case IPV6_MULTICAST_HOPS:
4325                  hlim = mtod(*mp, u_int *);
4326                  (*mp)->m_len = sizeof(u_int);
4327                  if (im6o == NULL)
4328                          *hlim = ip6_defmcasthlim;
4329                  else
4330                          *hlim = im6o->im6o_multicast_hlim;
4331                  return (0);
4332
4333          case IPV6_MULTICAST_LOOP:
4334                  loop = mtod(*mp, u_int *);
4335                  (*mp)->m_len = sizeof(u_int);
4336                  if (im6o == NULL)
4337                          *loop = ip6_defmcasthlim;
4338                  else
4339                          *loop = im6o->im6o_multicast_loop;
4340                  return (0);
4341
4342          default:
```

```
4343                      return (EOPNOTSUPP);
4344              }
4345      }
```
—— ip6_output.c

4299–4308 `m_get()` tries to allocate a new mbuf to store the return value of the `getsockopt()` call. Note that because the FreeBSD kernel has restructured socket option framework to avoid the use of the intermediate mbuf, there is actually no need for an mbuf to store the return value. However, the KAME implementation still uses an mbuf here for portability with other BSD variants.

4313–4345 The appropriate option value is copied into the allocated mbuf based on the given socket option name. The default value for an option is returned if that option has never been set before. For the `IPV6_MULTICAST_IF` option, the index of the outgoing interface stored in `im6o_multicast_ifp` is returned. For the `IPV6_MULTICAST_HOPS` option, the hop limit stored in `im6o_multicast_hlim` is returned. For the `IPV6_MULTICAST_LOOP` option, the Boolean value stored in `im6o_multicast_loop` that controls whether outgoing multicast packets should be looped back to local listeners is returned. An `EOPNOTSUPP` error is returned if unsupported option type is encountered.

4.7.3 `ip6_freemoptions()` Function

The `ip6_freemoptions()` function releases all dynamically allocated multicast options of a socket.

Listing 4-69
—— ip6_output.c
```
4317      /*
4318       * Discard the IP6 multicast options.
4319       */
4320      void
4321      ip6_freemoptions(im6o)
4322              struct ip6_moptions *im6o;
4323      {
4324              struct in6_multi_mship *imm;
4325
4326              if (im6o == NULL)
4327                      return;
4328
4329              while ((imm = im6o->im6o_memberships.lh_first) != NULL) {
4330                      LIST_REMOVE(imm, i6mm_chain);
4331                      in6_leavegroup(imm);
4332              }
4333              free(im6o, M_IPMOPTS);
4334      }
```
—— ip6_output.c

The function iterates through each entry of the `im6o_memberships` list, calling function `in6_leavegroup()` to perform the necessary steps to leave a multicast group. Then the memory for the option structure is released.

4.8 IPv6 Raw Socket Options: `ip6_raw_ctloutput()` Function

The `ip6_raw_ctloutput()` function is a dedicated processing function for handling the `IPV6_CHECKSUM` raw IPv6 socket option.

Listing 4-70

_____ ip6_output.c

```
3055    int
3056    ip6_raw_ctloutput(so, sopt)
3057            struct socket *so;
3058            struct sockopt *sopt;
3067    {
3068            int error = 0, optval, optlen;
3069            const int icmp6off = offsetof(struct icmp6_hdr, icmp6_cksum);
3073            struct in6pcb *in6p = sotoin6pcb(so);
3076            int level, op, optname;
3080            struct proc *p;
```

_____ ip6_output.c

3055–3080 so points to the socket and sopt contains information about the socket option. icmp6off is set to the offset length from the top of the icmp6_hdr{} structure to the checksum field, which is 2. Variable p is necessary for checking privilege of the caller, but this variable is effectively unused here. The reason is ip6_raw_ctloutput() is always called within the context of a raw socket and the owner of a raw socket must already have the necessary privilege level in order to open the socket in the first place.

Listing 4-71

_____ ip6_output.c

```
3087            if (sopt) {
3088                    level = sopt->sopt_level;
3089                    op = sopt->sopt_dir;
3090                    optname = sopt->sopt_name;
3091                    optlen = sopt->sopt_valsize;
3095                    p = sopt->sopt_p;
3097            } else {
3098                    panic("ip6_ctloutput: arg soopt is NULL");
3099            }
```

_____ ip6_output.c

3087–3099 The socket option parameters are extracted. The function name in the panic message is inaccurate but was not fixed when this code was copied out of the ip6_ctloutput() function.

Listing 4-72

_____ ip6_output.c

```
3104            if (level != IPPROTO_IPV6) {
3109                    return (EINVAL);
3110            }
```

_____ ip6_output.c

3104–3110 The socket option level must be IPPROTO_IPV6. This check should have been done by the caller and thus is actually redundant here.

Listing 4-73

_____ ip6_output.c

```
3112            switch (optname) {
3113            case IPV6_CHECKSUM:
3114                    /*
3115                     * For ICMPv6 sockets, no modification allowed for checksum
3116                     * offset, permit "no change" values to help existing apps.
3117                     *
```

```
3118                        * XXX 2292bis says: "An attempt to set IPV6_CHECKSUM
3119                        * for an ICMPv6 socket will fail."
3120                        * The current behavior does not meet 2292bis.
3121                        */
```
———————————————————————————————— *ip6_output.c*

3112–3121 This function only supports the IPV6_CHECKSUM option. The code comment indicates that the implementation allows the set operation on this option for an ICMPv6 raw socket, which does not conform to the specification, but this behavior remains for supporting old applications that assume the allowance of the set capability.

Listing 4-74
———————————————————————————————— *ip6_output.c*
```
3122                    switch (op) {
3124                    case SOPT_SET:
3128                            if (optlen != sizeof(int)) {
3129                                    error = EINVAL;
3130                                    break;
3131                            }
3133                            error = sooptcopyin(sopt, &optval, sizeof(optval),
3134                                            sizeof(optval));
3135                            if (error)
3136                                    break;
```
———————————————————————————————— *ip6_output.c*

3122–3136 The argument to this socket option must be an integer. The value is copied to the local variable `optval` if the length validation succeeds.

Listing 4-75
———————————————————————————————— *ip6_output.c*
```
3140                    if ((optval % 2) != 0) {
3141                            /* the API assumes even offset values */
3142                            error = EINVAL;
```
———————————————————————————————— *ip6_output.c*

3140–3142 Odd integer values as an offset are rejected as required by [RFC3542].

Listing 4-76
———————————————————————————————— *ip6_output.c*
```
3143                    } else if (so->so_proto->pr_protocol ==
3144                            IPPROTO_ICMPV6) {
3145                            if (optval != icmp6off)
3146                                    error = EINVAL;
```
———————————————————————————————— *ip6_output.c*

3143–3146 The application must provide the standard offset to the checksum field for an ICMPv6 raw socket if the application were to specify an offset. This behavior is not fully compliant to [RFC3542] that disallows any set operation on ICMPv6 raw sockets.

Listing 4-77
———————————————————————————————— *ip6_output.c*
```
3147                    } else
3148                            in6p->in6p_cksum = optval;
3149                    break;
```
———————————————————————————————— *ip6_output.c*

3147–3149 The offset value to the checksum field is stored in the PCB for later use.

Listing 4-78

```
——————————————————————————————————————————————ip6_output.c
3152                     case SOPT_GET:
3156                             if (so->so_proto->pr_protocol == IPPROTO_ICMPV6)
3157                                     optval = icmp6off;
3158                             else
3159                                     optval = in6p->in6p_cksum;
3160
3162                             error = sooptcopyout(sopt, &optval, sizeof(optval));
3168                             break;
——————————————————————————————————————————————ip6_output.c
```

3152–3168 The get operation retrieves the offset value to the checksum field from the PCB and returns it to the application. Note that the `in6p_cksum` member is initialized to -1, which means the kernel will perform any checksum operation on a raw socket for both inbound and outbound packets.

Listing 4-79

```
——————————————————————————————————————————————ip6_output.c
3170                     default:
3171                             error = EINVAL;
3172                             break;
3173                     }
——————————————————————————————————————————————ip6_output.c
```

3170–3173 An invalid operation will trigger an `EINVAL` error being returned, but this default case statement is actually redundant because the caller should have performed the necessary validation.

Listing 4-80

```
——————————————————————————————————————————————ip6_output.c
3174                       break;
3175
3176           default:
3177                   error = ENOPROTOOPT;
3178                   break;
——————————————————————————————————————————————ip6_output.c
```

3176–3178 An `ENOPROTOOPT` error is returned if an option other than `IPV6_CHECKSUM` is encountered.

Listing 4-81

```
——————————————————————————————————————————————ip6_output.c
3179           }
3185
3186           return (error);
3187   }
——————————————————————————————————————————————ip6_output.c
```

3179–3187 If everything is okay, the default error code, 0, is returned to indicate the success of this operation.

4.9   ICMPv6 Socket Options: `icmp6_ctloutput()` Function

The `icmp6_ctloutput()` function is called from `rip6_ctloutput()` to handle ICMPv6 specific socket options (see Figure 4-1). `ICMP6_FILTER` is the only option in this category that is defined in [RFC3542].

Listing 4-82

─── *icmp6.c*

```
3262    int
3264    icmp6_ctloutput(so, sopt)
3265            struct socket *so;
3266            struct sockopt *sopt;
3274    {
3275            int error = 0;
3276            int optlen;
3278            struct inpcb *inp = sotoinpcb(so);
3279            int level, op, optname;
3280
3281            if (sopt) {
3282                    level = sopt->sopt_level;
3283                    op = sopt->sopt_dir;
3284                    optname = sopt->sopt_name;
3285                    optlen = sopt->sopt_valsize;
3286            } else
3287                    level = op = optname = optlen = 0;
3294
3295            if (level != IPPROTO_ICMPV6) {
3300                    return EINVAL;
3301            }
3302
3303            switch (op) {
3304            case PRCO_SETOPT:
3305                    switch (optname) {
3306                    case ICMP6_FILTER:
3307                        {
3308                            struct icmp6_filter *p;
3309
3310                            if (optlen != sizeof(*p)) {
3311                                    error = EMSGSIZE;
3312                                    break;
3313                            }
3315                            if (inp->in6p_icmp6filt == NULL) {
3316                                    error = EINVAL;
3317                                    break;
3318                            }
3319                            error = sooptcopyin(sopt, inp->in6p_icmp6filt, optlen,
3320                                    optlen);
3331                            break;
3332                        }
3333
3334                    default:
3335                            error = ENOPROTOOPT;
3336                            break;
3337                    }
3342                    break;
3343
3344            case PRCO_GETOPT:
3345                    switch (optname) {
3346                    case ICMP6_FILTER:
3347                        {
3349                            if (inp->in6p_icmp6filt == NULL) {
3350                                    error = EINVAL;
3351                                    break;
3352                            }
```

```
3353                              error = sooptcopyout(sopt, inp->in6p_icmp6filt,
3354                                        sizeof(struct icmp6_filter));
3369                          break;
3370                      }
3371
3372                  default:
3373                          error = ENOPROTOOPT;
3374                          break;
3375                  }
3376                  break;
3377          }
3378
3379          return (error);
3380   }
```
——— icmp6.c

3262–3300 Whereas the caller has already verified sopt, validation on sopt is performed here again. The option parameters are then extracted from sopt. An EINVAL error is returned if the socket level is not IPPROTO_ICMPV6.

3303–3313 The ICMP6_FILTER option takes a fixed length of an icmp6_filter{} structure as the argument. An EMSGSIZE error is returned if the option length is invalid.

> *Note*: EMSGSIZE is not a very appropriate error code. EINVAL would be better here.

> *Note*: From the API point of view, icmp6_filter{} is an opaque structure; applications do not have to (or even should not) care about its actual implementation.

3315–3318 If the pointer to the filter specification were NULL, an EINVAL error would be returned. Note that this should actually be impossible to happen, since the rip6_attach() function allocates the memory for this member when it creates the PCB. Even though there is a bug in rip6_attach(), icmp6_ctloutput() can never be called with in6p_icmp6filt being NULL.

3319–3332 sooptcopyin() transfers the given filter specification to the corresponding PCB.

3334–3342 An ENOPROTOOPT error is returned for all other option names.

3344–3370 For the get operation, an EINVAL error would be returned if icmp6filt is NULL (again, this should be impossible). Otherwise, sooptcopyout() transfers the stored specification to sopt for returning back to the application.

3372–3376 For option names other than ICMP6_FILTER, an error of ENOPROTOOPT will be returned.

3378–3380 Unless sooptcopyin() or sooptcopyout() fails, which is unlikely to happen, 0 will be returned indicating that the operation was successful.

4.10   Delivering Incoming Information: ip6_savecontrol() Function

The transport layer input routine calls ip6_savecontrol() when the application to which the incoming packets are destined has informed the kernel to notify the application either when certain types of information are present in the incoming packets, or of certain information for every packet to the application. For example, an application may request the kernel for notification when some IPv6 extension headers are present, or the application may request the kernel to always return the hop limit value back to the application.

The information passed from the upper layer is stored in the `ip6_recvpktopts{}` structure shown in Listing 4-83.

Listing 4-83

```
                                                              ip6_var.h
202   struct ip6_recvpktopts {
203           struct mbuf *head;          /* mbuf chain of data passed to a user */
204
205   #ifdef SO_TIMESTAMP
206           struct mbuf *timestamp;     /* timestamp */
207   #endif
208           struct mbuf *hlim;          /* received hop limit */
209           struct mbuf *pktinfo;       /* packet information of rcv packet */
210           struct mbuf *hbh;           /* HbH options header of rcv packet */
211           struct mbuf *dest;          /* Dest opt header of rcv packet */
212           struct mbuf *rthdr;         /* Routing header of rcv packet */
213   };
                                                              ip6_var.h
```

202–213 The packet information is actually stored in a chain of mbuf blocks. The head member points to the head of the chain. Each of the remaining structure members point to a single mbuf if and only if the information requested by the application is present in the incoming packet.

Note: The old advanced API defined in [RFC2292] required to remember the previous information for optimization, the behavior that was deprecated in [RFC3542]. This structure was introduced to keep the previous set of information. However, the code described in this book basically conforms to [RFC3542] and the optimization was removed, and so there is actually no need to keep the separate structure. In fact, this feature has been removed in later versions of the implementation for simplicity.

Listing 4-84

```
                                                              ip6_input.c
1583  /*
1584   * Create the "control" list for this pcb.
1585   * The function will not modify mbuf chain at all.
1586   *
1587   * with KAME mbuf chain restriction:
1588   * The routine will be called from upper layer handlers like tcp6_input().
1589   * Thus the routine assumes that the caller (tcp6_input) have already
1590   * called IP6_EXTHDR_CHECK() and all the extension headers are located in the
1591   * very first mbuf on the mbuf chain.
1592   */
1593  void
1594  ip6_savecontrol(in6p, ip6, m, ctl)
1596          struct inpcb *in6p;
1600          struct ip6_hdr *ip6;
1601          struct mbuf *m;
1602          struct ip6_recvpktopts *ctl;
                                                              ip6_input.c
```

1583–1602 `in6p` points to the PCB that corresponds to the receiving socket. `ip6` points to the IPv6 header of the incoming packet. Mbuf m holds the entire packet. The `ctl` member is a control structure containing the optional information from this function to the caller.

Listing 4-85
_____ ip6_input.c

```
1603    {
1604    #define IS2292(x, y)          ((in6p->in6p_flags & IN6P_RFC2292) ? (x) : (y))
1605            struct mbuf **mp;
1613            struct proc *p = curproc;        /* XXX */
1619            int privileged = 0;
```
_____ ip6_input.c

1604–1619 The `IS2292()` macro returns true if and only if the application requested the old [RFC2292] style option. The code has a bug: `curproc` is a meaningless pointer because this function runs in an interrupt context (see discussions below).

Listing 4-86
_____ ip6_input.c

```
1621            if (ctl == NULL)          /* validity check */
1622                    return;
1623            bzero(ctl, sizeof(*ctl)); /* XXX is it really OK? */
1624            mp = &ctl->head;
```
_____ ip6_input.c

1621–1624 This function assumes the caller passes a non-NULL control structure or else the function terminates immediately.

Listing 4-87
_____ ip6_input.c

```
1626
1631            if (p && !suser(p))
1632                    privileged++;
```
_____ ip6_input.c

1631–1632 The intention of the privilege check here is to determine whether the receiving process is run by a superuser. As explained above, however, referring to a process by means of p in the interrupt context is wrong. As we will soon see, the privilege check is to ensure that only privileged applications can receive Hop-by-Hop or Destination options headers. However, such privilege validation is not necessary because `ip6_ctloutput()` should have already verified the necessary privilege level at the time when the application set the corresponding socket options (see Listing 4-8).

Listing 4-88
_____ ip6_input.c

```
1643    #ifdef SO_TIMESTAMP
1644            if ((in6p->in6p_socket->so_options & SO_TIMESTAMP) != 0) {
1645                    struct timeval tv;
1646
1647                    microtime(&tv);
1648                    *mp = sbcreatecontrol((caddr_t) &tv, sizeof(tv),
1649                                    SCM_TIMESTAMP, SOL_SOCKET);
1650                    if (*mp) {
1651                            /* always set regradless of the previous value */
```

```
1652                                    ctl->timestamp = *mp;
1653                                    mp = &(*mp)->m_next;
1654                            }
1655                    }
1656    #endif
```
─── ip6_input.c

1643–1656 If the application requested the packet timestamp of each received packet, then
the timeval{} structure tv is set to the current time maintained in the kernel. Function
sbcreatecontrol() allocates a separate mbuf and copies the values in tv to the mbuf
data buffer. The mbuf chain is adjusted.

Listing 4-89
─── ip6_input.c
```
1658            /* RFC 2292 sec. 5 */
1659            if ((in6p->in6p_flags & IN6P_PKTINFO) != 0) {
1660                    struct in6_pktinfo pi6;
1661
1662                    bcopy(&ip6->ip6_dst, &pi6.ipi6_addr, sizeof(struct in6_addr));
1663                    in6_clearscope(&pi6.ipi6_addr);          /* XXX */
1664                    pi6.ipi6_ifindex = (m && m->m_pkthdr.rcvif)
1665                                        ? m->m_pkthdr.rcvif->if_index
1666                                        : 0;
1667
1668                    *mp = sbcreatecontrol((caddr_t) &pi6,
1669                                          sizeof(struct in6_pktinfo),
1670                                          IS2292(IPV6_2292PKTINFO, IPV6_PKTINFO),
1671                                          IPPROTO_IPV6);
1672                    if (*mp) {
1673                            ctl->pktinfo = *mp;
1674                            mp = &(*mp)->m_next;
1675                    }
1676            }
```
─── ip6_input.c

1658–1676 If the application requested the packet information of each received packet, the
in6_pktinfo{} structure is filled with the destination address and the identifier of the
receiving interface.

      The scope zone ID may be embedded in a nonglobal scope destination address,
which should not be visible to the application. Function ip6_clearscope() removes
the zone ID from the address.

      Function sbcreatecontrol() prepares a new mbuf and stores the request
packet information. The new mbuf is linked into the mbuf chain.

Listing 4-90
─── ip6_input.c
```
1678            if ((in6p->in6p_flags & IN6P_HOPLIMIT) != 0) {
1679                    int hlim = ip6->ip6_hlim & 0xff;
1680
1681                    *mp = sbcreatecontrol((caddr_t) &hlim, sizeof(int),
1682                                          IS2292(IPV6_2292HOPLIMIT, IPV6_HOPLIMIT),
1683                                          IPPROTO_IPV6);
1684                    if (*mp) {
1685                            ctl->hlim = *mp;
1686                            mp = &(*mp)->m_next;
1687                    }
1688            }
```
─── ip6_input.c

1678–1688 If the application requested the hop limit value of each received packet, the Hop Limit value is copied from the IPv6 header to a new mbuf and that mbuf is then linked to the mbuf chain.

Listing 4-91

ip6_input.c
```
1690                if ((in6p->in6p_flags & IN6P_TCLASS) != 0) {
1691                    u_int32_t flowinfo;
1692                    int v;
1693
1694                    flowinfo = (u_int32_t)ntohl(ip6->ip6_flow & IPV6_FLOWINFO_MASK);
1695                    flowinfo >>= 20;
1696
1697                    v = flowinfo & 0xff;
1698                    *mp = sbcreatecontrol((caddr_t) &v, sizeof(v),
1699                                    IPV6_TCLASS, IPPROTO_IPV6);
1700                    if (*mp) {
1701                        ctl->hlim = *mp;
1702                        mp = &(*mp)->m_next;
1703                    }
1704                }
```
ip6_input.c

1690–1704 If the application requested the 8-bit Traffic Class value of each incoming packet, that value is copied from the IPv6 header to a new mbuf. Since the Traffic Class field is not aligned at a natural byte boundary, bitwise operations are necessary for its extraction from the IPv6 header.

       The `hlim` member is overridden at line 1701, and this is a bug. However, the overwrite is harmless because the use of the `hlim` member in the KAME implementation has been deprecated as part of the migration to [RFC3542].

Listing 4-92

ip6_input.c
```
1706                /*
1707                 * IPV6_HOPOPTS socket option. We require super-user privilege
1708                 * for the option, but it might be too strict, since there might
1709                 * be some hop-by-hop options which can be returned to normal user.
1710                 * See RFC 2292 section 6.
1711                 */
1712                if ((in6p->in6p_flags & IN6P_HOPOPTS) != 0 && privileged) {
```
ip6_input.c

1706–1712 If the application with the superuser privilege requested the Hop-by-Hop options header (when included) of each incoming packet, the following code will prepare the data for passing to the application. As code comments indicate, the superuser privilege requirement is too restrictive but is imposed by the implementation for performance reasons (see also Listing 4-8).

Listing 4-93

ip6_input.c
```
1713                /*
1714                 * Check if a hop-by-hop options header is contatined in the
1715                 * received packet, and if so, store the options as ancillary
1716                 * data. Note that a hop-by-hop options header must be
1717                 * just after the IPv6 header, which fact is assured through
1718                 * the IPv6 input processing.
```

```
1719                         */
1720                         struct ip6_hdr *ip6 = mtod(m, struct ip6_hdr *);
1721                         if (ip6->ip6_nxt == IPPROTO_HOPOPTS) {
1722                                 struct ip6_hbh *hbh;
1723                                 int hbhlen = 0;
1727
1729                                 hbh = (struct ip6_hbh *)(ip6 + 1);
1730                                 hbhlen = (hbh->ip6h_len + 1) << 3;
1746
1747                                 /*
1748                                  * XXX: We copy the whole header even if a
1749                                  * jumbo payload option is included, which
1750                                  * option is to be removed before returning
1751                                  * in the RFC 2292.
1752                                  * Note: this constraint is removed in
1753                                  * 2292bis.
1754                                  */
1755                                 *mp = sbcreatecontrol((caddr_t)hbh, hbhlen,
1756                                                       IS2292(IPV6_2292HOPOPTS,
1757                                                              IPV6_HOPOPTS),
1758                                                       IPPROTO_IPV6);
1759                                 if (*mp) {
1760                                         ctl->hbh = *mp;
1761                                         mp = &(*mp)->m_next;
1762                                 }
1766                         }
1767                 }
```
――― *ip6_input.c*

1720–1721 A Hop-by-Hop options header, if contained, can only appear just after the IPv6 header. Thus, a check on the Next Header field of the IPv6 header suffices in determining whether the Hop-by-Hop options header is present.

Note: The current implementation does not always reject a Hop-by-Hop options header appearing after a header other than the IPv6 header. In any event, the implementation of this function is correct: It should not care about the invalid case and should not pass an ill-ordered Hop-by-Hop options header to the application.

1722–1767 The IPv6 input routine has ensured the entire Hop-by-Hop options header fit in the first mbuf. Therefore, the start address and the length of the header is simply passed to the `sbcreatecontrol()` function to copy the header content to a separate mbuf. [RFC2292] required that some Hop-by-Hop options including the Jumbo Payload option be removed before passing the options header to the application. However, the KAME implementation intentionally skips that process due to possible overhead. [RFC3542] has removed that constraint; thus, the implementation is compliant with the latest RFC.

Listing 4-94
――― *ip6_input.c*
```
1769              if ((in6p->in6p_flags & (IN6P_RTHDR | IN6P_DSTOPTS)) != 0) {
1770                      struct ip6_hdr *ip6 = mtod(m, struct ip6_hdr *);
1771                      int nxt = ip6->ip6_nxt, off = sizeof(struct ip6_hdr);
1772
1773                      /*
1774                       * Search for destination options headers or routing
1775                       * header(s) through the header chain, and stores each
1776                       * header as ancillary data.
```

```
1777                         * Note that the order of the headers remains in
1778                         * the chain of ancillary data.
1779                         */
1780                        while (1) {          /* is explicit loop prevention necessary? */
```
                                                                    ip6_input.c

1769–1780 Destination options headers and the Routing headers can appear at any position
and for any number of times in the received packet. Thus, a necessary step is to go through
the entire packet until a transport layer header is found in order to pass all these headers
to the application as requested.

Variable nxt is set to the Next Header field of the IPv6 header, and the while
loop iterates through all extension headers, updating nxt.

Listing 4-95
                                                                    ip6_input.c
```
1781                        struct ip6_ext *ip6e = NULL;
1782                        int elen;
1786
1787                        /*
1788                         * if it is not an extension header, don't try to
1789                         * pull it from the chain.
1790                         */
1791                        switch (nxt) {
1792                        case IPPROTO_DSTOPTS:
1793                        case IPPROTO_ROUTING:
1794                        case IPPROTO_HOPOPTS:
1795                        case IPPROTO_AH: /* is it possible? */
1796                                break;
1797                        default:
1798                                goto loopend;
1799                        }
```
                                                                    ip6_input.c

1791–1799 The headers of interest are the Destination options header, the Routing header, the
Hop-by-Hop options header, and the Authentication header (AH). Any other header types
will terminate the while loop, which includes the Encapsulated Security Payload (ESP)
header because information cannot be interpreted after the ESP header. The reassembly
process would have removed the Fragment header if it were present in the packet. The
same logic applies to the AH, but a sanity check is done for it.

Listing 4-96
                                                                    ip6_input.c
```
1802                        if (off + sizeof(*ip6e) > m->m_len)
1803                                goto loopend;
1804                        ip6e = (struct ip6_ext *)(mtod(m, caddr_t) + off);
```
                                                                    ip6_input.c

1802–1804 The while loop will terminate if the first mbuf is too short to hold the common
part of the extension headers. ip6e points to the extension header with respect to the
current offset.

Listing 4-97
                                                                    ip6_input.c
```
1805                        if (nxt == IPPROTO_AH)
1806                                elen = (ip6e->ip6e_len + 2) << 2;
1807                        else
```

```
1808                                        elen = (ip6e->ip6e_len + 1) << 3;
1809                         if (off + elen > m->m_len)
1810                                        goto loopend;
```
_____ ip6_input.c

1805–1810 nxt specifies the type of the extension header we are now looking at. The header
length is calculated based on the semantics of the length field (note that the AH has
a different definition of header length calculation). If the current mbuf does not store
the entire header, the process is terminated. Again, this behavior should be reasonable,
assuming the logic in the IPv6 input routine.

Listing 4-98
_____ ip6_input.c

```
1829                         switch (nxt) {
1830                         case IPPROTO_DSTOPTS:
1831                         {
1832                                 if (!(in6p->in6p_flags & IN6P_DSTOPTS))
1833                                         break;
1834
1835                                 /*
1836                                  * We also require super-user privilege for
1837                                  * the option. See comments on IN6_HOPOPTS.
1838                                  */
1839                                 if (!privileged)
1840                                         break;
1841
1842                                 *mp = sbcreatecontrol((caddr_t)ip6e, elen,
1843                                                         IS2292(IPV6_2292DSTOPTS,
1844                                                                 IPV6_DSTOPTS),
1845                                                                 IPPROTO_IPV6);
1846                                 if (ctl->dest == NULL)
1847                                         ctl->dest = *mp;
1848                                 if (*mp)
1849                                         mp = &(*mp)->m_next;
1850                                 break;
1851                         }
```
_____ ip6_input.c

1829–1840 If this header is a Destination options header, the application wanted to see it, and
the application has the superuser privilege, then the following part will copy the header
data to pass it to the application. Again the privilege check is too strict, but this is based
on an implementation decision.

1842–1851 Function `sbcreatecontrol()` copies the Destination options header content
into a separate mbuf. The new mbuf is linked into the buffer chain. The appropriate field
in `ip6_recvpktopts{}` is initialized if this header is the first Destination options header
encountered.

Listing 4-99
_____ ip6_input.c

```
1852                         case IPPROTO_ROUTING:
1853                         {
1854                                 if (!in6p->in6p_flags & IN6P_RTHDR)
1855                                         break;
1856
1857                                 *mp = sbcreatecontrol((caddr_t)ip6e, elen,
1858                                                         IS2292(IPV6_2292RTHDR,
1859                                                                 IPV6_RTHDR),
1860                                                                 IPPROTO_IPV6);
```

```
1861                              if (ctl->rthdr == NULL)
1862                                      ctl->rthdr = *mp;
1863                              if (*mp)
1864                                      mp = &(*mp)->m_next;
1865                              break;
1866                      }
```
_____ ip6_input.c

1852–1866 The similar process logic for retrieving the option header content applies to the Routing header.

Listing 4-100
_____ ip6_input.c

```
1867                      case IPPROTO_HOPOPTS:
1868                      case IPPROTO_AH: /* is it possible? */
1869                              break;
1870
```
_____ ip6_input.c

1867–1870 Other extension headers are skipped.

Listing 4-101
_____ ip6_input.c

```
1871                      default:
1872                              /*
1873                               * other cases have been filtered in the above.
1874                               * none will visit this case.  here we supply
1875                               * the code just in case (nxt overwritten or
1876                               * other cases).
1877                               */
1881                              goto loopend;
1882
1883                      }
```
_____ ip6_input.c

1871–1883 The default case statement should not occur because these conditions have been eliminated at the beginning of the `while` loop (recall Listing 4-95). These conditions are explicitly considered here again for safety because the `while` loop is long and unintentional error can happen.

Listing 4-102
_____ ip6_input.c

```
1884
1885                      /* proceed with the next header. */
1886                      off += elen;
1887                      nxt = ip6e->ip6e_nxt;
1888                      ip6e = NULL;
1893              }
1894      loopend:
1895              ;
1896      }
1904 #undef IS2292
1905 }
```
_____ ip6_input.c

1885–1905 The offset and the Next Header values are updated based on the current header, and the loop continues to search for other possible headers to be passed to the application.

Socket Options and Ancillary Data Examples

This chapter describes the relationships among various structures that are required for Internet Protocol version 6 (IPv6) User Datagram Protocol (UDP) packet transmission to illustrate how IPv6 socket options and ancillary data objects work as defined in the advanced socket API specification.

5.1 Example of the Send Path

Assume an application has specified the following socket options for a UDP socket:

- Set the hop limit for outgoing multicast packets to 8 through the `IPV6_MULTICAST_HOPS` socket option.
- Set the Traffic Class for outgoing packets to 1 through the `IPV6_TCLASS` socket option.
- Set a Hop-by-Hop options header for outgoing packets through the `IPV6_HOPOPTS` socket option.

Now, the application sends UDP datagram to the socket with the following set of ancillary data:

- Set the Traffic Class value 8 using the `IPV6_TCLASS` ancillary data type.
- Set a Destination options header using the `IPV6_DSTOPTS` ancillary data type.

Figure 5-1 shows the contents of some relevant arguments to function `udp6_output()`.

FIGURE 5-1

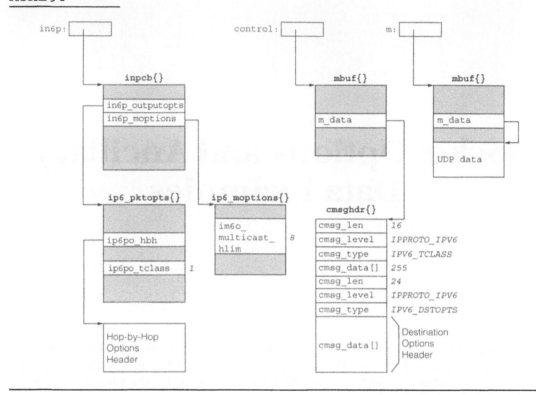

At the beginning of udp6_output().

Function udp6_output() calls ip6_setpktoptions() with its local variable opt in order to construct the packet options by merging the sticky options with the ancillary data objects.

Figure 5-2 shows the data structures at the point of calling ip6_output() after merging the options and ancillary data. As the figure shows, opt contains the Hop-by-Hop options header that was specified as a socket option and the Destination options header that was specified in the ancillary data object. Note that the Traffic Class value stored in opt is the value that was specified in the ancillary data object rather than the value set via the socket option.

The ip6_pktopts{} structure stored in opt and the ip6_moptions{} structure pointed from the PCB are passed to ip6_output() along with the UDP packet.

Figure 5-3 shows the content of some relevant arguments to ip6_output() at the entrance of the function. m0 points to the UDP packet with the IPv6 header, opt points to the ip6_pktopts{} structure, and im6o points to the ip6_moptions{} structure.

ip6_output() constructs a complete packet from these arguments. Since some extension headers are provided, the packet is split up at the boundary between the IPv6 and the UDP headers. The two extension headers are copied from the ip6_pktopts{} structure and are inserted between the IPv6 and UDP headers. The Traffic Class and Hop Limit fields of the IPv6

FIGURE 5-2

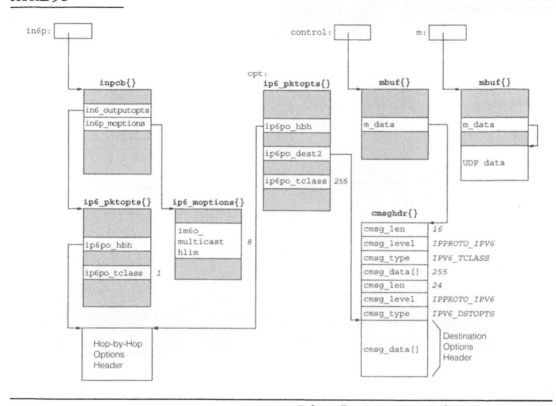

Before calling `ip6_output()` *from* `udp6_output()`.

header are filled with values from the `ip6_pktopts{}` structure and the `ip6_moptions{}` structure, respectively. Figure 5-4 shows the complete packet.

5.2   Example of the Receive Path

Our next example illustrates the construction of ancillary data objects from the received packet based on the socket options that were set in advance.

Suppose an application has requested the following information on a UDP socket, if available, from each received UDP packet along with the packet data:

- The destination address and the receiving interface by means of the `IPV6_RECVPKTINFO` option
- The IPv6 Hop-by-Hop options header by means of the `IPV6_RECVHOPOPTS` option
- The IPv6 Routing headers by means of the `IPV6_RECVRTHDR` option

Now, assume an IPv6 UDP packet containing a Routing header arrives and `udp6_input()` calls `ip6_savecontrol()` to construct ancillary data objects based on the specified values.

FIGURE 5-3

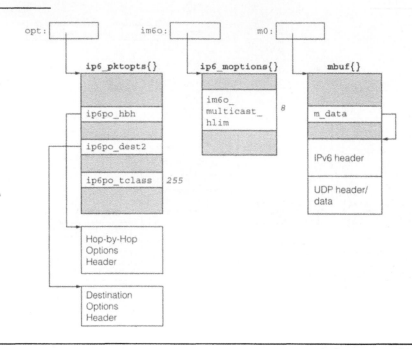

At the entrance of `ip6_output()`.

FIGURE 5-4

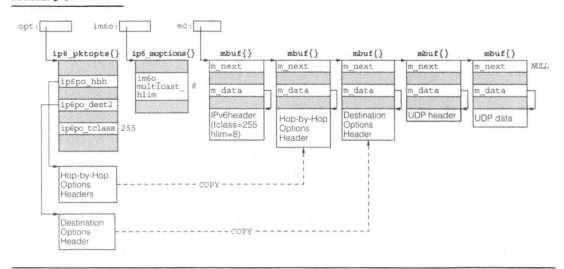

The complete outgoing packet with options.

FIGURE 5-5

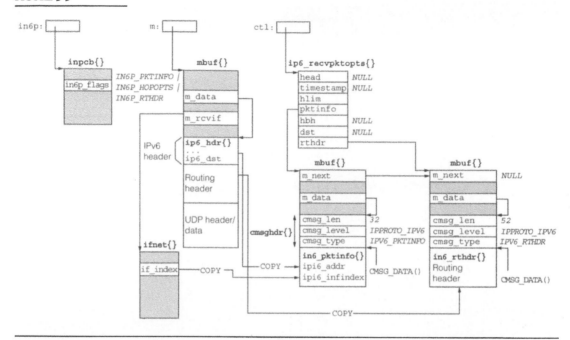

After constructing ancillary data objects in `ip6_savecontrol()`.

Figure 5-5 shows the contents of the various data structures after the ancillary data objects have been built.

in6p points to the PCB structure of the receiving socket. The flag bits in the in6p_flags member are set to mark the types of information requested by the application.

m is the mbuf structure containing the arriving packet. Note that in this figure the mbuf is depicted as if the base mbuf structure could contain the entire packet for simplicity. However, we would actually need an mbuf cluster, according to the length of the packet.

ctl is passed from udp6_input() to store the ancillary data objects, which will then be passed to the application via the receiving socket. Based on the content of the arriving packet and the flag bits in in6p_flags, two new mbufs are created to store ancillary data objects for IPV6_PKTINFO and IPV6_RTHDR.

The IPv6 destination address and the receiving interface index are copied into cmsg_data of the first mbuf as the in6_pktinfo{} structure. Similarly, the content of the Routing header from the packet is copied into cmsg_data of the second mbuf. Notice that no mbuf for the IN6P_HOPOPTS flag is created since the arriving packet does not contain a Hop-by-Hop options header.

Implementation of Library Functions: libinet6

In this chapter, we will show the implementation of some basic application programming interfaces (API) library functions with detailed explanation. Specifically, we describe the following four functions:

- `inet_pton()`
- `inet_ntop()`
- `getaddrinfo()`
- `getnameinfo()`

These are conversion functions between host names or textual addresses and Internet Protocol version 6 (IPv6) addresses in binary forms. The reason we are concentrating on these is that they are complicated and interesting due to the variety of IPv6 address representation. This also means learning these functions will help understand IPv6 addresses per se.

Table 6-1 summarizes source code files described in this chapter.

TABLE 6-1

File	Description
`${KAME}/kame/kame/libinet6/getaddrinfo.c`	`getaddrinfo()` and `gai_strerror()` functions
`${KAME}/kame/kame/libinet6/getnameinfo.c`	`getnameinfo()` function
`${KAME}/kame/kame/libinet6/inet_pton.c`	`inet_pton()` function
`/usr/src/lib/libc/net/inet_ntop.c`	`inet_ntop()` function

123

6.1   `inet_pton()` and `inet_pton6()` Functions

The `inet_pton()` function is the simplest function to use to convert a textual representation of IP addresses into the binary form. Unlike its predecessors, such as `inet_aton()`, `inet_pton()` supports multiple address families (i.e. it performs the address conversion according to the address family.) Listing 6-1 shows the main part of the `inet_pton()` function.

Listing 6-1

── inet_pton.c

```
80    int
81    inet_pton(af, src, dst)
82            int af;
83            const char *src;
84            void *dst;
85    {
86            switch (af) {
87            case AF_INET:
88                    return (inet_pton4(src, dst));
90            case AF_INET6:
91                    return (inet_pton6(src, dst));
93            default:
94                    errno = EAFNOSUPPORT;
95                    return (-1);
96            }
97            /* NOTREACHED */
98    }
```

── inet_pton.c

The main part of `inet_pton()` is simple: it only contains a `switch` statement that invokes the appropriate subroutine based on the given address family. As shown in the source code, this function currently supports `AF_INET` and `AF_INET6`. For other address families, −1 will be returned and `errno` will be set to `EAFNOSUPPORT`.

Listing 6-2 shows function `inet_pton6()`, which handles the `AF_INET6` address family and converts a textual representation of an IPv6 address into its binary form. Function `inet_pton6()` supports the various textual representations of addresses. In this function, the following macro constants will be used.

Name	Value	Description
NS_INADDRSZ	4	The size of an IPv4 address
NS_IN6ADDRSZ	16	The size of an IPv6 address
NS_INT16SZ	2	`sizeof(u_int16_t)`

Listing 6-2

── inet_pton.c

```
164    static int
165    inet_pton6(src, dst)
166            const char *src;
167            u_char *dst;
168    {
169            static const char xdigits_l[] = "0123456789abcdef",
170                              xdigits_u[] = "0123456789ABCDEF";
171            u_char tmp[NS_IN6ADDRSZ], *tp, *endp, *colonp;
172            const char *xdigits, *curtok;
```

```
173                    int ch, saw_xdigit;
174                    u_int val;
175
176                    memset((tp = tmp), '\0', NS_IN6ADDRSZ);
177                    endp = tp + NS_IN6ADDRSZ;
178                    colonp = NULL;
179                    /* Leading :: requires some special handling. */
180                    if (*src == ':')
181                            if (*++src != ':')
182                                    return (0);
183                    curtok = src;
184                    saw_xdigit = 0;
185                    val = 0;
186                    while ((ch = *src++) != '\0') {
187                            const char *pch;
188
189                            if ((pch = strchr((xdigits = xdigits_l), ch)) == NULL)
190                                    pch = strchr((xdigits = xdigits_u), ch);
191                            if (pch != NULL) {
192                                    val <<= 4;
193                                    val |= (pch - xdigits);
194                                    if (val > 0xffff)
195                                            return (0);
196                                    saw_xdigit = 1;
197                                    continue;
198                            }
199                            if (ch == ':') {
200                                    curtok = src;
201                                    if (!saw_xdigit) {
202                                            if (colonp)
203                                                    return (0);
204                                            colonp = tp;
205                                            continue;
206                                    } else if (*src == '\0') {
207                                            return (0);
208                                    }
209                                    if (tp + NS_INT16SZ > endp)
210                                            return (0);
211                                    *tp++ = (u_char) (val >> 8) & 0xff;
212                                    *tp++ = (u_char) val & 0xff;
213                                    saw_xdigit = 0;
214                                    val = 0;
215                                    continue;
216                            }
217                            if (ch == '.' && ((tp + NS_INADDRSZ) <= endp) &&
218                                inet_pton4(curtok, tp) > 0) {
219                                    tp += NS_INADDRSZ;
220                                    saw_xdigit = 0;
221                                    break;          /* '\0' was seen by inet_pton4(). */
222                            }
223                            return (0);
224                    }
225                    if (saw_xdigit) {
226                            if (tp + NS_INT16SZ > endp)
227                                    return (0);
228                            *tp++ = (u_char) (val >> 8) & 0xff;
229                            *tp++ = (u_char) val & 0xff;
230                    }
231                    if (colonp != NULL) {
232                            /*
233                             * Since some memmove()'s erroneously fail to handle
234                             * overlapping regions, we'll do the shift by hand.
235                             */
236                            const int n = tp - colonp;
237                            int i;
238
239                            if (tp == endp)
240                                    return (0);
```

```
241                for (i = 1; i <= n; i++) {
242                        endp[- i] = colonp[n - i];
243                        colonp[n - i] = 0;
244                }
245                tp = endp;
246        }
247        if (tp != endp)
248                return (0);
249        memcpy(dst, tmp, NS_IN6ADDRSZ);
250        return (1);
251    }
```
_____ inet_pton.c

6.1.1   Initial Setup

176–178 inet_ntop() uses a temporary work buffer buf to store intermediate conversion results. This buffer is zero-cleared and tp points to the head of this buffer while endp marks the end of this buffer to prevent buffer overrun. colonp will be non-NULL if and only if the input string contains a double colon (::), in which case colonp will specify the position in the output buffer where the expansion of the double colon should start.

180–182 A special case where the input starts with "::" is caught here in order to make the main parser simple. If the first character is a colon, then a valid input must start with "::". Otherwise, parsing the input fails here and 0 will be returned, indicating an error as described in Section 2.4.

183–185 During the parsing, curtok points to the location of the head of the last hexadecimal character that the parser has seen. It will eventually be used as an input to inet_pton4() in case the input contains a textual representation of an IPv4 address. saw_xdigit is a flag that indicates the parser has just recognized some hexadecimal string when nonzero. val stores temporary results of a hexadecimal value in the input.

6.1.2   Handle Hexadecimal String

186–198 The parser iterates through the entire input string character by character and assigns each character to ch. Inside the loop, the parser first checks whether the character is a hexadecimal number. If it is, pch has a non-NULL value pointing to the corresponding position in either the xdigits_l or the xdigits_u array. Then, val is updated with the character just recognized. Note that pch − xdigits is the integer corresponding to the recognized character. The temporary variable must not exceed the maximum value of a 16-bit integer (0xffff) in a valid textual representation. Otherwise, parsing fails and 0 will be returned. saw_xdigit marks the fact that the parser just parsed a hexadecimal character.

6.1.3   Handle Colon

199–205 If the parser encounters a colon, the parser saves the position immediately after the colon in curtok. If saw_xdigit is false, this means the parser is at the head of input which starts with "::" or else the parser has parsed another colon after a hexadecimal string. In the former case, colonp must be NULL; otherwise, the input string contains two sets of "::," which is an invalid textual representation. The parser stores the colon position in the corresponding output buffer in colonp.

206–208 The parser is looking at the single colon that follows a hexadecimal string if `saw_xdigit` is true. Thus, this position must not be the end of input.

209–216 At this position, the parser has a parsed hexadecimal value terminated by a colon, which should be a 16-bit integer. The input string is invalid if the temporary buffer does not have space to store the value. Otherwise, the value is stored in the next 16 bits of the output buffer and `tp` is incremented accordingly. `saw_xdigit` is reset to false. `val` is also cleared.

6.1.4   Handle an IPv4 Address

217–223 If the parser is looking at a period "`.`" character, the parser has encountered the beginning of a textual representation of an IPv6 address embedding an IPv4 address. In this case, the output buffer must have the space to store the address whose length is `NS_INADDRSZ`. If enough space is given, `inet_pton4()` is called to parse the text. `saw_xdigit` is cleared on successful return of `inet_pton4()`. Note that the loop terminates because an IPv4 address can only appear at the end of the original IPv6 address string.

6.1.5   Process the Last Hexadecimal Value

225–230 If `saw_xdigit` is true after exiting from the loop, there is still a hexadecimal value that is not yet stored in the output buffer. The remaining value is stored if there is enough space left in the buffer.

6.1.6   Fill Zero for a Double Colon

231–246 The parser has encountered a double colon if `colonp` is non-NULL. Since parsing of the input string is complete, the parser can determine the length for which the double colon should be expanded.

236–237 This part calculates n, the length of the stored value in the output buffer that corresponds to the part of input after the double colon.

239–240 There is no available space left to expand the double colon if the end of the output buffer is reached. Note that `inet_pton()` without this check would allow input strings such as,

`1111:2222:3333:4444::5555:6666:7777:8888`,

which is an invalid string as an IPv6 address.

241–245 The last n bytes of the output buffer are shifted to the end of the buffer. `tp` is set to `endp` to mark the end of the output buffer after expanding the double colon.

6.1.7   Postprocess

247–250 The input string is too short to be valid if the parser has not reached the end of the output buffer. Otherwise the conversion is successful and the converted value is copied from the temporary buffer into the buffer provided by the caller.

Note: Despite the careful coding, this code still has a controversial behavior. Since it accepts any hexadecimal string less than or equal to 0xffff, it does not impose a limitation on the length of the string. Thus, for example, it will accept 00000 (five zeros) as a 16-bit integer. You may think this is a bug, but this is actually intentional. In fact, [RFC3513] only says each piece separated by colons is a 16-bit hexadecimal value. This ambiguity was then discussed in the IETF, and a new version of the address architecture document [RFC4291] clearly specifies that each 16-bit value is up to four hexadecimal digits. Newer implementations of `inet_pton()` were also updated so that it would not allow the above example.

6.1.8 `inet_pton6()` Example

We illustrate the inner workings of `inet_pton6()` through an example to help gain solid understanding of the function. Suppose that this function is called with an input "2001:db8::1234". In lines 176–185, pointers and buffers are initialized as depicted in Figure 6-1.

After parsing the first colon, the first piece of 16-bit value, 0x2001, is copied to the output buffer (`tmp`). `src` and `tp` are incremented accordingly (Figure 6-2).

Similarly, after reading the second colon, the next piece of 16-bit value, 0x0db8, is copied (Figure 6-3). These processes correspond to lines 169–180 and 191–197 of Listing 6-2.

FIGURE 6-1 ──────

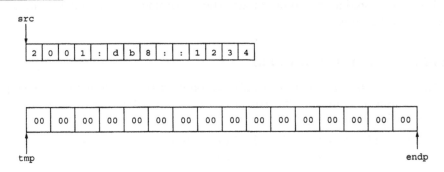

FIGURE 6-2 ──────

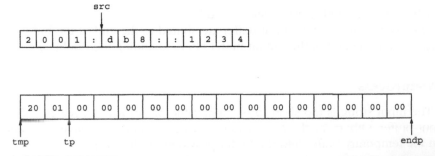

FIGURE 6-3

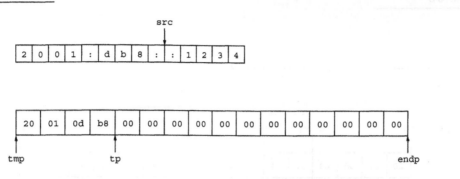

FIGURE 6-4

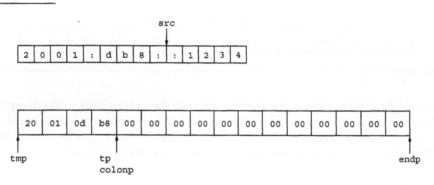

FIGURE 6-5

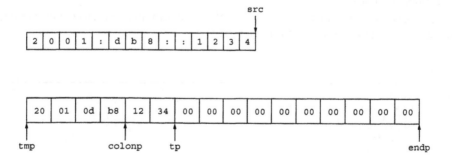

Then, the parser encounters a double colon. colonp is set to the location where tp currently points, which corresponds to lines 183–186 (Figure 6-4).

Eventually, the parser completely parses the input and the 16-bit piece after the double colon is copied to the output buffer, which corresponds to lines 225–230 (Figure 6-5).

FIGURE 6-6

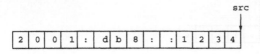

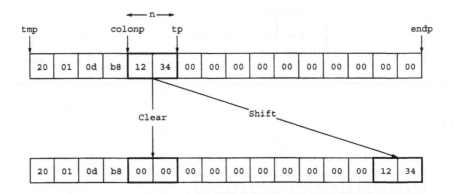

The parser must now expand the double colon in the output buffer. The length n of data that needs to be shifted toward the end of the buffer is `tp - colonp`, which equals to 2 bytes in this example. These 2 bytes are shifted toward the end of the output buffer and the original space is filled with zeros, which corresponds to lines 231–246 as in Figure 6-6.

6.2   `inet_ntop()` and `inet_ntop6()` Functions

The `inet_ntop()` function performs the reverse function of `inet_pton()`, which takes an IP address in the binary form and converts it to a printable string. `inet_ntop()` supports multiple address families.

`inet_ntop()` is not a product by the KAME's implementation. However, we explain the implementation merged in FreeBSD for reference.

Listing 6-3

inet_ntop.c

```
47    const char *
48    inet_ntop(af, src, dst, size)
49          int af;
50          const void *src;
51          char *dst;
52          size_t size;
53    {
54          switch (af) {
55          case AF_INET:
56                  return (inet_ntop4(src, dst, size));
57          case AF_INET6:
58                  return (inet_ntop6(src, dst, size));
59          default:
60                  errno = EAFNOSUPPORT;
```

```
61                    return (NULL);
62          }
63          /* NOTREACHED */
64    }
```
_____ inet_ntop.c

47–64 Similar to `inet_pton()`, the main body of `inet_ntop()` is a dispatcher that invokes the right subroutine according to the address family. If the given address family is not supported in this implementation, −1 is returned and global variable `errno` is set to `EAFNOSUPPORT`.

Listing 6-4 shows function `inet_ntop6()`, which handles the `AF_INET6` address family.

Listing 6-4
_____ inet_ntop.c

```
99    static const char *
100   inet_ntop6(src, dst, size)
101         const u_char *src;
102         char *dst;
103         size_t size;
104   {
105         /*
106          * Note that int32_t and int16_t need only be "at least" large enough
107          * to contain a value of the specified size. On some systems, like
108          * Crays, there is no such thing as an integer variable with 16 bits.
109          * Keep this in mind if you think this function should have been coded
110          * to use pointer overlays. All the world's not a VAX.
111          */
112         char tmp[sizeof "ffff:ffff:ffff:ffff:ffff:ffff:255.255.255.255"], *tp;
113         struct { int base, len; } best, cur;
114         u_int words[NS_IN6ADDRSZ / NS_INT16SZ];
115         int i;
116
117         /*
118          * Preprocess:
119          *      Copy the input (bytewise) array into a wordwise array.
120          *      Find the longest run of 0x00's in src[] for :: shorthanding.
121          */
122         memset(words, '\0', sizeof words);
123         for (i = 0; i < NS_IN6ADDRSZ; i++)
124                 words[i / 2] |= (src[i] << ((1 - (i % 2)) << 3));
125         best.base = -1;
126         cur.base = -1;
127         for (i = 0; i < (NS_IN6ADDRSZ / NS_INT16SZ); i++) {
128                 if (words[i] == 0) {
129                         if (cur.base == -1)
130                                 cur.base = i, cur.len = 1;
131                         else
132                                 cur.len++;
133                 } else {
134                         if (cur.base != -1) {
135                                 if (best.base == -1 || cur.len > best.len)
136                                         best = cur;
137                                 cur.base = -1;
138                         }
139                 }
140         }
141         if (cur.base != -1) {
142                 if (best.base == -1 || cur.len > best.len)
143                         best = cur;
144         }
145         if (best.base != -1 && best.len < 2)
146                 best.base = -1;
147
148         /*
```

```
149                    * Format the result.
150                    */
151             tp = tmp;
152             for (i = 0; i < (NS_IN6ADDRSZ / NS_INT16SZ); i++) {
153                    /* Are we inside the best run of 0x00's? */
154                    if (best.base != -1 && i >= best.base &&
155                        i < (best.base + best.len)) {
156                            if (i == best.base)
157                                    *tp++ = ':';
158                            continue;
159                    }
160                    /* Are we following an initial run of 0x00s or any real hex? */
161                    if (i != 0)
162                            *tp++ = ':';
163                    /* Is this address an encapsulated IPv4? */
164                    if (i == 6 && best.base == 0 &&
165                        (best.len == 6 || (best.len == 5 && words[5] == 0xffff))) {
166                            if (!inet_ntop4(src+12, tp, sizeof tmp - (tp - tmp)))
167                                    return (NULL);
168                            tp += strlen(tp);
169                            break;
170                    }
171                    tp += sprintf(tp, "%x", words[i]);
172             }
173             /* Was it a trailing run of 0x00's? */
174             if (best.base != -1 && (best.base + best.len) ==
175                 (NS_IN6ADDRSZ / NS_INT16SZ))
176                    *tp++ = ':';
177             *tp++ = '\0';
178
179             /*
180              * Check for overflow, copy, and we're done.
181              */
182             if ((size_t)(tp - tmp) > size) {
183                    errno = ENOSPC;
184                    return (NULL);
185             }
186             strcpy(dst, tmp);
187             return (dst);
188     }
```
                                                                          ————— inet_ntop.c

6.2.1   Local Variables

112–115 The `tmp` buffer is the output buffer that is large enough to hold any valid textual representation of an IPv6 address. `words` is an array of eight 16-bit integers for storing each 16-bit portion of the given IPv6 address in binary form.

6.2.2   Copy the Address

122–124 The `words` buffer is initially zero-cleared. Then, each 16-bit portion of the address, which is in the network byte order, is copied into the array.

6.2.3   Find the Longest Zeros

125–126 This segment of code tries to find the longest continuous zeros in the address so that these zeros can be compressed as the double colon "::". Two instances of a structure of two integers defined at line 113 are used to track and compare the longest continuous zero blocks: `best` is the longest zero block that has been seen, while `cur` is the zero block currently under consideration. The `base` member of the structure specifies the starting location of the zero block in the `words` array, which has the −1 value as the initial state. The `len` member is the length of the zero block.

127–140 The `for` loop iterates through all the entries of the `words` buffer one at a time. If an array entry has the value of zero and the parser is not currently looking at zeros, then `cur.base` stores this array location and its `len` member is initialized to 1. If the entry value is zero and the parser is already processing zeros, the `len` member is simply incremented. If the parser encounters a nonzero array entry and `cur.base` contains a valid location, the current zero block is compared against the longest known zero block that is stored in `best`. `best` is updated with `cur` if either `best` has not been set or the current zero block is longer than what is stored in `best`, and then `cur` is reinitialized.

141–144 `cur.base` holds a valid location at the completion of the `for` loop if the address terminates with a sequence of zeros. `best` is replaced with `cur` if this sequence is the longest sequence in the address.

6.2.4 Check the Need for Compression

145–146 No compression can be done if the length of the zero sequence is less than 2. In this case, `best` is cleared.

6.2.5 Convert the Address

151–152 `tp` advances in the `tmp` buffer as the address is converted to textual representation. The `for` loop makes a single path to convert the address.

153–159 If `best.base` specifies a valid location and the `for` loop is at the start of the longest zero block, a colon is written out in the output buffer. There is no output written for the remaining bytes of the zero block.

160–162 The delimiter colon is written out, which may be the other colon for the double-colon compressed form.

163–170 The given address may be an IPv4-compatible IPv6 address if there are 12 consecutive zero bytes from the start of the address. The given address may be an IPv4-mapped IPv6 address if there are 10 consecutive zero bytes from the start of the address followed by 0xFFFF. In either case the remaining 32 bits are passed to function `inet_ntop4()` to obtain the textual representation of the IPv4 address. `tp` is then updated to point to the end of the resulting string.

Note: The condition for the IPv4-compatible address is incomplete, which is missing the IPv4 addresses that begin with zeros, for example, `0.0.1.2`, which will be converted to "`::102`" instead of "`::0.0.1.2`." However, such a case should not be a problem in practice because these types of addresses are rarely if at all used. In addition, the address space defined by the IPv4-compatible IPv6 addresses is inherently ambiguous because of the conflicting definition with the loopback address "`::1`." The loopback address would better be printed as "`::1`" instead of "`::0.0.0.1`."

173–177 If `best.base` specifies a valid zero block that terminates at the end of the address, only a single colon has been written out at line 157 in the `for` loop. The terminating colon is added here. The temporary buffer is terminated with the null character. Note that the output buffer is big enough to contain any textual representation of IPv6 addresses, including the terminating character.

6.2.6 Copy the Result

179–187 If the buffer given by the caller is too small to hold the resulting string, a NULL pointer is returned and global variable `errno` is set to `ENOSPC`. Otherwise, the content of the internal output buffer `tmp` is copied into the caller-supplied buffer.

6.3 `getaddrinfo()` Function

Function `getaddrinfo()` is a name to address conversion function used by the majority of dual-stack applications. Specifically, it retrieves a list of "address information" for a given host name and service name, whose elements are pairs of addresses and port numbers. In addition to the definition given in [RFC3493], the KAME implementation of `getaddrinfo()` supports extensions such as the preferred extended format for IPv6 scoped addresses specified in [RFC4007] and the destination address selection algorithm specified in [RFC3484].

In the description below, we generally assume `AF_INET` and `PF_INET` are identical and so are `AF_INET6` and `PF_INET6` and so on, as indicated in [RFC3493]. In general, we will use the `AF_xxx` notation with the exception that we will refer to `PF_xxx` when the corresponding source code uses those definitions.

6.3.1 `afd{}` Structure

In the following discussion, a dedicated structure called `afd{}` (shown in Listing 6-5) will be used several times. It contains a list of generic information for each supported address family.

Listing 6-5

getaddrinfo.c

```
153    static const struct afd {
154            int a_af;
155            int a_addrlen;
156            int a_socklen;
157            int a_off;
158            const char *a_addrany;
159            const char *a_loopback;
160            int a_scoped;
161    } afdl [] = {
163            {PF_INET6, sizeof(struct in6_addr),
164             sizeof(struct sockaddr_in6),
165             offsetof(struct sockaddr_in6, sin6_addr),
166             in6_addrany, in6_loopback, 1},
168            {PF_INET, sizeof(struct in_addr),
169             sizeof(struct sockaddr_in),
170             offsetof(struct sockaddr_in, sin_addr),
171             in_addrany, in_loopback, 0},
172            {0, 0, 0, 0, NULL, NULL, 0},
173    };
```

getaddrinfo.c

FIGURE 6-7

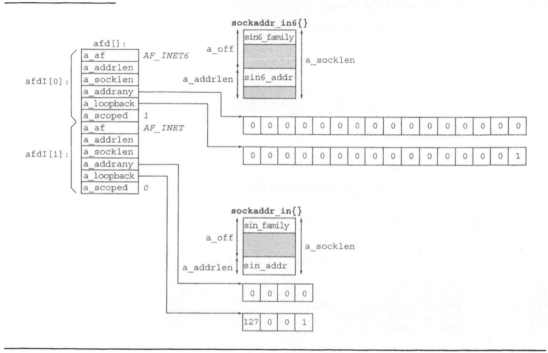

Predefined afd{} structures for AF_INET and AF_INET6.

153–160 a_addrlen is the length of the address and a_socklen is the length of the socket
address structure for the corresponding address family. a_off is the offset from the start
of the socket address structure to the address field in the structure. a_addrany and
a_loopback are the addresses in the binary form that represent the all-zero and the
loopback addresses for the address family. The latter is expected to be the address for
the host named "localhost." a_scoped specifies whether the address family supports
the notion of scoped addresses. This field is actually intended to support IPv6 scoped
addresses in explore_numeric_scope() to be discussed in Listing 6-12.

161–173 A static array afdl contains the definitions for the AF_INET6 and the AF_INET
address families. Figure 6-7 shows some of the values of these structures.

6.3.2 getaddrinfo() Overview

The getaddrinfo() function is a large function that invokes complex subroutines. We
describe the overall function structure followed by a detailed description of each subroutine.
Listing 6-6 shows the overall structure of getaddrinfo().

Listing 6-6

getaddrinfo.c
```
420   int
421   getaddrinfo(hostname, servname, hints, res)
422        const char *hostname, *servname;
```

```
423              const struct addrinfo *hints;
424              struct addrinfo **res;
425    {
426              struct addrinfo sentinel;
427              struct addrinfo *cur;
428              int error = 0;
429              struct addrinfo ai, ai0, *afai;
430              struct addrinfo *pai;
431              const struct afd *afd;
432              const struct explore *ex;
433              struct addrinfo *afailist[sizeof(afdl)/sizeof(afdl[0])];
434              struct addrinfo *afai_unspec;
435              int pass, found;
436              int numeric = 0;
437
438              /* ensure we return NULL on errors */
439              *res = NULL;
440
441              memset(afailist, 0, sizeof(afailist));
442              afai_unspec = NULL;
443
444              memset(&sentinel, 0, sizeof(sentinel));
445              cur = &sentinel;
446              pai = &ai;
447              pai->ai_flags = 0;
448              pai->ai_family = PF_UNSPEC;
449              pai->ai_socktype = ANY;
450              pai->ai_protocol = ANY;
451              pai->ai_addrlen = 0;
452              pai->ai_canonname = NULL;
453              pai->ai_addr = NULL;
454              pai->ai_next = NULL;

       ----------------------------------------------------
/* validate argument */

/* handle NULL or numeric host name */

/* handle FQDN host name */

/* reorder results */
       ----------------------------------------------------

732    bad:
733              if (afai_unspec)
734                      freeaddrinfo(afai_unspec);
735              for (afd = afdl; afd->a_af; afd++) {
736                      if (afailist[afd - afdl])
737                              freeaddrinfo(afailist[afd - afdl]);
738              }
739              if (!*res)
740                      if (sentinel.ai_next)
741                              freeaddrinfo(sentinel.ai_next);
742              return error;
743    }
```
_____getaddrinfo.c

6.3.3 Initialization

438–454 `afailist` is an array of pointers each of whose entries points to an `addrinfo{}` structure of a supported address family. It has two entries in the KAME implementation, one for `AF_INET` and one for `AF_INET6`. This array will be used to store the results for a NULL or numeric host name. `afai_unspec` will be used to store temporary results for an fully qualified domain name (FQDN) host name. `sentinel` will be used to reorder the results. `pai` will store hint parameters that are given by the caller.

6.3.4 Postprocess

732–742 Temporary resources are freed. `*res` points to `sentinel.ai_next` if function `getaddrinfo()` returns successfully. Otherwise a nonempty list referenced by `sentinel.ai_next` is freed.

6.3.5 Parameters Validation

The first main section of `getaddrinfo()`, shown in Listing 6-7, validates the parameters that are passed in from the caller.

Listing 6-7

getaddrinfo.c

```
456         if (hostname == NULL && servname == NULL)
457                 return EAI_NONAME;
458         if (hints) {
459                 /* error check for hints */
460                 if (hints->ai_addrlen || hints->ai_canonname ||
461                     hints->ai_addr || hints->ai_next)
462                         ERR(EAI_BADHINTS); /* xxx */
463                 if (hints->ai_flags & ~AI_MASK)
464                         ERR(EAI_BADFLAGS);
465                 switch (hints->ai_family) {
466                 case PF_UNSPEC:
467                 case PF_INET:
469                 case PF_INET6:
471                         break;
472                 default:
473                         ERR(EAI_FAMILY);
474                 }
475                 memcpy(pai, hints, sizeof(*pai));
476
477                 /*
478                  * if both socktype/protocol are specified, check if they
479                  * are meaningful combination.
480                  */
481                 if (pai->ai_socktype != ANY && pai->ai_protocol != ANY) {
482                         for (ex = explore; ex->e_af >= 0; ex++) {
483                                 if (!MATCH_FAMILY(pai->ai_family, ex->e_af,
484                                     WILD_AF(ex)))
485                                         continue;
486                                 if (!MATCH(pai->ai_socktype, ex->e_socktype,
487                                     WILD_SOCKTYPE(ex)))
488                                         continue;
489                                 if (!MATCH(pai->ai_protocol, ex->e_protocol,
490                                     WILD_PROTOCOL(ex)))
491                                         continue;
492
493                                 /* matched */
494                                 break;
495                         }
496
497                         if (ex->e_af < 0) {
498                                 ERR(EAI_BADHINTS);
499                         }
500                 }
501         }
502
503 #if defined(AI_ALL) && defined(AI_V4MAPPED)
```

```
504          /*
505           * post-2553: AI_ALL and AI_V4MAPPED are effective only against
506           * AF_INET6 query. They need to be ignored if specified in other
507           * occassions.
508           */
509          switch (pai->ai_flags & (AI_ALL | AI_V4MAPPED)) {
510          case AI_V4MAPPED:
511          case AI_ALL | AI_V4MAPPED:
512                  if (pai->ai_family != AF_INET6)
513                          pai->ai_flags &= ~(AI_ALL | AI_V4MAPPED);
514                  break;
515          case AI_ALL:
517                  /* illegal */
518                  ERR(EAI_BADFLAGS);
522                  break;
523          }
524  #endif
525
526          /*
527           * check for special cases. (1) numeric servname is disallowed if
528           * socktype/protocol are left unspecified. (2) servname is disallowed
529           * for raw and other inet{,6} sockets.
530           */
531          if (MATCH_FAMILY(pai->ai_family, PF_INET, 1)
533           || MATCH_FAMILY(pai->ai_family, PF_INET6, 1)
535              ) {
536                  ai0 = *pai;          /* backup *pai */
537
538                  if (pai->ai_family == PF_UNSPEC) {
540                          pai->ai_family = PF_INET6;
544                  }
545                  error = get_portmatch(pai, servname);
546                  if (error)
547                          ERR(error);
548
549                  *pai = ai0;
550          }
551
552          ai0 = *pai;
```
—— getaddrinfo.c

456–457 According to [RFC3493], at least one of `hostname` and `servname` must be a non-NULL pointer. Otherwise, an error of `EAI_NONAME` will be returned.

458–462 [RFC3493] also requires that every member of the `hints` structure other than `ai_flags`, `ai_family`, `ai_socktype`, and `ai_protocol` be set to zero or a NULL pointer. Otherwise, an error of `EAI_BADHINTS` will be returned. Note that `EAI_BADHINTS` is not a standard error code and is specific to the KAME implementation (see Table 2-3).

463–464 `AI_MASK` combines all of the supported flags for `ai_flags`. The definition of `AI_MASK` is as follows:

```
#define AI_MASK \
(AI_PASSIVE | AI_CANONNAME | AI_NUMERICHOST | AI_ADDRCONFIG)
```

An `EAI_BADFLAGS` error is returned if an unsupported flag is specified in `ai_flags` of the `hints` structure. Note the implementation does not completely conform to [RFC3493], which also defines `AI_NUMERICSERV`, `AI_V4MAPPED`, and `AI_ALL`.

465–474 An `EAI_FAMILY` error is returned if `ai_family` has an unsupported address family value.

475   Validation completes and the `hints` structure is copied in `pai`.

481–500 If both the socket type `ai_socktype` and the protocol `ai_protocol` fields have values, the coherence of the combination against the `explore` array is checked. For example, the combination of `SOCK_STREAM` socket type and `IPPROTO_UDP` is illegal and is rejected here. In this case, an `EAI_BADHINTS` error will be returned.

The definition of the `explore{}` structure is given in Listing 6-8.

Listing 6-8

_____getaddrinfo.c
```
175     struct explore {
176             int e_af;
177             int e_socktype;
178             int e_protocol;
179             const char *e_protostr;
180             int e_wild;
181     #define WILD_AF(ex)              ((ex)->e_wild & 0x01)
182     #define WILD_SOCKTYPE(ex)        ((ex)->e_wild & 0x02)
183     #define WILD_PROTOCOL(ex)        ((ex)->e_wild & 0x04)
184     };
```
_____getaddrinfo.c

The supported combinations of socket type and protocol for each address family are given in Table 6-2. As shown in the table, this implementation takes stream control transmission protocol (SCTP) into account. SCTP is a new transport protocol defined in [RFC2960], and its technical details are beyond the scope of this book. For our discussion below, it is enough to understand that SCTP is a stream-based transport protocol like transmission control protocol (TCP).

The values for `e_protostr` are omitted because these values are not used in the source code. The "wild flags" column specifies which field of the address family, socket type, and protocol is allowed to have a wildcard ("any") value during matching. For example, the fifth row shows `SOCK_RAW` does not match if a wildcard is specified for the socket type.

We now turn back to Listing 6-7.

TABLE 6-2

Address family	SocketType	Protocol	Wild flags
INET6	SOCK_DGRAM	UDP	AF | SOCK | PROTO
INET6	SOCK_STREAM	SCTP	AF | SOCK | PROTO
INET6	SOCK_STREAM	TCP	AF | SOCK | PROTO
INET6	SOCK_SEQPACKET	SCTP	AF | SOCK | PROTO
INET6	SOCK_RAW	ANY	AF | PROTO
INET	SOCK_DGRAM	UDP	AF | SOCK | PROTO
INET	SOCK_STREAM	SCTP	AF | SOCK | PROTO
INET	SOCK_STREAM	TCP	AF | SOCK | PROTO
INET	SOCK_SEQPACKET	SCTP	AF | SOCK | PROTO
INET	SOCK_RAW	ANY	AF | PROTO

503–524 [RFC3493] clarifies that the AI_ALL and the AI_V4MAPPED flags are only meaningful for an AF_INET6 socket. Therefore, these flags are cleared for an AF_INET socket. The code also regards the case where only AI_ALL is specified as an error. However, this treatment of AI_ALL does not conform to [RFC3493], which simply ignores the case.

531–552 If the specified address family is PF_INET, PF_INET6, or PF_UNSPEC, function get_portmatch() checks whether servname is a valid service name for the given protocol family. get_portmatch() will return an error code if there is a mismatch. For simplicity, the code assumes PF_INET6 when PF_UNSPEC is specified, but this behavior is incorrect because there is no guarantee that PF_INET and PF_INET6 have the same service name space.

6.3.6   Converting NULL or Numeric Host Name

The second main section of getaddrinfo() shown in Listing 6-9 handles either the NULL or the numeric host names.

Listing 6-9

_____ getaddrinfo.c

```
554                 /*
555                  * NULL hostname, or numeric hostname.
556                  * If numeric representation of AF1 can be interpreted as FQDN
557                  * representation of AF2, we need to think again about the code below.
558                  */
559                 found = 0;
560                 for (afd = afdl; afd->a_af; afd++) {
561                         *pai = ai0;
562
563                         if (!MATCH_FAMILY(pai->ai_family, afd->a_af, 1))
564                                 continue;
565
566                         if (pai->ai_family == PF_UNSPEC)
567                                 pai->ai_family = afd->a_af;
568
569                         if (hostname == NULL) {
570                                 /*
571                                  * filter out AFs that are not supported by the kernel
572                                  * XXX errno?
573                                  */
574                                 if (!addrconfig(pai->ai_family))
575                                         continue;
576                                 error = explore_null(pai, servname,
577                                     &afailist[afd - afdl]);
578                         } else
579                                 error = explore_numeric_scope(pai, hostname, servname,
580                                     &afailist[afd - afdl]);
581
582                         if (!error && afailist[afd - afdl])
583                                 found++;
584                 }
585                 if (found) {
586                         numeric = 1;
587                         goto globcopy;
588                 }
589
590                 if (hostname == NULL)
591                         ERR(EAI_NONAME);        /* used to be EAI_NODATA */
592                 if (pai->ai_flags & AI_NUMERICHOST)
593                         ERR(EAI_NONAME);
```

_____ getaddrinfo.c

559–567 The for loop compares each supported address family against the address family given in the hints. If the given address family is unspecified, it will be set to the value in the afd entry that is based on the current loop index.

569–577 Function addrconfig() will check whether the current address family is available on the node if the caller does not specify a host name. If the address family is available, function explore_null() is called to return either the "any" or the "loopback" address depending on the type of socket, that is, the socket being passive or active.

578–580 If the caller specifies a host name, function explore_numeric_scope() is called to try to convert the host name assuming the host name is in the numeric format.

582–584 The found variable indicates whether a numeric address has been obtained. If so, the resolved address information has been stored in afailist[afd - afdl].

585–588 The conversion process terminates if at least one address is found. Variable numeric is set to 1 to mark the fact that the case of FQDN host names has not been explored.

590–593 No attempts succeeded so far. If the caller did not provide a host name or the AI_NUMERICHOST flag was specified, there is no need to explore the case of FQDN host names. An error of EAI_NONAME will simply be returned.

6.3.7 explore_null() Function

The explore_null() function returns either the "any address" or the address of "localhost," together with the port number for the given service name back to the caller.

Listing 6-10

getaddrinfo.c

```
1235    /*
1236     * hostname == NULL.
1237     * passive socket -> anyaddr (0.0.0.0 or ::)
1238     * non-passive socket -> localhost (127.0.0.1 or ::1)
1239     */
1240    static int
1241    explore_null(pai, servname, res)
1242            const struct addrinfo *pai;
1243            const char *servname;
1244            struct addrinfo **res;
1245    {
1246            const struct afd *afd;
1247            struct addrinfo *cur;
1248            struct addrinfo sentinel;
1249            int error;
1250
1251            *res = NULL;
1252            sentinel.ai_next = NULL;
1253            cur = &sentinel;
1254
1255            /*
1256             * if the servname does not match socktype/protocol, ignore it.
1257             */
1258            if (get_portmatch(pai, servname) != 0)
1259                    return 0;
1260
1261            afd = find_afd(pai->ai_family);
1262            if (afd == NULL)
1263                    return 0;
```

```
1264
1265            if (pai->ai_flags & AI_PASSIVE) {
1266                    GET_AI(cur->ai_next, afd, afd->a_addrany);
1267                    /* xxx meaningless?
1268                     * GET_CANONNAME(cur->ai_next, "anyaddr");
1269                     */
1270                    GET_PORT(cur->ai_next, servname);
1271            } else {
1272                    GET_AI(cur->ai_next, afd, afd->a_loopback);
1273                    /* xxx meaningless?
1274                     * GET_CANONNAME(cur->ai_next, "localhost");
1275                     */
1276                    GET_PORT(cur->ai_next, servname);
1277            }
1278            cur = cur->ai_next;
1279
1280            *res = sentinel.ai_next;
1281            return 0;
1282
1283    free:
1284            if (sentinel.ai_next)
1285                    freeaddrinfo(sentinel.ai_next);
1286            return error;
1287    }
```
_____ getaddrinfo.c

1251–1253 `*res` is initialized to NULL in case of failure. `sentinel.ai_next` will have a pointer to a valid result. This function is actually simple enough that we could have written it without using the `sentinel` parameter.

1255–1259 `get_portmatch()` checks whether `servname` is a valid service name for the protocol family. The function fails and returns if the service name is invalid. The caller interprets the empty `addrinfo` chain as a failure.

1261–1263 `find_afd()` iterates through the `afdl` array to find an appropriate `afd` entry for the given address family.

1265–1270 The caller wants the "any address" if the `AI_PASSIVE` flag is set, which is suitable for binding with a listening socket. The `GET_AI()` macro allocates a new `addrinfo{}` structure and initializes it with information from the `afd` structure and its `a_addrany` member. Then, the `GET_PORT()` macro converts `servname` to a 16-bit integer and sets that value into the port field of `ai_next.ai_addr`. The code jumps to the `free` label if either of `GET_xxx()` macros fails.

Note that when this code was first written, the specification was not clear on how the `AI_CANONNAME` flag should be processed for a NULL host name. Thus, the code is commented out for `AI_CANONNAME`. Then, [RFC3493] clarifies that this flag is only meaningful for non-NULL host names.

1271–1277 The caller wants the address for "local hosts" if the `AI_PASSIVE` flag is not set. The process is identical to the previous case except that the `a_loopback` member is used instead.

1278–1287 On success, `*res` is set to point to the newly created `addrinfo{}` structure and 0 is returned to the caller.

1283–1287 Any allocated memory is freed when an error occurs, and the appropriate error code is returned to the caller.

6.3.8 `explore_numeric()` Function

The `explore_numeric()` and `explore_numeric_scope()` functions try to convert a host name assuming it is in a numeric form. The latter also supports the extension of the textual representation of IPv6 addresses for scoped addresses. In fact, `explore_numeric()` acts as a backend function of `explore_numeric_scope()` in this implementation. We first explain the `explore_numeric()` function in Listing 6-11.

Listing 6-11

getaddrinfo.c

```
1289    /*
1290     * numeric hostname
1291     */
1292    static int
1293    explore_numeric(pai, hostname, servname, res, ohostname)
1294            const struct addrinfo *pai;
1295            const char *hostname;
1296            const char *servname;
1297            struct addrinfo **res;
1298            const char *ohostname;
1299    {
1300            const struct afd *afd;
1301            struct addrinfo *cur;
1302            struct addrinfo sentinel;
1303            int error;
1304            char pton[PTON_MAX];
1305
1306            *res = NULL;
1307            sentinel.ai_next = NULL;
1308            cur = &sentinel;
1309
1310            afd = find_afd(pai->ai_family);
1311            if (afd == NULL)
1312                    return 0;
1313
1314            switch (afd->a_af) {
1315    #if 0 /*X/Open spec*/
1316            case AF_INET:
1317                    if (inet_aton(hostname, (struct in_addr *)pton) == 1) {
1318                            if (pai->ai_family == afd->a_af ||
1319                                pai->ai_family == PF_UNSPEC /*?*/) {
1320                                    GET_AI(cur->ai_next, afd, pton);
1321                                    GET_PORT(cur->ai_next, servname);
1322                                    while (cur && cur->ai_next)
1323                                            cur = cur->ai_next;
1324                            } else
1325                                    ERR(EAI_FAMILY);           /*xxx*/
1326                    }
1327                    break;
1328    #endif
1329            default:
1330                    if (inet_pton(afd->a_af, hostname, pton) == 1) {
1331                            if (pai->ai_family == afd->a_af ||
1332                                pai->ai_family == PF_UNSPEC /*?*/) {
1333                                    GET_AI(cur->ai_next, afd, pton);
1334                                    GET_PORT(cur->ai_next, servname);
1335                                    if ((pai->ai_flags & AI_CANONNAME)) {
1336                                            /*
1337                                             * Set the numeric address itself as
1338                                             * the canonical name, based on a
1339                                             * clarification in rfc2553bis-03.
1340                                             */
```

```
1341                                          GET_CANONNAME(cur->ai_next, ohostname);
1342                                 }
1343                             while (cur && cur->ai_next)
1344                                 cur = cur->ai_next;
1345                       } else
1346                             ERR(EAI_FAMILY);          /* XXX */
1347                    }
1348                break;
1349          }
1350
1351       *res = sentinel.ai_next;
1352       return 0;
1353
1354    free:
1355    bad:
1356          if (sentinel.ai_next)
1357                freeaddrinfo(sentinel.ai_next);
1358       return error;
1359    }
```
—— getaddrinfo.c

1306–1312 The initialization of the variables is similar to `explore_null()`. As already explained, this implementation of this function could be simplified by eliminating `sentinel`. Additionally, the validation by `find_afd()` is redundant because the caller has already performed that validation.

1314–1328 [RFC3493] requires `getaddrinfo()` to accept the IPv4 numeric addresses that are in the class-based address form, for example, "10" for "`10.0.0.0.`" This requirement means function `inet_pton()` cannot be used as the backend conversion function because `inet_pton()` does not accept class-based address by definition. Thus, `inet_aton()` should be used instead for the `AF_INET` address family. As shown in Listing 6-11, however, this segment of code is disabled. The reason is that at the time when that code was written, [RFC2553] was not clear on the treatment of class-based IPv4 addresses.

Similar to `explore_null()`, on the successful return of `inet_aton()`, `GET_AI()` allocates a new `addrinfo{}` entry to store the converted host name followed by `GET_PORT()`, which sets an appropriate port number in the appropriate field of the `ai_addr` member.

The `while` loop starting at line 1322 is meaningless and can be ignored here because the `ai_next` member must never be non–NULL.

1330–1349 For all the address families other than `AF_INET`, function `inet_pton()` can simply be used for the conversion. (Note: in this particular code, `inet_pton()` is also used for `AF_INET` due to the preprocessor condition at line 1315.) On success, `GET_AI()` allocates a new `addrinfo{}` entry to store the converted host name followed by `GET_PORT()` that sets an appropriate port number in the appropriate field of the `ai_addr` member. The same converted host name is used as the "canonical" name (i.e. it is also copied into the `ai_canonname` field of the `addrinfo{}` structure when the `AI_CANONNAME` flag is set in the `hints{}` structure.)

1351–1352 `*res` stores the conversion results, which can be NULL if either `inet_aton()` or `inet_pton()` failed.

1354–1356 The allocated `addrinfo{}` entry is freed on error, and an appropriate error code is returned to the caller.

Now, it is time to describe the `explore_numeric_scope()` function, shown in Listing 6-12.

Listing 6-12

```
1361    /*
1362     * numeric hostname with scope
1363     */
1364    static int
1365    explore_numeric_scope(pai, hostname, servname, res)
1366            const struct addrinfo *pai;
1367            const char *hostname;
1368            const char *servname;
1369            struct addrinfo **res;
1370    {
1374            const struct afd *afd;
1375            struct addrinfo *cur;
1376            int error;
1377            char *cp, *hostname2 = NULL, *scope, *addr;
1378            struct sockaddr_in6 *sin6;
1379
1380            afd = find_afd(pai->ai_family);
1381            if (afd == NULL)
1382                    return 0;
1383
1384            if (!afd->a_scoped)
1385                    return explore_numeric(pai, hostname, servname, res, hostname);
1386
1387            cp = strchr(hostname, SCOPE_DELIMITER);
1388            if (cp == NULL)
1389                    return explore_numeric(pai, hostname, servname, res, hostname);
1390
1403            /*
1404             * Handle special case of <scoped_address><delimiter><scope id>
1405             */
1406            hostname2 = strdup(hostname);
1407            if (hostname2 == NULL)
1408                    return EAI_MEMORY;
1409            /* terminate at the delimiter */
1410            hostname2[cp - hostname] = '\0';
1411            addr = hostname2;
1412            scope = cp + 1;
1414
1415            error = explore_numeric(pai, addr, servname, res, hostname);
1416            if (error == 0) {
1417                    u_int32_t scopeid;
1418
1419                    for (cur = *res; cur; cur = cur->ai_next) {
1420                            if (cur->ai_family != AF_INET6)
1421                                    continue;
1422                            sin6 = (struct sockaddr_in6 *)(void *)cur->ai_addr;
1423                            if (ip6_str2scopeid(scope, sin6, &scopeid) == -1) {
1424                                    free(hostname2);
1425                                    freeaddrinfo(*res);
1426                                    *res = NULL;
1427                                    return(EAI_NONAME); /* XXX: is return OK? */
1428                            }
1429                            sin6->sin6_scope_id = scopeid;
1430                    }
1431            }
1432
1433            free(hostname2);
1434
1435            if (error && *res) {
1436                    freeaddrinfo(*res);
1437                    *res = NULL;
```

```
1438            }
1439            return error;
1441    }
```
_____getaddrinfo.c

1380–1387 As in `explore_null()`, `find_afd()` provides the `afd` entry for the given address family. If this does not have scoped addresses, `explore_numeric()` does the job. In this implementation, `explore_numeric()` will simply be used for the `AF_INET` family. Then, `strchr()` searches for the delimiter character in case `hostname` is formatted in the extended representation. As specified in [RFC4007], the delimiter is the percent character ("%"). If `hostname` does not contain the delimiter, it is enough to pass `hostname` to `explore_numeric()`.

1406–1415 If `hostname` contains the delimiter character, a copy of `hostname` is made and stored in `hostname2`. `hostname2` is then divided into two parts: the address and the scope zone ID. The address part is passed to `explore_numeric()` for conversion.

1416–1431 If `explore_numeric()` succeeds, the entire `addrinfo{}` entries are examined in the `for` loop. For each `AF_INET6` entry function `ip6_str2scopeid()` (see Listing 6-13) is called to parse the scope zone ID. `scopeid` contains a 32-bit scope zone ID on successful return from `ip6_str2scopeid()`, which is then set into the `sin6_scope_id` field of the `sockaddr_in6{}` structure. An `EAI_NONAME` error is returned on failure after freeing the necessary resources.

1433–1441 Temporary resources are freed and an appropriate error code is returned.

6.3.9 `ip6_str2scopeid()` Function

Function `ip6_str2scopeid()` converts a textual representation of a given scope zone index into a 32-bit integer.

Listing 6-13
_____getaddrinfo.c
```
1653    /* convert a string to a scope identifier. XXX: IPv6 specific */
1654    static int
1655    ip6_str2scopeid(scope, sin6, scopeid)
1656            char *scope;
1657            struct sockaddr_in6 *sin6;
1658            u_int32_t *scopeid;
1659    {
1660            u_long lscopeid;
1661            struct in6_addr *a6 = &sin6->sin6_addr;
1662            char *ep;
1663
1664            /* empty scopeid portion is invalid */
1665            if (*scope == '\0')
1666                    return -1;
1667
1668            if (IN6_IS_ADDR_LINKLOCAL(a6) || IN6_IS_ADDR_MC_LINKLOCAL(a6) ||
1669                IN6_IS_ADDR_MC_NODELOCAL(a6)) {
1670                    /*
1671                     * We currently assume a one-to-one mapping between links
1672                     * and interfaces, so we simply use interface indices for
1673                     * like-local scopes.
1674                     */
1675                    *scopeid = if_nametoindex(scope);
```

```
1676                       if (*scopeid == 0)
1677                               goto trynumeric;
1678                       return 0;
1679             }
1680
1681             /* still unclear about literal, allow numeric only - placeholder */
1682             if (IN6_IS_ADDR_SITELOCAL(a6) || IN6_IS_ADDR_MC_SITELOCAL(a6))
1683                     goto trynumeric;
1684             if (IN6_IS_ADDR_MC_ORGLOCAL(a6))
1685                     goto trynumeric;
1686             else
1687                     goto trynumeric;           /* global */
1688
1689             /* try to convert to a numeric id as a last resort */
1690     trynumeric:
1691             errno = 0;
1692             lscopeid = strtoul(scope, &ep, 10);
1693             *scopeid = (u_int32_t)(lscopeid & 0xffffffffUL);
1694             if (errno == 0 && ep && *ep == '\0' && *scopeid == lscopeid)
1695                     return 0;
1696             else
1697                     return -1;
1698     }
```
——getaddrinfo.c

1664–1666 The function terminates immediately on an empty string.

1668–1679 The implementation allows the interface names to be used as zone identifiers for link-local and interface-local addresses. From an architectural perspective, however, links can be larger in scope than interfaces. Nevertheless, the implementation assumes one-to-one mapping between links and interfaces, and thus it makes sense to use interface names under this assumption.

Note that macro IN6_IS_ADDR_MC_NODELOCAL() identifies the interface-local multicast addresses. The API standard follows an older version of the address architecture that has the notion of node-local but was replaced with interface-local (see the note for Table 2.4).

The interface index for the given interface name is simply used as the zone ID when interface names are used as zone IDs. Function if_nametoindex() does the conversion. Strictly speaking, this conversion is not sufficient because the specification requires encoding the scope type (e.g. a "link") into each zone ID to ensure uniqueness among all zone identifiers.

1681–1687 There are no valid strings except numeric IDs defined as scope zone IDs for scopes that are larger than the link scope.

1690–1698 [RFC4007] specifies that an implementation that supports the extended format must at least support numeric zone IDs. strtoul() attempts to convert the string to an integer. On success, the result from strtoul() is returned along with a 0 error code. Otherwise, −1 is returned to indicate the failure.

6.3.10   Example: Convert an IPv6 Link-Local Address to the Extended Format

Figure 6-8 depicts how getaddrinfo() converts the string "fe80::1234\%ne0" to the corresponding sockaddr_in6{} structure. Figure 6-8 concentrates on the conversion process performed in explore_numeric_scope() and its backend functions.

FIGURE 6-8

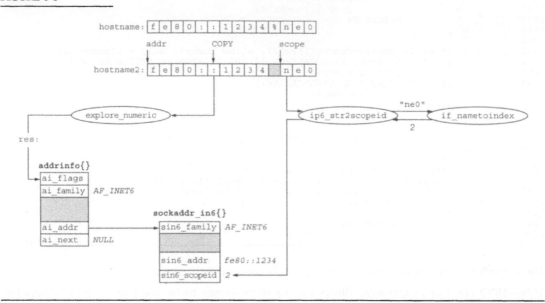

Convert `fe80::1234%ne0` *by* `getaddrinfo()`.

The hostname variable stores the string "fe80::1234\%ne0." Function `explore_numeric_scope()` first makes a copy of the string in `hostname2` and then divides the string in `hostname2` into the address part and the scope zone ID part.

The address part is passed to `explore_numeric()`, which returns an `addrinfo{}` chain in variable `res` that has a single entry. The `ai_addr` member of the `addrinfo{}` structure points to a `sockaddr_in6{}` structure whose `sin6_addr` member is `fe80::1234` in the binary form.

The scope zone ID part, "ne0," is passed to function `ip6_str2scopeid()` and then to function `if_nametoindex()` and is converted to the corresponding interface index as the link zone ID. We assume the interface identifier for the interface name "ne0" is 2 in this example.

The `explore_numeric_scope()` function finally sets the `sin6_scope_id` member of the `sockaddr_in6{}` structure pointed from the `addrinfo{}` structure to 2. The conversion process completes successfully and the `addrinfo{}` structure will be returned to the caller.

6.3.11   Converting FQDN Domain Names: `explore_fqdn()`

The third main section of `getaddrinfo()` shown in Listing 6-14 attempts to convert an alphabetical host name to an IP address by means of domain name server (DNS) resolution.

Listing 6-14

getaddrinfo.c

```
595        /*
596         * hostname as alphabetical name.
597         * first, try to query DNS for all possible address families.
```

```
598                 */
600                 /*
601                  * the operating systems support PF_UNSPEC lookup in explore_fqdn().
602                  */
603                 *pai = ai0;
604                 error = explore_fqdn(pai, hostname, servname, &afai_unspec);
```
—— getaddrinfo.c

603–604 `pai` is reinitialized to `ai0` in case `pai` has been modified. Function `explore_fqdn()` is called to perform the conversion procedure, which is shown in Listing 6-15.

Listing 6-15
—— getaddrinfo.c
```
4130   /*
4131    * FQDN hostname, DNS lookup
4132    */
4133   static int
4134   explore_fqdn(pai, hostname, servname, res)
4135           const struct addrinfo *pai;
4136           const char *hostname;
4137           const char *servname;
4138           struct addrinfo **res;
4139   {
4140           struct addrinfo *result;
4141           struct addrinfo *cur;
4142           int error = 0, i;
4143
4144           result = NULL;
4145           *res = NULL;
4146
4147           /*
4148            * if the servname does not match socktype/protocol, ignore it.
4149            */
4150           if (get_portmatch(pai, servname) != 0)
4151                   return 0;
4152
4153           if (!_hostconf_init_done)
4154                   _hostconf_init();
4155
4156           for (i = 0; i < MAXHOSTCONF; i++) {
4157                   if (!_hostconf[i].byname)
4158                           continue;
4159                   error = (*_hostconf[i].byname)(pai, hostname, &result);
4160                   if (error != 0)
4161                           continue;
4162                   for (cur = result; cur; cur = cur->ai_next) {
4163                           GET_PORT(cur, servname);
4164                           /* canonname should already be filled. */
4165                   }
4166                   *res = result;
4167                   return 0;
4168           }
4169
4170   free:
4171           if (result)
4172                   freeaddrinfo(result);
4173           return error;
4174   }
```
—— getaddrinfo.c

4144–4151 `get_portmatch()` verifies whether the given `servname` is meaningful for the given socket type and protocol. This validation should not fail here because the check has already been done for `AF_INET` and `AF_INET6` (Listing 6-16) and `get_portmatch()` unconditionally succeeds for other address families.

4153–4154 If this is the first time for the execution of `getaddrinfo()`, `_hostconf_init()` is called to parse the `/etc/host.conf` file and to construct the `_hostconf` array. This is an array of the `_hostconf{}` structure, each of which has a single member, `byname`, a method to convert a host name to an IP address.

Note that `_hostconf_init_done` is a static variable in the source file, which is set to 1 in `_hostconf_init()`. Since this variable is not protected from simultaneous accesses by multiple threads, this implementation of `getaddrinfo()` is not thread-safe, whereas [RFC3493] requires `getaddrinfo()` function to be so. This is the only part described in this book that breaks thread-safeness. It is not so hard to fix this particular part, but backend resolver routines are not thread-safe either and it is much harder to fix that part.

The content of `/etc/host.conf` in the default installation of FreeBSD is as follows.

Listing 6-16

── */etc/host.conf*

```
# First try the /etc/hosts file
hosts
# Now try the nameserver next.
bind
# If you have YP/NIS configured, uncomment the next line
# nis
```

── */etc/host.conf*

Each line specifies a method for converting host names into addresses with decreasing preference. A line that begins with the pound sign is a comment line. As commented in the file, the static database stored in the host's `/etc/hosts` file is examined first, followed by DNS resolution. If the last line is uncommented, YP/NIS can also be available, although this function is not enabled in this `getaddrinfo()` implementation by default.

The supported name resolution method functions that are set in the `_hostconf` array are

- hosts `_files_getaddrinfo()`
- bind `_dns_getaddrinfo()`
- nis `_nis_getaddrinfo()`

4156–4168 Each iteration of the `for` loop invokes the `byname` method in the current `_hostconf` array entry with the given host name until a method succeeds. The `result` variable will then point to a chain of `addrinfo{}` structures containing the conversion result. The `GET_PORT()` macro sets the port value for the given `servname` in the appropriate field of the `ai_addr` member of each `addrinfo{}` structure. Finally, `*res` is set to `result` and the conversion procedure terminates.

This organization of loop is important from the performance point of view. Suppose that the application specifies the `AF_UNSPEC` for the `ai_family` member of the `hint` structure, indicating that the application wants both IPv4 and IPv6 addresses for the given host name. With the default configuration of `/etc/host.conf`, we first try to find both IPv4 and IPv6 addresses in the `/etc/hosts` file. We will only try using the DNS method when we cannot find either IPv4 or IPv6 addresses. A previous version of getaddrinfo() did this by a per-address family loop, first trying all the methods for a single address family, say IPv4, and then trying the methods for the other address family. Thus, even if the answer we wanted could be found in the /etc/hosts file, we could have tried DNS at least once, causing unnecessary delay.

4170–4173 If all the methods fail or an error occurs in the GET_PORT() macro, the incomplete result in the result chain is freed (if any), and an appropriate error is returned. In the former case, the error code returned by the last method is remembered and returned to the caller.

Note: GET_PORT() should actually not fail, because get_portmatch() already checks the validity of servname

6.3.12   Reorder the **addrinfo** Chain

The last main section of getaddrinfo() first constructs an addrinfo{} chain with the base information for all possible combinations of address family, socket type, and protocol. getaddrinfo() then rearranges the addrinfo{} chain based on the implementation-specific policy and, if applicable, the address selection algorithm per [RFC3484].

Listing 6-17

```
                                                               getaddrinfo.c
630   globcopy:
631           pass = 1;
632   copyagain:
633           for (ex = explore; ex->e_af >= 0; ex++) {
634                   *pai = ai0;
635
636                   if (pai->ai_family == PF_UNSPEC)
637                           pai->ai_family = ex->e_af;
638
639                   if (!MATCH_FAMILY(pai->ai_family, ex->e_af, WILD_AF(ex)))
640                           continue;
641                   if (!MATCH(pai->ai_socktype, ex->e_socktype, WILD_SOCKTYPE(ex)))
642                           continue;
643                   if (!MATCH(pai->ai_protocol, ex->e_protocol, WILD_PROTOCOL(ex)))
644                           continue;
645
646   #ifdef AI_ADDRCONFIG
647                   /*
648                    * If AI_ADDRCONFIG is specified, check if we are
649                    * expected to return the address family or not.
650                    */
651                   if ((pai->ai_flags & AI_ADDRCONFIG) != 0 &&
652                       !addrconfig(afd->a_af))
653                           continue;
654   #endif
655
656                   /*
657                    * XXX: Dirty hack.  Some passive applications only assume
658                    * a single entry returned and makes a socket for the head
659                    * entry.  In such a case, it would be safer to return
660                    * "traditional" socktypes (e.g. TCP/UDP) first.
661                    * We should, ideally, fix the applications rather than to
662                    * introduce the grotty workaround in the library, but we do
663                    * not want to break deployed apps just due to adding a new
664                    * protocol type.
```

```
665                         */
666                         if ((pai->ai_flags & AI_PASSIVE)) {
667                                 if (pass == 1 && ex->e_protocol == IPPROTO_SCTP)
668                                         continue;
669                                 if (pass == 2 && ex->e_protocol != IPPROTO_SCTP)
670                                         continue;
671                         }
672
673                         if (pai->ai_family == PF_UNSPEC)
674                                 pai->ai_family = ex->e_af;
675                         if (pai->ai_socktype == ANY && ex->e_socktype != ANY)
676                                 pai->ai_socktype = ex->e_socktype;
677                         if (pai->ai_protocol == ANY && ex->e_protocol != ANY)
678                                 pai->ai_protocol = ex->e_protocol;
679
680                         /*
681                          * if the servname does not match socktype/protocol, ignore it.
682                          */
683                         if (get_portmatch(pai, servname) != 0)
684                                 continue;
685
686                         if (afai_unspec)
687                                 afai = afai_unspec;
688                         else {
689                                 if ((afd = find_afd(pai->ai_family)) == NULL)
690                                         continue;
691                                 /* XXX assumes that afd points inside afdl[] */
692                                 afai = afailist[afd - afdl];
693                         }
694                         if (!afai)
695                                 continue;
696
697                         error = explore_copy(pai, afai, &cur->ai_next);
698
699                         while (cur && cur->ai_next)
700                                 cur = cur->ai_next;
701                 }
702         if ((pai->ai_flags & AI_PASSIVE) && ++pass <= 2)
703                 goto copyagain;
704
705         /* XXX inhibit errors if we have the result */
706         if (sentinel.ai_next)
707                 error = 0;
708
709         /*
710          * ensure we return either:
711          * - error == 0, non-NULL *res
712          * - error != 0, NULL *res
713          */
714         if (error == 0) {
715                 if (sentinel.ai_next) {
716                         /*
717                          * If the returned entry is for an active connection,
718                          * and the given name is not numeric, reorder the
719                          * list, so that the application would try the list
720                          * in the most efficient order.
721                          */
722                         if (hints == NULL || !(hints->ai_flags & AI_PASSIVE)) {
723                                 if (!numeric)
724                                         (void)reorder(&sentinel);
725                         }
726                         *res = sentinel.ai_next;
727                         error = 0;
728                 } else
729                         error = EAI_FAIL;
730         }
731
732  bad:
```

```
733                if (afai_unspec)
734                        freeaddrinfo(afai_unspec);
735                for (afd = afdl; afd->a_af; afd++) {
736                        if (afailist[afd - afdl])
737                                freeaddrinfo(afailist[afd - afdl]);
738                }
739                if (!*res)
740                        if (sentinel.ai_next)
741                                freeaddrinfo(sentinel.ai_next);
742                return error;
743        }
```
                                                              _____ getaddrinfo.c

630–644 The `for` loop examines all supported combinations of address family, socket type, and protocol. `pai` is reinitialized with `ai0`, a copy of the hint parameters. Unless `pai` matches the address family, the socket type, and the protocol, this combination is ignored (see Table 6-2, page 139).

646–654 A combination is ignored if the `AI_ADDRCONFIG` flag is specified, but the node does not support the address family that is currently being examined.

656–670 If the `AI_PASSIVE` flag is specified in the hint, the loop considers non-SCTP protocols in the first pass. The loop is then repeated and only SCTP is considered in the second pass. The reason for this complicated process is that some legacy applications assume that the `AI_PASSIVE` flag will cause `getaddrinfo()` to return at most one `addrinfo{}` structure for a fixed combination of address family and socket type. If `getaddrinfo()` happens to return an `addrinfo()` chain beginning with one for SCTP to such an application, then the application will try to open an SCTP socket only. This is probably not the result that the application wants and an undesirable side effect is likely to happen.

673–684 If some parameters are unspecified in the hint structure, specific values from the `explore{}` structure are substituted. Then, `get_portmatch()` checks to see whether `servname` is a valid service name for the given socket type and protocol family.

686–695 If `hostname` has been successfully resolved as an alphabetical name (typically an FQDN), `afai_unspec` should be non-NULL and will be used in the following process. Otherwise, `find_afd()` identifies the corresponding `afd{}` structure and `afai` is set to point to the corresponding `addrinfo{}` structure in the `afailist` array that has been initialized in the second main section of `getaddrinfo()` (see Listing 6-9).

697–701 At this point, `afai` contains a chain of `addrinfo{}` structures in each of which the `ai_addr` member is the `sockaddr{}` structure corresponding to the given `hostname`. `explore_copy()` makes a copy of the chain for the socket type and protocol that is being examined by the current iteration of the `for` loop. Then, the `while` loop resets the `cur` pointer to point to the last entry of the copied chain to ensure that `explore_copy()` concatenates each new copy at the end of intermediate results.

Note: The code here has a bug. If `explore_copy()` fails after several successes, the error will be cleared just after the loop because `sentinel.ai_next` is non-NULL (see below).

702–703 Another iteration of the loop is necessary if the `AI_PASSIVE` flag is specified (recall the discussion for lines 656 through 670).

705–706 An intermediate error is reset to 0 if there is a nonempty `addrinfo{}` chain.

714–727 `getaddrinfo()` finally tries to "optimize" the order of the `addrinfo{}` chain according to [RFC3484] when the following conditions are met:

- No error has been encountered thus far.

- A nonempty `addrinfo()` chain exists.

- The conversion is not for a passive socket.

- `hostname` is an alphabetical name not numeric.

A separate function `reorder()` performs the reordering of the `addrinfo{}` chain. `sentinel` will be modified accordingly. Then, `*res` is set to point to the result chain.

728–730 The `addrinfo{}` chain may still be empty even when there is no explicit error because some functions called by `getaddrinfo()` can fail without indicating a particular error. Since [RFC3493] specifies that `getaddrinfo()` return a nonempty chain on success, an error of `EAI_FAIL` is assigned here.

733–743 This part is shared by both erroneous and successful cases. All of the temporary resources are freed. If no `addrinfo{}` chain is going to be returned but we have an intermediate nonempty result, it is also freed.

6.3.13 `reorder()` Function

The `reorder()` function shown in Listing 6-19, which is called from the body of `getaddrinfo()`, sorts the `addrinfo{}` chain in the preferred order according to both local policies and the address selection rules defined in [RFC3484].

Function `reorder()` uses a separate structure, `ai_order{}` shown in Listing 6-18 for performing the necessary sorting. Each `ai_order{}` structure corresponds to a single `addrinfo{}` entry.

Listing 6-18

getaddrinfo.c

```
219    struct ai_order {
220            union {
221                    struct sockaddr_storage aiou_ss;
222                    struct sockaddr aiou_sa;
223            } aio_src_un;
224    #define aio_srcsa aio_src_un.aiou_sa
225            u_int32_t aio_srcflag;
226            int aio_srcscope;
227            int aio_dstscope;
228            struct policyqueue *aio_srcpolicy;
229            struct policyqueue *aio_dstpolicy;
230            struct addrinfo *aio_ai;
231            int aio_matchlen;
232    };
```
getaddrinfo.c

219–231 The `aio_src_un` union stores the socket address structure of the source address that would be used for the corresponding `addrinfo{}` entry as the destination. This is a union of `sockaddr_storage{}` and `sockaddr{}` in order to support all possible address families. `aio_srcflag` holds flags representing properties of the source address. Currently, `AIO_SRCFLAG_DEPRECATED` flag is the only available flag, which indicates that the source address is an IPv6 deprecated address. `aio_srcscope` and `aio_dstscope` specify the address scope type of the source and destination addresses, respectively. These two fields are integers that map to the "scope" field of IPv6 multicast addresses. For example, value 2 refers to the link-local scope and value 8 refers to the organization-local (multicast) scope, and so forth. Notice that the notion of scopes also applies to IPv4 addresses as specified in [RFC3484]. `aio_srcpolicy` and `aio_dstpolicy` point to entries of the policy table as defined in [RFC3484], which are the most suitable policies for the source and destination addresses, respectively. `aio_ai` points to the corresponding `addrinfo{}` entry in the given chain. `aio_matchlen` is the bit length of the source address that matches the destination address. This value will be used as a "tiebreaker" in the comparison for sorting.

We now explain the `reorder()` function.

Listing 6-19

_____getaddrinfo.c

```
745    static int
746    reorder(sentinel)
747            struct addrinfo *sentinel;
748    {
749            struct addrinfo *ai, **aip;
750            struct ai_order *aio;
751            int i, n;
752            struct policyhead policyhead;
753
754            /* count the number of addrinfo elements for sorting. */
755            for (n = 0, ai = sentinel->ai_next; ai != NULL; ai = ai->ai_next, n++)
756                    ;
757
758            /*
759             * If the number is small enough, we can skip the reordering process.
760             */
761            if (n <= 1)
762                    return(n);
763
764            /* allocate a temporary array for sort and initialization of it. */
765            if ((aio = malloc(sizeof(*aio) * n)) == NULL)
766                    return(n);           /* give up reordering */
767            memset(aio, 0, sizeof(*aio) * n);
768
769            /* retrieve address selection policy from the kernel */
770            TAILQ_INIT(&policyhead);
771            get_addrselectpolicy(&policyhead);
772
773            for (i = 0, ai = sentinel->ai_next; i < n; ai = ai->ai_next, i++) {
774                    aio[i].aio_ai = ai;
775                    aio[i].aio_dstscope = gai_addr2scopetype(ai->ai_addr);
776                    aio[i].aio_dstpolicy = match_addrselectpolicy(ai->ai_addr,
777                                                            &policyhead);
778            }
779
780            /* perform sorting. */
781            qsort(aio, n, sizeof(*aio), comp_dst);
782
783            /* reorder the addrinfo chain. */
784            for (i = 0, aip = &sentinel->ai_next; i < n; i++) {
785                    *aip = aio[i].aio_ai;
786                    aip = &aio[i].aio_ai->ai_next;
787            }
```

```
788              *aip = NULL;
789
790              /* cleanup and return */
791              free(aio);
792              free_addrselectpolicy(&policyhead);
793              return(n);
794      }
```
_____ getaddrinfo.c

754–767 The number of addrinfo{} entries in the chain is first calculated and then stored in n. If the chain consists of a single entry, the expensive sorting operations are omitted. Otherwise, memory is allocated for an array of n ai_order{} structures, which is initialized with zeros.

769–771 get_addrselectpolicy() retrieves the address selection policy table from the kernel and copies the table to policyhead as a list of entries.

773–777 For each addrinfo{} entry of the given chain, a separate ai_order{} structure is allocated, whose aio_ai member is set to the addrinfo{} entry. Destination-related parameters are also set. gai_addr2scopetype() returns the scope type of the destination address. match_addrselectpolicy() returns the most suitable policy table entry for the destination address.

Note: This version of the code has a serious bug. A separate function named set_source() is expected to be called just after line 777 in order to fill in source-related fields of the ai_order structure. Older versions of this code had invoked set_source(), but this function call was removed by an accident. In examples shown below, however, we will assume these parameters are set correctly.

780–781 The ai_order array is then sorted in the preferred order according to the given parameters. comp_dst() compares the given two ai_order entries and returns the preferred entry.

783–788 The addrinfo{} chain starting at ai_next of sentinel is then reordered as sorted in the ai_order array.

790–794 Temporary resources are freed. This function finally returns the number of entries in the chain.

Note: In earlier versions of this implementation, the return value is used for code that updates the corresponding statistics purposes. In this version, n is unused.

6.3.14 comp_dst() Function

The comp_dst() function is the comparison method called via qsort(). Listing 6-20 shows the function.

Listing 6-20
_____ getaddrinfo.c

```
1023    static int
1024    comp_dst(arg1, arg2)
1025            const void *arg1, *arg2;
```

```
1026    {
1027                const struct ai_order *dst1 = arg1, *dst2 = arg2;
1028
1029                /*
1030                 * Rule 1: Avoid unusable destinations.
1031                 * XXX: we currently do not consider if an appropriate route exists.
1032                 */
1033                if (dst1->aio_srcsa.sa_family != AF_UNSPEC &&
1034                    dst2->aio_srcsa.sa_family == AF_UNSPEC) {
1035                        return(-1);
1036                }
1037                if (dst1->aio_srcsa.sa_family == AF_UNSPEC &&
1038                    dst2->aio_srcsa.sa_family != AF_UNSPEC) {
1039                        return(1);
1040                }
1041
1042                /* Rule 2: Prefer matching scope. */
1043                if (dst1->aio_dstscope == dst1->aio_srcscope &&
1044                    dst2->aio_dstscope != dst2->aio_srcscope) {
1045                        return(-1);
1046                }
1047                if (dst1->aio_dstscope != dst1->aio_srcscope &&
1048                    dst2->aio_dstscope == dst2->aio_srcscope) {
1049                        return(1);
1050                }
1051
1052                /* Rule 3: Avoid deprecated addresses. */
1053                if (dst1->aio_srcsa.sa_family != AF_UNSPEC &&
1054                    dst2->aio_srcsa.sa_family != AF_UNSPEC) {
1055                        if (!(dst1->aio_srcflag & AIO_SRCFLAG_DEPRECATED) &&
1056                            (dst2->aio_srcflag & AIO_SRCFLAG_DEPRECATED)) {
1057                                return(-1);
1058                        }
1059                        if ((dst1->aio_srcflag & AIO_SRCFLAG_DEPRECATED) &&
1060                            !(dst2->aio_srcflag & AIO_SRCFLAG_DEPRECATED)) {
1061                                return(1);
1062                        }
1063                }
1064
1065                /* Rule 4: Prefer home addresses. */
1066                /* XXX: not implemented yet */
1067
1068                /* Rule 5: Prefer matching label. */
1070                if (dst1->aio_srcpolicy && dst1->aio_dstpolicy &&
1071                    dst1->aio_srcpolicy->pc_policy.label ==
1072                    dst1->aio_dstpolicy->pc_policy.label &&
1073                    (dst2->aio_srcpolicy == NULL || dst2->aio_dstpolicy == NULL ||
1074                     dst2->aio_srcpolicy->pc_policy.label !=
1075                     dst2->aio_dstpolicy->pc_policy.label)) {
1076                        return(-1);
1077                }
1078                if (dst2->aio_srcpolicy && dst2->aio_dstpolicy &&
1079                    dst2->aio_srcpolicy->pc_policy.label ==
1080                    dst2->aio_dstpolicy->pc_policy.label &&
1081                    (dst1->aio_srcpolicy == NULL || dst1->aio_dstpolicy == NULL ||
1082                     dst1->aio_srcpolicy->pc_policy.label !=
1083                     dst1->aio_dstpolicy->pc_policy.label)) {
1084                        return(1);
1085                }
1086
1088                /* Rule 6: Prefer higher precedence. */
1089                if (dst1->aio_dstpolicy &&
1090                    (dst2->aio_dstpolicy == NULL ||
1091                     dst1->aio_dstpolicy->pc_policy.preced >
1092                     dst2->aio_dstpolicy->pc_policy.preced)) {
1093                        return(-1);
1094                }
1095                }
1096                if (dst2->aio_dstpolicy &&
```

```
1097                    (dst1->aio_dstpolicy == NULL ||
1098                     dst2->aio_dstpolicy->pc_policy.preced >
1099                     dst1->aio_dstpolicy->pc_policy.preced)) {
1100                        return(1);
1101            }
1103
1104            /* Rule 7: Prefer native transport. */
1105            /* XXX: not implemented yet */
1106
1107            /* Rule 8: Prefer smaller scope. */
1108            if (dst1->aio_dstscope >= 0 &&
1109                dst1->aio_dstscope < dst2->aio_dstscope) {
1110                    return(-1);
1111            }
1112            if (dst2->aio_dstscope >= 0 &&
1113                dst2->aio_dstscope < dst1->aio_dstscope) {
1114                    return(1);
1115            }
1116
1117            /*
1118             * Rule 9: Use longest matching prefix.
1119             * We compare the match length in a same AF only.
1120             */
1121            if (dst1->aio_ai->ai_addr->sa_family ==
1122                dst2->aio_ai->ai_addr->sa_family) {
1123                        if (dst1->aio_matchlen > dst2->aio_matchlen) {
1124                                return(-1);
1125                        }
1126                        if (dst1->aio_matchlen < dst2->aio_matchlen) {
1127                                return(1);
1128                        }
1129            }
1130
1131            /* Rule 10: Otherwise, leave the order unchanged. */
1132            return(-1);
1133    }
```
——— getaddrinfo.c

This function basically just performs the pairwise comparison of two `aio_ai` entries corresponding to two different `addrinfo{}` entries, as described in [RFC3484]. We just make comments where an explicit note is necessary.

[RFC3484] says in its Rule 1 that if one destination is known to be reachable while the other is known to be unreachable, the former should be preferred. However, it is generally difficult to know whether a particular destination is reachable or not, especially in a user-space program. Thus, this implementation only checks to see if each destination has a source address in Rule 1.

A couple of rules are not yet supported in this implementation. One is Rule 4 that prefers destinations that would have Mobile IPv6 home addresses as the source address. The other one is Rule 7 that prefers destinations that are reached over native IPv6 networks, that is, nontunneling networks. It is generally difficult to detect if a particular destination is reached over a tunnel, and thus this rule is not implemented.

6.3.15 Other Subroutines for `getaddrinfo()`

`getaddrinfo()` depends on many subroutines that are not yet described. These functions are summarized in Table 6-3. The essential implementation of `getaddrinfo()` that we have described in detail should allow the reader to understand the details of these minor subroutines. All of the functions can be found in `getaddrinfo.c`.

TABLE 6-3

Function name	Function prototype and description
get_ai()	```static struct addrinfo *get_ai(const struct addrinfo *pai, const struct afd *afd, const char *addr);``` Allocates a new addrinfo{} structure and copies the parameters specified in pai and afd to the new structure; returns the pointer to the new structure; if memory allocation fails, returns a NULL pointer. This function allocates the entire memory for the addrinfo{} structure and the corresponding ai_addr space at once.
get_canonname()	```static int get_canonname(const struct addrinfo *pai, struct addrinfo *ai, const char *str);``` If the AI_CANONNAME flag is specified in pai, duplicates the string specified by str, and sets it to the ai_canonname member of ai. Returns 0 on success or EAI_MEMORY if memory allocation for the copied string fails.
get_port()	```static int get_port(struct addrinfo *ai, const char *servname, int matchonly);``` Converts the appropriate port value for servname and the protocol stored in ai and sets the corresponding port field of the ai_addr member of ai (sin6_port for IPv6) to the port value. If matchonly is nonzero, it just validates the parameters and keeps ai intact. Returns 0 on success, or EAI_xxx error codes.
get_portmatch()	```static int get_portmatch(const struct addrinfo *ai, const char *servname);``` This function is equivalent to get_port(ai, servname, 1).
copy_ai()	```static struct addrinfo *copy_ai(const struct addrinfo *pai);``` Allocates a new addrinfo{} structure and copies all the parameters from pai to the new structure; returns the pointer to the structure, or a NULL pointer
explore_copy()	```static int explore_copy(const struct addrinfo *pai, const struct addrinfo *src0, struct addrinfo **res);``` Copies the entire addrinfo{} chain stored in src0; values for ai_socktype and ai_protocol are copied from pai. On success, sets *res to the head of the copied chain and returns 0; otherwise, EAI_MEMORY will be returned.

(Continued)

TABLE 6-3 (*Continued*)

Function name	Function prototype and description
`find_afd()`	`static const struct afd *find_afd(int af);` This function iterates through the `afdl` array to find an appropriate `afd` entry for the given address family (see Section 6.3).
`addrconfig()`	`static int addrconfig(int af);` Returns 1 if the given address family (`af`) is available on the system, or returns 0. The current implementation simply checks if the system can open a `SOCK_DGRAM` socket for the address family and is almost meaningless.
`get_addrselectpolicy()`	`static void get_addrselectpolicy(struct policyhead *head);` Issues the `IPV6CTL_ADDRCTLPOLICY` sysctl to get the address selection policy, constructs a list of policy table entries, and sets head to the head of the list
`free_addrselectpolicy()`	`static void free_addrselectpolicy(struct policyhead *head);` Frees all resources allocated for head
`match_addrselectpolicy()`	`static struct policyqueue *match_addrselectpolicy(struct sockaddr *addr, struct policyhead *head);` Searches in the policy table from head for the entry that best matches addr; returns the pointer to the best match entry. If nothing is found, returns NULL.
`set_source()`	`static void set_source(struct ai_order *aio, struct policyhead *ph);` Gets the source address for the destination address stored in `aio` by trying to connect to the destination and then getting the local socket address, and sets related parameters in `aio`, referring to ph when necessary
`gai_addr2scopetype()`	`static int gai_addr2scopetype(struct sockaddr *sa);` Returns scope type number for the given socket address

Often the `get_xxx()` functions are used through wrapper macros, `GET_AI()`, `GET_CANONNAME()`, and `GET_PORT()`. On failure, these macros stop the procedure immediately, going to label free. `GET_AI()` also sets variable error to `EAI_NOMEMORY`.

A similar macro, `ERR()`, is often used, also. It takes an error code, sets the error variable to it, and goes to the bad label.

6.4 Address Ordering Examples

We will examine some examples in order to describe the address ordering procedure together with how the getaddrinfo() implementation itself works. In the following examples, we will concentrate on address families and addresses, ignoring socket types, protocols, and ports.

Consider a network depicted in Figure 6-9 where two hosts, a client and a server, are connected via the IPv4/IPv6 Internet. Both hosts have IPv4 and IPv6 addresses as shown in the figure. We assume all of the server's addresses are stored in the DNS.

Note that the server has a 6to4 address(*) as well as "normal" IPv6 addresses (i.e. non-6to4 address). This example is not common because 6to4 addresses are not necessary when normal global IPv6 addresses and IPv6 connectivity are available. This configuration is created purely for illustration and explanation.

> (*) 6to4 is a transition technology defined in [RFC3056], which is beyond the scope of this book. For the discussion here, it is enough to know that 6to4 addresses are identified by the prefix 2002::/16.

Let us assume an application program running on the client wants to communicate with the server either via IPv6 or via IPv4 and passes the server's host name to getaddrinfo().

getaddrinfo() calls the explore_fqdn() function, which makes several DNS queries (through its backend functions) to resolve IPv4 and IPv6 addresses. The ordering of the addrinfo{} chain at this stage depends on the details of the backend function and the ordering

FIGURE 6-9

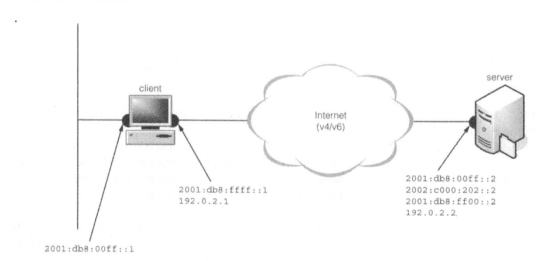

Example network topology with multiple candidates of address.

FIGURE 6-10

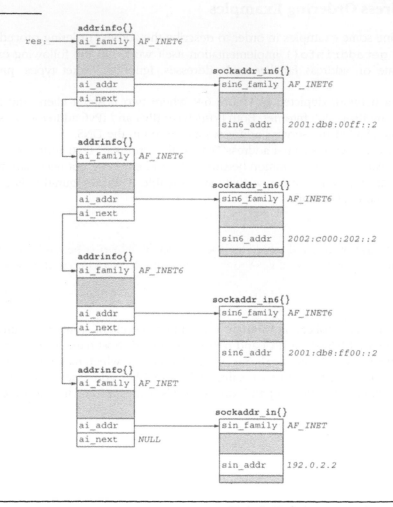

addrinfo{} chain constructed in `explore_fqdn()`.

of resource records provided by the DNS. In this example, we assume we have the chain as shown in Figure 6-10.

In the `for` loop of Listing 6-17, the `addrinfo{}` chain is copied to a separate chain beginning at `sentinel.ai_next`. Although the list could be reordered inside the `for` loop, the chain of this example does not change. In any event, the reordering at this stage does not matter because the `reorder()` function changes the list again regardless of the temporary result.

The `reorder()` function allocates an array of `ai_order{}`, filling in each entry with parameters to reorder the chain. Figure 6-11 shows the content of the array and the relationship between the array and the `addrinfo{}` chain before reordering.

FIGURE 6-11

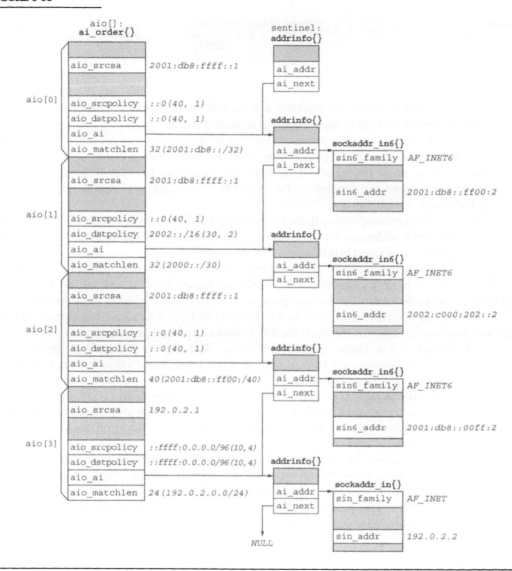

ai_order array before reordering.

Notice that the source address for the destination 2001:db8:00ff::2 should be 2001:db8:ffff::1, not 2001:db8:00ff::1, which is the longest match of bitwise comparison. The reason is that the former is assigned on the outgoing interface to the Internet while the latter is on an internal interface (source address selection Rule 5).

In this example, we assume the default policy table as defined in [RFC3484]. We can review the content of the policy table installed in the kernel by the **ip6addrctl** command. The following is an example output of this command.

% **ip6addrctl**

```
Prefix                          Prec Label      Use
::1/128                           50     0         0
::/0                              40     1     38940
2032::/16                         30     2         0
::/96                             20     3         0
::ffff:0.0.0.0/96                 10     4         0
```

The left-hand three columns are the table entries and the rightmost column shows statistics of how many times each entry is used, which is collected in the kernel.

In Figure 6-11, values for `aio_srcpolicy` and `aio_dstpolicy` should read like this: `::/0(40, 1)` means the key of the policy table entry for this address is `::/0`, and its precedence and matching label are 40 and 1, respectively. Also, the prefixes followed by values of `aio_matchlen` mean the longest prefix shared by the source and destination addresses, providing the match length value.

Note that the prefix corresponding to the IPv4-mapped IPv6 address (`::ffff:0.0.0.0/96`) simply represents IPv4 addresses for comparison purposes only. This is irrelevant to the usage of this type of address described in [RFC3493].

Figure 6-12 shows the result of reordering in the `reorder()` function. The given `addrinfo{}` chain is also reordered accordingly. In Figure 6-12, we show the `ai_order` members that tiebreak each pairwise comparison by dotted lines labeled with the rule number: `2001:db8:ff00::2` is preferred to `2001:db8:00ff::2` because the former has the longer matched source address (by Rule 9); `2001:db8:00ff::2` is preferred to `192.0.2.2` because the former has a higher precedence value (Rule 6); `192.0.2.2` is preferred to `2002:c000:202::2` because the former has the same precedence value for the source and destination while the latter does not (Rule 5).

If the application calling `getaddrinfo()` goes through the `addrinfo{}` chain, trying to connect to the address stored in each `addrinfo{}` entry until the attempt succeeds, which is the behavior of most of today's dual-stack applications, then the application will try the addresses in the preferred order.

The default policy table shown on page 164 prefers IPv6 communication over IPv4 communication. In some cases, however, an administrator might configure the host to prefer IPv4 communication instead, for example, when it is known that the quality of IPv6 connectivity is poorer than that of IPv4. This policy can be implemented by modifying the policy table. The administrator can create a new policy file with the following content:

```
::1/128                           50     0
::ffff:0.0.0.0/96                 45     4
::/0                              40     1
2002::/16                         30     2
::/96                             20     3
```

and then install the new policy file into the kernel using the **ip6addrctl** command:

```
# ip6addrctl install newpolicy
```

Note that installing a new policy table requires the superuser privilege.

Figure 6-13 is the reordering result for the previous network configuration with the new policy table. As shown in the figure, the pair of IPv4 addresses is most preferred.

FIGURE 6-12

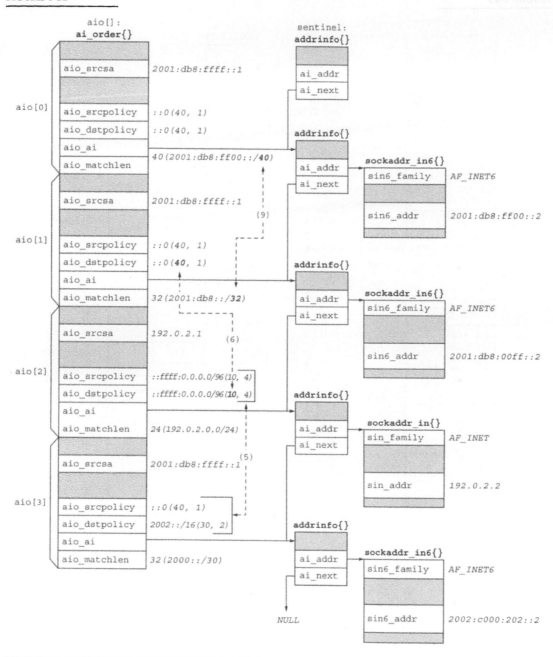

Result of address reordering.

FIGURE 6-13

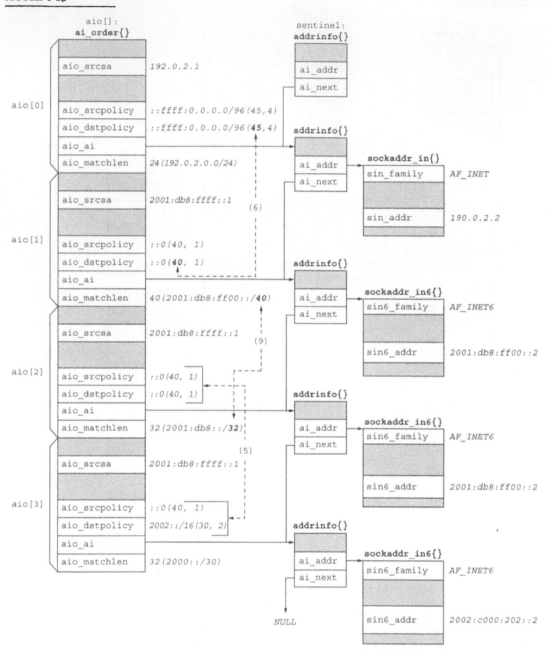

Reordering result preferring IPv4 communication.

6.5 `freeaddrinfo()` Function

The `freeaddrinfo()` function is the destructor of an `addrinfo{}` chain provided by `getaddrinfo()`.

Listing 6-21

```
387    void
388    freeaddrinfo(ai)
389            struct addrinfo *ai;
390    {
391            struct addrinfo *next;
392
393            do {
394                    next = ai->ai_next;
395                    if (ai->ai_canonname)
396                            free(ai->ai_canonname);
397                    /* no need to free(ai->ai_addr) */
398                    free(ai);
399                    ai = next;
400            } while (ai);
401    }
```

`freeaddrinfo()` iterates through the entire chain and frees resources for each `addrinfo{}` entry. Since the memory for `ai_addr` is allocated inside the `addrinfo{}` structure, freeing the `addrinfo{}` structure should be sufficient except for the memory pointed by `ai_canonname`. Note that this implementation assumes the argument `ai` is non-NULL. [RFC3493] is silent on this point and it is the application's responsibility to ensure the assumption.

6.6 `gai_strerror()` Function

The `gai_strerror()` function converts an error code from `getaddrinfo()` to a readable string.

Listing 6-22

```
300    static struct ai_errlist {
301            const char *str;
302            int code;
303    } ai_errlist[] = {
304            { "Success",                                     0, },
305    #ifdef EAI_ADDRFAMILY
306            { "Address family for hostname not supported",   EAI_ADDRFAMILY, },
307    #endif
308            { "Temporary failure in name resolution",        EAI_AGAIN, },
309            { "Invalid value for ai_flags",                  EAI_BADFLAGS, },
310            { "Non-recoverable failure in name resolution",  EAI_FAIL, },
311            { "ai_family not supported",                     EAI_FAMILY, },
312            { "Memory allocation failure",                   EAI_MEMORY, },
313    #ifdef EAI_NODATA
314            { "No address associated with hostname",         EAI_NODATA, },
315    #endif
316            { "hostname nor servname provided, or not known", EAI_NONAME, },
317            { "servname not supported for ai_socktype",      EAI_SERVICE, },
318            { "ai_socktype not supported",                   EAI_SOCKTYPE, },
319            { "System error returned in errno",              EAI_SYSTEM, },
320            { "Invalid value for hints",                     EAI_BADHINTS, },
321            { "Resolved protocol is unknown",                EAI_PROTOCOL, },
```

```
322                  /* backward compatibility with userland code prior to 2553bis-02 */
324                  { "Address family for hostname not supported",  1, },
325                  { "No address associated with hostname",        7, },
330                  { NULL,                                        -1, },
331          };

374     char *
375     gai_strerror(ecode)
376              int ecode;
377     {
378              struct ai_errlist *p;
379
380              for (p = ai_errlist; p->str; p++) {
381                      if (p->code == ecode)
382                              return (char *)p->str;
383              }
384              return "Unknown error";
385     }
```
——— getaddrinfo.c

330–331 gai_strerror() uses a separate local array, ai_errlist, as the database for the conversion, which is an array of structures of the same name. Each structure is simply an error code and the corresponding string. EAI_ADDRFAMILY and EAI_NODATA were deprecated by [RFC3493] and the corresponding definitions are disabled by default in this code. In order to provide binary backward compatibility, however, the old code values are kept at the end of this array. EAI_BADHINTS has never been defined in RFCs. This code is specific to this implementation. Such definition and usage are still acceptable because applications typically use the error codes as opaque values through the gai_strerror() function. Still, portable applications should not directly use the unofficial definition.

374–385 The for loop iterates through the entire ai_errlist array, looking for the entry that matches the given code. This function returns the corresponding error string if a match is found. Otherwise, the default string "Unknown error" will be returned.

6.7   getnameinfo() Function

In this section, we describe KAME's implementation of the getnameinfo() function. It implements the function specification as defined in [RFC3493] and it also supports the extended format for IPv6-scoped addresses specified in [RFC4007].

Similar to getaddrinfo(), getnameinfo() uses a supplemental structure named afd{} (see Listing 6-5). The afd{} structure for the getnameinfo() function is a subset of the same named structure for getaddrinfo().

Another supplemental structure for getnameinfo() is the sockinet{} structure, which holds the common fields of the sockaddr_in{} and sockaddr_in6{} structures. The only purpose of this structure is to provide the offset to the port number field of these structures. These structures are shown in Listing 6-23.

Listing 6-23

——— getnameinfo.c

```
70      static const struct afd {
71              int a_af;
72              int a_addrlen;
73              int a_socklen;
74              int a_off;
75      } afdl [] = {
```

```
77              {PF_INET6, sizeof(struct in6_addr), sizeof(struct sockaddr_in6),
78                      offsetof(struct sockaddr_in6, sin6_addr)},
80              {PF_INET, sizeof(struct in_addr), sizeof(struct sockaddr_in),
81                      offsetof(struct sockaddr_in, sin_addr)},
82              {0, 0, 0},
83      };
84
85      struct sockinet {
87              u_char  si_len;
89              u_char  si_family;
90              u_short si_port;
91      };
```
——————————————————————————————— getnameinfo.c

Through the following listings, we describe the details of the getnameinfo() function.

6.7.1 Initial Checks

Listing 6-24

——————————————————————————————— getnameinfo.c
```
99      int
100     getnameinfo(sa, salen, host, hostlen, serv, servlen, flags)
101             const struct sockaddr *sa;
103             socklen_t salen;
107             char *host;
108             size_t hostlen;
109             char *serv;
110             size_t servlen;
111             int flags;
112     {
113             const struct afd *afd;
114             struct servent *sp;
115             struct hostent *hp;
116             u_short port;
117             int family, i;
118             const char *addr;
119             u_int32_t v4a;
120             int h_error;
121             char numserv[512];
122             char numaddr[512];
123
124             if (sa == NULL)
125                     return EAI_FAIL;
126
128             if (sa->sa_len != salen)
129                     return EAI_FAIL;
131
132             family = sa->sa_family;
133             for (i = 0; afdl[i].a_af; i++)
134                     if (afdl[i].a_af == family) {
135                             afd = &afdl[i];
136                             goto found;
137                     }
138             return EAI_FAMILY;
139
140     found:
141             if (salen != afd->a_socklen)
142                     return EAI_FAIL;
```
——————————————————————————————— getnameinfo.c

124–129 An EAI_FAIL error is returned if the sockaddr{} structure is not provided or if the sa_len member of the structure is inconsistent with the given salen parameter.

132–138 The for loop searches for the appropriate afd{} structure for the given address family. An EAI_FAMILY error is returned if no entry is found.

140–142 An `EAI_FAIL` error is returned if the given `salen` value does not match the length of the corresponding `afd{}` structure.

6.7.2 Extract Port and Address

Listing 6-25

getnameinfo.c
```
144             /* network byte order */
145             port = ((const struct sockinet *)sa)->si_port;
146             addr = (const char *)sa + afd->a_off;
```
getnameinfo.c

144–146 The port number of the given `sockaddr{}` structure is extracted by casting `sa` to the generic `sockinet{}` structure. The address field is referred to from variable `addr` using the offset value from the head of the `sockaddr{}` structure provided by the corresponding `afd{}` structure. Note that the extracted number is expected to be passed to the `getservbyport()` function, where the port number is in the network byte order, and so `ntohs()` is not performed here.

6.7.3 Convert the Port Number

Listing 6-26

getnameinfo.c
```
148             if (serv == NULL || servlen == 0) {
149                     /*
150                      * do nothing in this case.
151                      * in case you are wondering if "&&" is more correct than
152                      * "||" here: rfc2553bis-03 says that serv == NULL OR
153                      * servlen == 0 means that the caller does not want the result.
154                      */
```
getnameinfo.c

148–154 If the buffer for the service name `serv` is a NULL pointer or if the length of the buffer is 0, then according to [RFC3493] the caller does not want a result for the service name.

Listing 6-27

getnameinfo.c
```
155             } else {
156                     if (flags & NI_NUMERICSERV)
157                             sp = NULL;
158                     else {
159                             sp = getservbyport(port,
160                                     (flags & NI_DGRAM) ? "udp" : "tcp");
161                     }
162                     if (sp) {
163                             if (strlen(sp->s_name) + 1 > servlen)
164                                     return EAI_MEMORY;
165                             strlcpy(serv, sp->s_name, servlen);
166                     } else {
167                             snprintf(numserv, sizeof(numserv), "%u", ntohs(port));
168                             if (strlen(numserv) + 1 > servlen)
169                                     return EAI_MEMORY;
170                             strlcpy(serv, numserv, servlen);
171                     }
172             }
```
getnameinfo.c

155–172 Unless the NI_NUMERICSERV flag is specified, getservbyport() is called to convert the port number to a servent{} structure, which contains a printable string for the number. If servent{} is found and the given buffer length is large enough to store the string with the terminating null character, the string is copied to the serv buffer. On failure in getting servent{}, the port number is converted to a digit string and is copied to the serv buffer if the buffer has enough space. In either case, the EAI_MEMORY error is returned if the given buffer is not big enough.

Note: EAI_MEMORY is not an appropriate error in such a case. EAI_OVERFLOW, which is newly defined in [RFC3493], would be better. The same note applies to the other code below.

Note: getservbyport() that is provided in FreeBSD targeted in this book is not thread-safe. Consequently, getnameinfo() is not thread-safe either.

6.7.4 Consideration for Special Addresses

The rest of this function tries to convert the address to a printable string. As part of the preprocess operation, some special addresses are explicitly considered to avoid meaningless operation such as issuing DNS queries for nonexistence records. This validation process is not documented in the API specification but is useful in terms of reducing resolution time and network traffic.

Listing 6-28

————————————————————————————————getnameinfo.c

```
174              switch (sa->sa_family) {
175              case AF_INET:
176                      v4a = (u_int32_t)
177                          ntohl(((const struct sockaddr_in *)sa)->sin_addr.s_addr);
178                      if (IN_MULTICAST(v4a) || IN_EXPERIMENTAL(v4a))
179                              flags |= NI_NUMERICHOST;
180                      v4a >>= IN_CLASSA_NSHIFT;
181                      if (v4a == 0)
182                              flags |= NI_NUMERICHOST;
183                      break;
185              case AF_INET6:
186                  {
187                      const struct sockaddr_in6 *sin6;
188                      sin6 = (const struct sockaddr_in6 *)sa;
189                      switch (sin6->sin6_addr.s6_addr[0]) {
190                      case 0x00:
191                              if (IN6_IS_ADDR_V4MAPPED(&sin6->sin6_addr))
192                                      ;
193                              else if (IN6_IS_ADDR_LOOPBACK(&sin6->sin6_addr))
194                                      ;
195                              else
196                                      flags |= NI_NUMERICHOST;
197                              break;
198                      default:
199                              if (IN6_IS_ADDR_LINKLOCAL(&sin6->sin6_addr)) {
200                                      flags |= NI_NUMERICHOST;
201                              }
202                              else if (IN6_IS_ADDR_MULTICAST(&sin6->sin6_addr))
203                                      flags |= NI_NUMERICHOST;
204                              break;
205                      }
```

```
206                }
207            break;
209        }
```

174–209 For the following addresses, `getnameinfo()` will simply try to convert them to textual representation as numeric addresses. Additional processes for DNS-based conversion will be suppressed.

- IPv4 multicast addresses
- Class E IPv4 addresses (`240.0.0.0 − 255.255.255.255`)
- IPv4 addresses beginning with 0x00
- IPv6 addresses beginning with 0x00 except IPv4-mapped IPv6 addresses and the loopback address
- IPv6 link-local addresses
- IPv6 multicast addresses

The `NI_NUMERICHOST` flag is set for the above addresses as if the caller originally intended to retrieve only numeric results.

6.7.5   Convert the Address

Listing 6-29

getnameinfo.c
```
210        if (host == NULL || hostlen == 0) {
211            /*
212             * do nothing in this case.
213             * in case you are wondering if "&&" is more correct than
214             * "||" here: rfc2553bis-03 says that host == NULL or
215             * hostlen == 0 means that the caller does not want the result.
216             */
```
getnameinfo.c

210–216 If the buffer for the host name `host` is a NULL pointer or if the length of the buffer is 0, then according to [RFC3493] the caller does not want a result for the host name.

Listing 6-30

getnameinfo.c
```
217        } else if (flags & NI_NUMERICHOST) {
218            int numaddrlen;
219
220            /* NUMERICHOST and NAMEREQD conflicts with each other */
221            if (flags & NI_NAMEREQD)
222                return EAI_NONAME;
223
224            switch(afd->a_af) {
226            case AF_INET6:
227            {
228                int error;
229
230                if ((error = ip6_parsenumeric(sa, addr, host,
231                                              hostlen, flags)) != 0)
232                    return(error);
233                break;
```

```
234                     }
236             default:
237                     if (inet_ntop(afd->a_af, addr, numaddr, sizeof(numaddr))
238                         == NULL)
239                             return EAI_SYSTEM;
240                     numaddrlen = strlen(numaddr);
241                     if (numaddrlen + 1 > hostlen) /* don't forget terminator */
242                             return EAI_MEMORY;
243                     strlcpy(host, numaddr, hostlen);
244                     break;
245             }
```
                                                            —————————— getnameinfo.c

217–222 As commented at line 220, the simultaneous use of both NI_NUMERICHOST and
NI_NAMEREQD flags contradicts each other. This implementation throws an error of
EAI_NONAME when both the flags are specified.

224–234 For an IPv6 address, a separate function ip6_parsenumeric() will convert the
address into textual representation. inet_ntop() is not appropriate here because it
cannot handle IPv6 scoped addresses well.

236–245 For addresses of other address families, inet_ntop() converts the name to a textual
string in the local numaddr buffer. Since inet_ntop() does not need a temporary
resource and we already know the address should be valid (Listing 6-24), inet_ntop()
should not fail here. If it ever happens, an error of EAI_SYSTEM is returned, indicating
the unexpected result. After the conversion, the result is copied to the host buffer with
the terminating NULL character if the given buffer length is enough to store the entire
result. Otherwise, the EAI_MEMORY error is returned.

Listing 6-31
                                                            —————————— getnameinfo.c
```
246             } else {
248                     hp = getipnodebyaddr(addr, afd->a_addrlen, afd->a_af, &h_error);
257
258                     if (hp) {
259     #if 0
260                             /*
261                              * commented out, since "for local host" is not
262                              * implemented here - see RFC2553 p30
263                              */
264                             if (flags & NI_NOFQDN) {
265                                     char *p;
266                                     p = strchr(hp->h_name, '.');
267                                     if (p)
268                                             *p = '\0';
269                             }
270     #endif
271                             if (strlen(hp->h_name) + 1 > hostlen) {
273                                     freehostent(hp);
275                                     return EAI_MEMORY;
276                             }
277                             strlcpy(host, hp->h_name, hostlen);
279                             freehostent(hp);
```
                                                            —————————— getnameinfo.c

246–248 getipnodebyaddr() tries to convert the address to an FQDN, often by DNS
reverse lookups. Note that [RFC3493] obsoletes this function and is not expected to
be called from applications. getipnodebyaddr() was once implemented and was
used by getnameinfo() as a backend function. Note that getipnodebyaddr() is

a thread-safe function and it is safe to use it as a backend without breaking the thread-safeness of the `getnameinfo()` implementation.

258–270 According to [RFC3493], the `NI_NOFQDN` flag means that only the node name portion of the FQDN should be returned for local hosts (see Table 2-2). However, this implementation intentionally disables this part; otherwise the code would return the first label of the FQDN, that is, the part before the first period. The reason behind the current implementation is due to the fact that the meaning of "for local hosts" is vague. If an application only wants to get the first label, the application will have to truncate the result from `getnameinfo()`.

271–277 As was done before, the result host name is copied to the host variable with the terminating NULL character. If the buffer is too short, an `EAI_MEMORY` error is returned.

Listing 6-32
─── getnameinfo.c

```
281                     } else {
282                             if (flags & NI_NAMEREQD)
283                                     return EAI_NONAME;
284                             switch(afd->a_af) {
286                             case AF_INET6:
287                             {
288                                     int error;
289
290                                     if ((error = ip6_parsenumeric(sa, addr, host,
291                                                             hostlen,
292                                                             flags)) != 0)
293                                             return(error);
294                                     break;
295                             }
297                             default:
298                                     if (inet_ntop(afd->a_af, addr, host,
299                                         hostlen) == NULL)
300                                             return EAI_SYSTEM;
301                                     break;
302                             }
303                     }
304             }
305             return(0);
306     }
```
─── getnameinfo.c

281–303 At this point, `getipnodebyaddr()` has failed. An `EAI_NONAME` error is returned if the `NI_NAMEREQD` flag is specified. Otherwise, either `ip6_parsenumeric()` or `inet_ntop()` will try converting the address to textual representation similar to the case where `NI_NUMERICHOST` is specified.

6.7.6 `ip6_parsenumeric()` Function

`ip6_parsenumeric()` is called by `getnameinfo()`, which converts an IPv6 address into printable textual representation taking into consideration the address scopes.

Listing 6-33
─── getnameinfo.c

```
309     static int
310     ip6_parsenumeric(sa, addr, host, hostlen, flags)
311             const struct sockaddr *sa;
312             const char *addr;
313             char *host;
```

```
314              size_t hostlen;
315              int flags;
316   {
317              int numaddrlen;
318              char numaddr[512];
319
320              if (inet_ntop(AF_INET6, addr, numaddr, sizeof(numaddr)) == NULL)
321                      return EAI_SYSTEM;
322
323              numaddrlen = strlen(numaddr);
324              if (numaddrlen + 1 > hostlen) /* don't forget terminator */
325                      return EAI_MEMORY;
326              strlcpy(host, numaddr, hostlen);
327
328              if (((const struct sockaddr_in6 *)sa)->sin6_scope_id) {
329                      char zonebuf[MAXHOSTNAMELEN];
330                      int zonelen;
331
332                      zonelen = ip6_sa2str(
333                          (const struct sockaddr_in6 *)(const void *)sa,
334                          zonebuf, sizeof(zonebuf), flags);
335                      if (zonelen < 0)
336                              return EAI_MEMORY;
337                      if (zonelen + 1 + numaddrlen + 1 > hostlen)
338                              return EAI_MEMORY;
339
340                      /* construct <numeric-addr><delim><zoneid> */
341                      memcpy(host + numaddrlen + 1, zonebuf,
342                          (size_t)zonelen);
343                      host[numaddrlen] = SCOPE_DELIMITER;
344                      host[numaddrlen + 1 + zonelen] = '\0';
345              }
346
347              return 0;
348   }
```
——getnameinfo.c

320–326 inet_ntop() converts the IPv6 address into textual representation and stores the result into the local buffer numaddr. inet_ntop() should succeed because all the input is known to be valid. The length of the converted string is set in numaddrlen, and strlcpy() copies the string to the host, ensuring it is terminated by a NULL character. (Using strlcpy() is actually redundant because inet_ntop() should have null-terminated the original string.)

328–345 If a nonzero value is specified in the sin6_scope_id field of the socket address structure, which should be a sockaddr_in6{} structure, ip6_sa2str() is called to convert the ID value to textual representation. The result is stored in a local buffer zonebuf. If the conversion succeeds and the buffer for the entire host name has enough space to store the address with the ID string, then the delimiter character ("%") followed by the string is appended to the textual representation of the address. The EAI_MEMORY error is returned if something unexpected happens.

6.7.7 ip6_sa2str() Function

The ip6_sa2str() function, shown in Listing 6-34, is called by ip6_parsenumeric().

Listing 6-34
——getnameinfo.c
```
350   /* ARGSUSED */
351   static int
```

```
352    ip6_sa2str(sa6, buf, bufsiz, flags)
353            const struct sockaddr_in6 *sa6;
354            char *buf;
355            size_t bufsiz;
356            int flags;
357    {
358            unsigned int ifindex;
359            const struct in6_addr *a6;
360            int n;
361
362            ifindex = (unsigned int)sa6->sin6_scope_id;
363            a6 = &sa6->sin6_addr;
364
365    #ifdef NI_NUMERICSCOPE
366            if ((flags & NI_NUMERICSCOPE) != 0) {
367                    n = snprintf(buf, bufsiz, "%u", sa6->sin6_scope_id);
368                    if (n < 0 || n >= bufsiz)
369                            return -1;
370                    else
371                            return n;
372            }
373    #endif
374
375            /* if_indextoname() does not take buffer size.  not a good api... */
376            if ((IN6_IS_ADDR_LINKLOCAL(a6) || IN6_IS_ADDR_MC_LINKLOCAL(a6) ||
377                IN6_IS_ADDR_MC_NODELOCAL(a6)) && bufsiz >= IF_NAMESIZE) {
378                    char *p = if_indextoname(ifindex, buf);
379                    if (p) {
380                            return(strlen(p));
381                    }
382            }
383
384            /* last resort */
385            n = snprintf(buf, bufsiz, "%u", sa6->sin6_scope_id);
386            if (n < 0 || n >= bufsiz)
387                    return -1;
388            else
389                    return n;
390    }
```
—— getnameinfo.c

365–373 If the NI_NUMERICSCOPE flag is defined and specified, the application wanted to convert the ID part into numeric representation. snprintf() does the conversion and returns the length of the string (excluding the terminating NULL character) on success. This function returns −1 if the conversion fails. Note that NI_NUMERICSCOPE is not officially defined in [RFC3493]. Applications should avoid using the flag.

375–382 The KAME implementation supports interface names such as "ne0" as scope zone indices for the interface-local scope (multicast only). Additionally, the implementation assumes a one-to-one mapping between links and interfaces and allows interface names as zone indices for this scope type. In these cases, the sin6_scope_id value is assumed to be an interface index and is passed to if_indextoname() to convert the value to an interface name. If the conversion succeeds, the interface name will be used as a printable representation. The sin6_scope_id value is handled as an opaque value in that the process continues even if if_indextoname() fails.

384–389 For scope types other than interface-local and link-local, or in the case where if_indextoname() fails above, the sin6_scope_id value is converted to a digit string similar to the case where the NI_NUMERICSCOPE flag is specified.

6.8 Other Library Functions

As shown in Chapters 2 and 3, the API specifications define several other library functions. KAME's implementation provides almost all of them, and we could describe those line-by-line. However, since the implementation is quite trivial and may not be very interesting, we simply give a list of files that implement these library functions.

When needed, the source code is available in the accompanying CD-ROM. [Ste94] also provides implementation of if_xxx() functions explained in Section 2.2.

The additional library functions defined in [RFC3493] are listed in Table 6-4. All files are located under the ${KAME}/kame/kame/libinet6/ directory.

The additional library functions defined in [RFC3542] are listed in Table 6-5. All files are located under the ${KAME}/kame/kame/libinet6/ directory.

TABLE 6-4

Function	File
if_indextoname()	if_indextoname.c
if_nametoindex()	if_nametoindex.c
if_freenameindex()	if_nameindex.c
if_nameindex()	if_nameindex.c

TABLE 6-5

Function	File
inet6_rth_space()	rthdr.c
inet6_rth_init()	rthdr.c
inet6_rth_add()	rthdr.c
inet6_rth_reverse()	rthdr.c
inet6_rth_segments()	rthdr.c
inet6_rth_getaddr()	rthdr.c
inet6_opt_init()	ip6opt.c
inet6_opt_append()	ip6opt.c
inet6_opt_finish()	ip6opt.c
inet6_opt_set_val()	ip6opt.c
inet6_opt_next()	ip6opt.c
inet6_opt_find()	ip6opt.c
inet6_opt_get_val()	ip6opt.c
rresvport_af()	rresvport_af.c
rcmd_af()	rcmd.c
rexec_af()	(not implemented)

References

Most of the references for this book are RFCs. Some specifications are in the process of standardization or revision, for which Internet Drafts are referred to. Both types of documents are freely available from the IETF web page: http://www.ietf.org. Note, however, that an Internet Draft is a work-in-progress material, which may expire or may have become an RFC by the time this book is published. There are WWW or FTP sites on the Internet that provide a copy of old versions of Internet Drafts when necessary. At the time of this writing, the KAME project's FTP server provides this service, which is located at ftp://ftp.kame.net/pub/internet-drafts/.

The following list of references are categorized into three parts: The first part consists of non-IETF references; the second part is a list of RFC referred to or mentioned in this book; the last part is a reference list of Internet Drafts.

[LiAdv07]	IPv6 Advanced Protocols Implementation
[LiCore06]	IPv6 Core Protocols Implementation
[RFC2292]	W. Stevens and M. Thomas, "Advanced Sockets API for IPv6," RFC2292, February 1998.
[RFC2373]	R. Hinden and S. Deering, "IP Version 6 Addressing Architecture," RFC2373, July 1998.
[RFC2460]	S. Deering and R. Hinden, "Internet Protocol, Version 6 (IPv6) Specification," RFC2460, December 1998.
[RFC2553]	R. Gilligan, et al., "Basic Socket Interface Extensions for IPv6," RFC2553, March 1999.
[RFC2710]	S. Deering, et al., "Multicast Listener Discovery (MLD) for IPv6," RFC2710, October 1999.
[RFC2894]	M. Crawford, "Router Renumbering for IPv6," RFC2894, August 2000.
[RFC2960]	R. Stewart, et al., "Stream Control Transmission Protocol," RFC2960, October 2000.

[RFC3041]   T. Narten and R. Draves, "Privacy Extensions for Stateless Address Auto-configuration in IPv6," RFC3041, January 2001.

[RFC3056]   B. Carpenter and K. Moore, "Connection of IPv6 Domains via IPv4 Clouds," RFC3056, February 2001.

[RFC3484]   R. Draves, "Default Address Selection for Internet Protocol version 6 (IPv6)," RFC3484, February 2003.

[RFC3493]   R. Gilligan, et al., "Basic Socket Interface Extensions for IPv6," RFC3493, February 2003.

[RFC3513]   R. Hinden and S. Deering, "Internet Protocol Version 6 (IPv6) Addressing Architecture," RFC3513, April 2003.

[RFC3542]   W. Stevens, et al., "Advanced Sockets Application Program Interface (API) for IPv6," RFC3542, May 2003.

[RFC3678]   D. Thaler, et al., "Socket Interface Extensions for Multicast Source Filters," RFC3678, January 2004.

[RFC3879]   C. Huitema and B. Carpenter, "Deprecating Site Local Addresses," RFC3879, September 2004.

[RFC4007]   S. Deering, et al., "IPv6 Scoped Address Architecture," RFC4007, March 2005.

[RFC4193]   R. Hinden and B. Haberman, "Unique Local IPv6 Unicast Addresses," RFC4193, October 2005.

[RFC4291]   R. Hinden and S. Deering, "IP Version 6 Addressing Architecture," RFC4291, February 2006.

[Ste94]   W. Stevens and G. Wright, "TCP/IP Illustrated, Volume 2: The Implementation," Addison-Wesley, 1994.

[V4MAPPED]   C. Metz and J. Hagino, "IPv4-Mapped Address API Considered Harmful," Internet Draft: draft-cmetz-v6ops-v4mapped-api-harmful-01.txt, October 2003.

Index

Printed and bound by CPI Group (UK) Ltd, Croydon, CR0 4YY

03/10/2024

01040319-0014